Nandita Haksar is a human rights lawyer and campaigner and writer. Haksar was a member of the first fact-finding team to visit Manipur to document the violations being committed by the Indian security forces. On the basis of the fact-finding report, she filed the first cases against the Armed Forces (Special Powers) Act, 1958 in 1983 on behalf of the victims of human rights violations in Manipur.

Her first case, *Sebastian M. Hongray vs Union of India*, led to the landmark Supreme Court judgement on the award of compensation in cases of custodial death.

She lived in Manipur from 1988 to 1991 in connection with another human rights case. This was the time the first refugees were coming into India after the military crackdown in Myanmar in 1990. She filed cases on behalf of the refugees and set precedents in refugee law in India. She once again took up the cause of refugees, especially from Myanmar, after the military coup in February 2021.

Haksar has also taken part in the Indo-Naga peace talks. Her experience has given her a ringside view of the working of the state and of the human rights movement. She has travelled and written extensively on the Northeast, and has published many articles and books, such as *Rogue Agent: How India's Military Intelligence Betrayed the Burmese Resistance* (2009); *The Judgement that Never Came: Army Rule in North East India* (co-authored with Sebastian Hongray, 2011); *ABC of Naga Culture and Civilization: A Resource Book* (2013); *Across the Chicken Neck: Travels in the Northeast India* (2015); *The Exodus Is Not Over: Migrations from the Ruptured Homelands of Northeast India* (2016); and *Kuknalim: Naga Armed Resistance: Testimonies of Leaders, Pastors, Healers and Soldiers* (2019). She has also authored a book of memoirs, *Flavours of Nationalism: A Memoir with Recipes for Love, Hate and Friendship* (2018).

SHOOTING THE SUN

Why Manipur Was Engulfed by Violence and the Government Remained Silent

NANDITA HAKSAR

SPEAKING TIGER BOOKS LLP
125A, Ground Floor, Shahpur Jat, near Asiad Village,
New Delhi 110049

First published by Speaking Tiger Books 2023

Copyright © Nandita Haksar 2023

ISBN: 978-93-5447-703-4
eISBN: 978-93-5447-701-0

10 9 8 7 6 5 4 3 2 1

The moral right of the author has been asserted.

I dedicate this book to the memory of M.K. Binodini,
who may not agree with everything I have said,
but we would have discussed our disagreements over tea, for me,
and paan, for Sebastian.

Aunty, I so wish you were here with us.

I also dedicate this book to all those
who have suffered physical and emotional trauma.
May each of you get justice and find peace.

'When the bright sun fell by the arrow…he was afraid and hid himself in the earth in a great cave by the big village near his father Pakhangba and his mother Senamehi. Then the Meithei land was dark by day and dark by night. The fields and the whole countryside looked to the Gods for pity because the day remained not. Weeds grew. Women that used to go to the fields went no more, women that used to toil in the fields went no more. The ten kings…these ten gods knew not how to look for the place where the sun was.'

—*Numit Kappa*, 'Shooting the Sun',
one of the oldest Meitei epics, translated
by T.C. Hodson in *The Meitheis*
(London: 1908), pp. 126–27

CONTENTS

District Map of Manipur

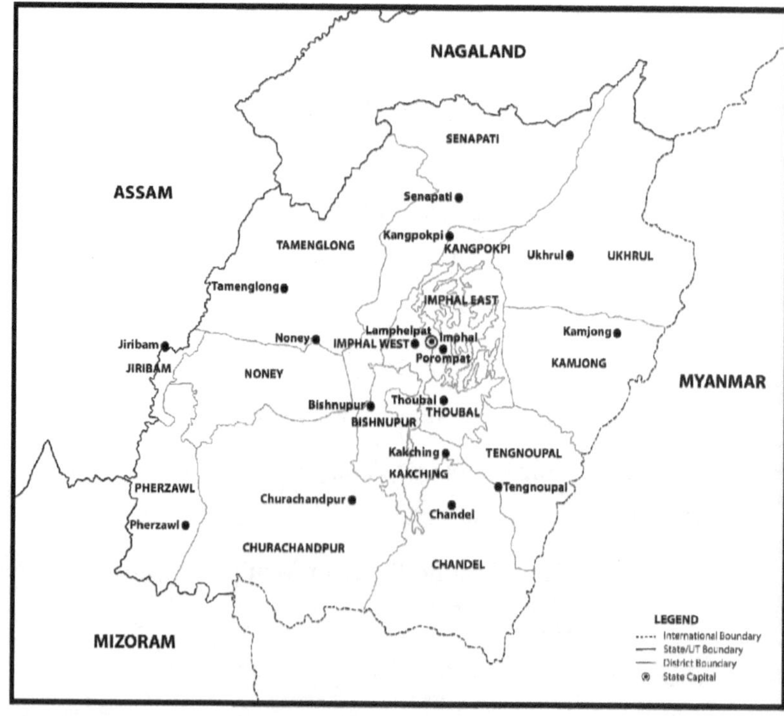

Reproduced from the boundaries given on Maps of India (available at www.mapsofindia.com/maps/manipur/manipur.htm).

A Prelude

Where Have All the Flowers Gone?

The stories of Manipur that this book tells are violent, cruel and infused with unadulterated savagery. The hate and rage in them is tangible and there is no way to make the stories any less brutal.

The reports coming out of the state since May 2023 have eclipsed everything else there is to know about this magnificent place, its cultural as well as biological diversity. Almost as if wanting to remind us of these aspects of its beauty, three new species of flowers revealed themselves in Kakching. Never recorded before, the bright yellow flowering plants growing up to eight feet exhibit a wide range of pharmacological properties—anti-inflammatory, anti-cancer, anti-diabetic, anti-hepatotoxic, anti-diarrheal, carminative, diuretic, anti-rheumatic, hypotensive, antioxidant, anti-microbial, anti-viral and insecticidal.

Manipur is a place where many flowers have bloomed, literally and metaphorically. More than five centuries ago a Meitei king, Charairongba (1697–1709), wrote a book called *Leiron* (*lei* means flower). He describes more than a hundred flowers, edible plants and medicinal herbs and relates stories associated with each plant.

Here are some descriptions of the flowers he gives:

> Lei Kabok: it is a white flower that remains ever fresh and is not eaten by worms…an ideal present for boys and girls to give to each other to show their love; Nongleishang: this flower grows in an enchanted forest in the remote hills and is associated with folk stories; Santhong Maiba Lei: it is believed that this flower was a gift of the gods…[i]t seems to be sprinkled with silver dust and it has silvery sword-like leaves…used by ancient priests and priestess[es] for religious offerings; Kusum Lei: this flower was brought to Manipur by the Muslims…the petals of the flowers look as if they are made from gold and the leaves resemble the teeth of a tiger; Singut Yenga Lei: this is a flower associated with a story of friendship and love of two women who turned themselves into two reeds so that during the dry season they may be burnt together and become ash and they may rise to the sky in the form of smoke; and Thambal: this is the lotus flower which grows in the Waithou Lake and is believed to grow from the pit of Nongda Lairen Pakhangba's[1] stomach.[2]

The description of the flowers includes information about the plants from the Hills as well as the Valley and those associated with folk stories of tribal people and also of the Muslims in Manipur.

I learnt much about Meitei culture when I was living in Manipur from 1988 to 1991. It was Maharaj Kumari Binodini, the daughter of the Manipur Kingdom's monarch, Sir Maharaj Churachand Singh, who told me of the pre-Hindu Sanamahi religion and even took me to meet a famous *maibi*, a woman priestess.

I was in the state to represent the Nagas in a case of large-scale human rights violations committed by the Indian security forces in the Poumai Naga-inhabited areas of Senapati district during the counter-insurgency operation codenamed Bluebird (1987). M.K. Binodini mobilized many well-known artists and writers in support of the case and campaign against the Armed Forces (Special Powers) Act, 1958.

A Meitei sub-divisional officer, N. Surendra Singh gave me all the relevant files from his SDO's office which documented the human rights violations being committed during Operation Bluebird. (Many of these documents were field reports sent by him in the form of telegrams to the district administration.) He paid with his life for his act of courage.[3]

The Superintendent of Jails was a man from the Kuki community. He helped me, among other things, by allowing me access to my clients in jail. He also came to my aid when I took up the case of the Burmese refugees who had started coming into Manipur after the military crackdown in Myanmar in 1988.

Meiteis, Nagas and Kukis were all extremely sympathetic to the Burmese refugees who had crossed to Manipur in the wake of crackdown. It was quite inspiring, because I knew there had been long wars with Burma in the past. I was deeply moved once again when I went to the Manipur High Court in 2021, in the midst of the Covid pandemic, after a gap of more than two decades, to once more represent some refugees who had fled to Manipur after the military coup in Myanmar in February that year. I was overwhelmed by the support, for both me and the cause I had taken up, by so many of my old friends and acquaintances (again, across communities).

This is not to say that I was, or am, not aware of the divisions and conflicts between the communities living in Manipur. After all, I was still called a *mayang* (a derogatory word for 'outsider').[4] There have been deadly conflicts between the communities many times in the past. What we saw in 2023, however, was different. This time, even the security forces were divided down ethnic lines, with the Manipur police and commandos identifying with the Meiteis, and the central forces, especially the Assam Rifles, identifying with the Kukis. There were even clashes between the police and the central forces.

For months, the violence showed no signs of ending. President's Rule[5] has had to be imposed during past conflicts, for instance, during the Naga–Kuki clashes in 1993. However, this time the calls for the imposition of President's Rule by various organizations and parties both within Manipur as well as from all corners of the country fell on deaf ears. The violence affected everyone in Manipur, from school children to those dependent on the internet for their livelihood, and from cultivators to lawyers. But it is clear that the violence was overwhelmingly directed at the Kuki-Zo.

The Kuki group of tribes in Manipur includes the Gangte, Hmar, Kom, Paite, Thadou, Vaiphei and Zo. With the exception of the Thadous, all the other communities have disowned the term Kuki and call themselves by their own names. Many prefer to refer to themselves as Zomi. The Thadou Kuki are numerically the largest community and have played a dominant role in Kuki politics. In Manipur, the Kuki-Zo are concentrated in the Churachandpur district, which has the highest literacy rate in the state, although they have villages in all the Naga-majority areas as well as the Valley.

The Meiteis use the term Khonjai to refer to the Kukis, but more recently a consensus seems to have developed among the Kuki tribes of Manipur to use the compound term Kuki-Zo to refer to themselves. It is therefore the term I choose to employ, interchangeably with Kuki, in this book.

The term 'Kuki', we may note, is an exonym. It was likely used by the Bengalis to refer to the tribes living in some of these regions of India and Myanmar. During British rule, all communities and tribes that were not included in the Naga group of tribes were called Kuki. They divided the Kukis into 'Old Kukis' and 'New Kukis', the former having largely identified themselves with the Naga group of tribes in the years since. What are called Kukis on this side of the border are called 'Chins' by the Burmese. Although the Kuki-Chin-Mizo-Zo group of tribes are recognized as separate tribes, they have many similarities of culture and language.

This affinity has been at the root of accusations against the Kuki-Zo of being 'outsiders'—accusations which came to be thrown around with disturbing conviction as Manipur erupted like a volcano in May 2023. Official figures record 175 deaths, the destruction of nearly five thousand homes, and the displacement of tens of thousands of people. The liquid-hot lava of hate and anger destroyed everything in its path, burning all bridges between communities. It may take a very long time indeed to build new ones.

Peace can only return if the truth is acknowledged. But there isn't one simple and straightforward truth that needs to be acknowledged. The story is complex. If this book is able to convey a fraction of the complexity of the identity politics playing out in Manipur, and help those outside understand and engage with issues in a more meaningful manner, it would have accomplished its purpose.

The title of this book refers to *Numit Kappa* or 'Shooting the Sun', the oldest Meitei epic written in the period of the earliest monarchs of the Ningthouja dynasty of Manipur in the first century AD. It speaks of a time when there were two suns in the sky but one was shot dead and the other hid himself in a cave and plunged the land into darkness. Then the people prayed to the sun to come out of the cave, and it finally did, shining over the land once again.

This book is written in the hope that the sun will shine again over Manipur—upon all its people equally.

CHAPTER ONE

Shooting the Sun

'I'm just an ordinary Indian from Manipur living a retired life. The state is now "stateless". Life and property can be destroyed anytime by anyone, just like in Libya, Lebanon, Nigeria, Syria, etc.'

—a post on X (formerly Twitter) by
Lt Gen (Retd) L. Nishikanta Singh, June 16, 2023

Imphal, the capital of Manipur, was described by the advancing Japanese during the Second World War as *Takane no hana*, or a flower on the lofty height. Imphal is bounded in the north and north-west by the Imphal River and the Langol Hills, respectively. Here, in the Langol, is the Game Village and Langol Housing Complex. The houses are mostly small government quarters, occupied largely by tribals working in the lower ranks within the administration.

It was in one these houses, allotted to an officer in the Sports Authority of India, that I lived for a while. I was representing Poumai Nagas, victims of human rights violations committed by personnel of the Assam Rifles, a central paramilitary force, in 1987.

The house had two bedrooms, a small toilet and bathroom and a kitchen. There were times when the water came for an hour every three days; I learnt all about water harvesting during my stay. Our neighbours fetched water from the stream down the hill and cheerfully carried the heavy buckets back up, chatting and laughing. Despite the problems and difficulties I faced, the days spent in Langol were among the happiest in my life. The air was fresh and I was surrounded by nature. There was a vegetable garden at the back and further back were the hills. Even the fifteen-to-twenty-minute motorcycle ride from Langol to the Sessions Court went past green paddy fields.

Langol would be enveloped in silence at night and I slept peacefully. Only during the rainy season would the silence be broken by the croaking of frogs. I used to sit watching local boys carrying flashlights and buckets to catch them.

One of my neighbours was a young lawyer, Khupchinpau. He was a Paite, of the Kuki-Zo community. We used to meet in the court complex and also in Langol. But the meeting I remember most vividly was at the railway station in Dimapur, Nagaland. I had gone there to catch a train back to Delhi since there were no trains in Manipur at the time. As I entered the platform I found Khupchinpau. He greeted me with a broad smile.

'What are you doing here?'

'I am trying to catch a train. But what are *you* doing here?' I noticed he had no luggage.

His face lit up and he announced: 'I have brought my villagers to see a train. They have not seen a train.'

I joined him and his villagers in sharing the excitement of seeing the train.

All these memories came rushing back on Sunday, August 6, 2023. That was the day I read with both shock and disbelief that Langol Game Village had been subjected to mortar attacks the previous day. Then I read that most people living in the government quarters had long shifted to relief camps when the houses were set on fire on May 4.

I watched a video someone had uploaded online. There was no sound but the camera panned the area and one could see figures dressed in black running across the paddy fields. Orange flames were leaping out of the houses and black smoke enveloped the trees.

My thoughts went to Khupchinpau. Where was he? I had last met him so many years ago; more than two decades, in fact. The memory of him at the railway station still filled me with joy, but also unease.

I made a few phone calls to friends in Imphal. Khupchinpau was safe in Churachandpur.

He had left Langol long ago and moved to a locality called Paite Veng. It was a locality where many members of both the Paite and Meitei communities had built their dream houses with their life savings. Paite Veng was attacked on May 3, 2023, the first day of the violence in Manipur. I had seen photographs of the locality with burnt homes. Some reports said forty homes and one church had been burnt down there. One comment on Twitter read: 'Is it even possible and legitimate to rechristen a place after driving out the residents? This is a locality (Paite Veng) in Imphal, where [the] Zomi community lived until they were driven out on 3rd May, and houses burnt. Now it's been renamed "Kwakeithel Ningthemki"—a Meitei name.'

I got Khupchinpau's mobile number. While I knew he was in Churachandpur, I had no idea of the circumstances of his escape. I just sent a message saying I was thinking of him.

He replied: 'Hello, thank you for calling me... What is going on in our world?'

*

Something almost diabolical appeared to be unfolding before us. I could not put my finger on it, but something left me deeply at unease. Manipur was the home of my husband, Sebastian, and in a way mine, too.

There's a visual which has got stuck in my mind:

A young man wearing a dark teal-coloured full-sleeved T-shirt paired with brown track pants and a camouflage tactical vest. He is looking at the camera holding a machete in one hand and in the other hand he is holding something that has been blurred deliberately. The photo was said to be of one Ramesh, who is alleged to have beheaded a man called David Theik from the Hmar community.

Ramesh was later identified as Mairembam Romesh Mangang, a security detail of Shanti Kumar alias Sanisam Premchandra Singh, the Bharatiya Janata Party member of Manipur's legislative assembly from the Kumbi constituency. It has been reported that 'Kumbi is known to be a hotspot of Meitei insurgent groups where politicians conduct...financial dealings with underground groups'.[6]

The blurred portion of the image is in fact a human head, freshly severed from the body. Later photos showed the head spiked on a fence.

Beyond the horror of the brutal act is a question: why?

There was nothing remarkable about the life of David Theik. He was from a village called Langza in Churachandpur district. He went to school and was passionate about football. He played for several village tournaments.

David could not continue his studies after school because his family was too poor to support him. His mother had died when he was six years old and his father had physical disabilities, so it fell to David to shoulder the responsibility of supporting his father and younger brother. Driven by poverty and lack of employment, David, like so many tribal boys from Manipur, went to Mumbai in search of a job, joining the ranks of the migrant workers from the Northeast. He worked as a waiter in a hotel. Perhaps he lost his job during the Covid pandemic or he was homesick, and so he returned.

David was happy to be back among the green fields and the familiar sight of the distant hills, finally able to breathe the fresh air in his village. But he knew he had to go back to Mumbai, and was indeed planning to, when suddenly the state was engulfed in violence.

The majority of the population in Langza village are from the Hmar[7] community, who are Christians. The surrounding villages have a mix of tribal and non-tribal populations. The non-tribal are the Meiteis, who are mostly Vaishnavite. There had never been any clash between the two communities. But this time the villagers in Langza felt a need to set up a village defence force. The Hmar tribe fell within the Kuki-Zo group of tribes who seemed to be the prime targets of violence.

The villagers in Langza took turns to keep watch. On July 1, 2023, David Theik had volunteered for the job. David helped a woman and her two children escape that day when the village was attacked by armed Meitei mobs.

The next day, on July 2, the mob came again. They went around looting and destroying homes. Twenty-six houses and three churches (belonging to the Independent Church of India, Evangelical Assembly Church and Reformed Presbyterian Church) were burnt down. David and his friend, who was with him keeping watch, went into hiding before the latter went to fetch a scooter. But while his friend was away looking for their means of escape, David was caught by the mob. The crowd put a rope around his neck and dragged him to a field. Instead of shooting him, they tortured him for four hours. They gouged out an eye and savagely cut off his limbs.

When a group of Hmar tribal youth went to Langza to collect the remains of 34-year-old David Theik they found the village destroyed, the mud and thatch houses pulled apart and tin roofs mangled and heaps of ashes still smouldering. All the youth could recover of David was a few bones and charred bits of flesh.

In the annals of Kuki-Zo history, David Theik is a now a celebrated *pasaltha*, a hero in the tradition of the warriors of the past who gave up their lives keeping their villages safe from attack.

But the question remains: why was Langza attacked and why was David Theik the subject of such brutality?

David Theik's uncle, Buonkhawlien, told Saptarshi Basak of *The Quint* that the attack was carried out by 'Meitei terrorists'. It was this uncle who had filed the FIR at the Churachandpur police station against 'unknown persons' with 'unauthorized possession of firearms'. The case was later transferred to Bishnupur police station and was being investigated but no arrests had been made when the report was published. (Churachandpur police station is Kuki-dominated while the Bishnupur station is Meitei-dominated.)

A narrative has been put forward that regards Mizo-Chin-Kukis 'outsiders', 'foreigners'. Some say they are all illegal migrants. How can Khupchinpau or David Theik be called foreigners? They had been born in India and grew up here. They were Indian citizens.

*

Then there was the bizarre incident which occurred in parliament in August 2023.

K. Vanlalvena, the member of parliament from Mizoram, claimed that his mic was switched off during a speech in the Rajya Sabha on August 10. He was speaking on the Manipur issue. He said he opposed calling the 'tribal people of Manipur as Myanmarese'.

The Rajya Sabha MP posted this on his Twitter account:

'I raised Manipur issue at Parliament session [this] afternoon, i.e. the 10th Aug 2023. Hon'ble Chairman switched… off my microphone while I just began to speak. I continued my speech without microphone in the midst [of] roarings of Opp MPs.'

The strange thing about this was that the member of parliament belonged to the Mizo National Front, which is a member of the BJP-led National Democratic Alliance.

He was arguing that the 'Kuki-Zo tribes in Manipur belong to the Mizo community—they are our people. The troubles in Manipur state have not been created by the Maynmarese refugees but by the [central] and state governments. This was violence that was pre-planned by the Manipur government'.

But he was not allowed to speak, to represent his people in parliament. What is more, Chairman Jagdeep Dhankhar ordered that the words Vanlalvena did speak be expunged from the record.

*

I tried to put it all behind me, but I could not stop myself from reading about Manipur. Then one night, for the first time in many years, I had nightmares. Something was driving me to make sense of everything happening out there. I knew that even writing a book on Manipur, in the midst of this volatile situation, was a hazardous job. I also knew that the Manipur government had passed an order the previous year stating that no book on the state could be published without their consent. (The order passed in September 2022 stated that it had come to the government's notice that 'some books published on the history, culture, tradition and geography of the state contain material which may either distort facts or disturb the peaceful coexistence amongst various communities'. Hence the pre-censorship of books on that broad range of subjects.)

I have tried to stop myself from writing this book. Yet I find myself driven to do so. I have been fighting a little voice that keeps warning me that I am on a dangerous journey and it is better to turn back. But some questions haunt me day and night: Who was behind this violence, and more importantly, what was their motive? Who would gain from the destruction, arson and killings?

What lies at the root of this violence is identity politics, and everyone is party to it. I believe the tragedy of Manipur is very much like the story in Gabriel Garcia Marquez's *Chronicle of a Death Foretold*. The events kept unfolding rapidly, the conflicts becoming deadlier, and like in the novel, everyone knew the tragedy would take place, but no one was willing to prevent it.

I believe everyone involved has added to this situation; and this includes the state and central governments, political parties and the insurgents. And of course the intelligence agencies and perhaps foreign powers too. I also hold myself guilty for being attracted to identity politics for a time.

But while it is true that everyone has contributed to the tragedy taking place in Manipur, it is also true that there are hundreds of people living there, mostly from poor families, who even in the midst of this mayhem have quietly helped each other, often risking their own lives to save those of strangers. They are nameless, voiceless and anonymous. They are not organized but their existence keeps alive our faith in humanity. It is their example that inspires me.

CHAPTER TWO

Making of the Meitei Identity

It is an appeal from the helpless and
voiceless of our rotten society.
Now our society is going from bad
to worse because of the situation
that obtains. The people
have forgotten to share happiness and
enjoy their life because of the news in
the morning newspapers,
which are filled with news of terror,
massacre, rape, corruption…
How to end the suffering?

—*Shooting the Sun* (Numit Kappa),
a 2020 play by Nabakumar Nongmeikapam

In the *People of India* series published by the Anthropological Survey of India, Volume XXXI deals with Manipur. In the Foreword, there is an important observation, almost a prophecy of the things to come:

'The centrality of Meitei identity to Manipur is suggested by a number of identity-based movements. The Meitei are engaged in the process of definition of their identity at two levels. First, they have rediscovered and even reconstructed their script. Secondly, while Vaishnavism is still strong, they are re-stressing their pre-Vaishnava identities and reconstructing their older rituals, festivals, etc. In recent years, Manipur has been marked by the rise of a strong identity-based movement of the Meitei.'[8]

Identity movements have flourished in Northeast India, including in Manipur, for decades. There have been clashes and conflicts, too, all of them deadly. I had been witness to these myself and at least two friends of mine have been assassinated in these conflicts. And so, ever since the violence in Manipur began on May 3, 2023, I felt a growing disquiet and fear. Although I was physically in Delhi my mind was in Imphal, trying to make sense of what was happening.

The story of Vungzagin Valte, Tribal Affairs and Hills Minister of Manipur in the 2017–22 Bharatiya Janata Party government, is quite revealing. V. Valte, a Paite, is 61 years old and has been elected to the Manipur assembly thrice, once as a Congress candidate in 2012 and twice as that of the BJP (in 2017, the year he joined the party, and 2022), from the Thanlon constituency in Pherzawl district. He is the seniormost tribal MLA and advisor to the Chief Minister.

On May 4, he was on his way to the residence of the Chief Minister when his car was stopped by a mob. The attack was brutal. They gave him electric shocks and smashed his head with iron rods. They left him almost lifeless, unable to speak, and a cripple. His driver was also attacked brutally and he died. His PSO, or personal security officer, who was supposed to be guarding the MLA, was allowed to leave unharmed.

The MLA and his driver belonged to the Kuki-Zo community while the policeman guarding the MLA was a Meitei.

Valte's family managed to fly him to Delhi and he was admitted to a private hospital. His wife, Moinu Valte was in shock and was admitted to a hospital herself. When she was shifted to the general ward she received a call from the Chief Minister who told her not to worry.

In July, when the Delhi Commission for Women chairperson Swati Maliwal met the MLA, he could speak a little. He said he had gone to the Chief Minister to get an order passed to protect 'my people'. He said his people were not safe; the Chief Minister 'betrayed us', he said.[9]

The MLA's family said in an interview to Rajdeep Sardesai that they received no official financial assistance through the weeks and months they were in Delhi. Sardesai asked Moinu Valte whether the police had arrested anyone. She said 'they know everything' but they have not arrested anyone. The son, Joseph, said the attackers were people wearing black shirts but he did not name the organization they belonged to.

The FIR merely says that the attack was carried out by unknown people.

We do not know yet how many people have died in Manipur. Many bodies lie unclaimed in the morgue. The largest number are of people from the Kuki-Zo tribes but there are also some of the Meiteis. Even these dead bodies became the subject of political controversy.

The Meitei contention is that the bodies of dead Kukis were really those of infiltrators from Myanmar. Retired sessions judge Aribam Noutuneshwari openly accused the central government of deliberately ignoring the attacks by armed Kuki foreigners and militants against the Meiteis. He remarked bitterly that the Centre ought to bury the remains of the slain Kukis and establish Kukiland in Gujarat, Prime Minister Narendra Modi's state, if he and Union Home Minister Amit

Shah had such fondness for that tribal group. Noutuneshwari had a similar suggestion for the Chief Minister of Mizoram.[10]

In Delhi, Solicitor General of India Tushar Mehta submitted before the Supreme Court on August 1 that most of the unclaimed bodies were those of infiltrators who had come to India with a certain agenda.[11] In response, a Delhi-NCR-based women's organization of the Kuki-Hmar-Zomi community of Manipur demanded that the Solicitor General withdraw his remark. The statement of the UNAU Tribal Women's Forum, Delhi-NCR, read: 'Such a loose and unfounded remark from the solicitor general of the country is unbecoming, unacceptable and abhorrent. It is deeply hurtful to the families of the dead who, till today, are unable to perform the last rites of their loved ones.'[12]

But these brutal murders and assaults had not satiated people's hunger for death and destruction. The talented and popular Meitei singer, Jayenta Loukrakpam, known by his stage name Tapta, channelled his creativity into composing and singing a series of songs urging his people to kill Kukis. The first song he posted on the internet on July 7 included the following lyrics: 'Even if peace returns Meiteis will not stop this war; we will not have peace until every Kuki is killed.'

In a telephone conversation with Saptarshi Basak of *The Quint*, Tapta said he was writing from a war zone. He told Basak, 'They [the Kukis] have said that they will kill us. They are still preparing to attack. They started this war, we were living in peace. It was their solidarity march. Who all participated in that, do you know? They burned houses and killed people. In Churachandpur, in Moreh. They have guns; we don't have anything, not even guns. The indigenous Kuki militants plus migrant Kuki terrorists plus the Indian central force, all of them combined are attacking the Meiteis. What have Meiteis done wrong? We have not done anything. Meiteis are only defending [themselves]. They have guns, snipers and sophisticated automatic rifles. What do we have?'

The article was published on July 12, 2023. Authorities seemed not to have taken cognizance of the obvious hate speech in the song. An FIR was filed against Tapta by the Zomi Students' Federation for that controversial song, since the lyrics amounted to an incitement to violence. But that didn't stop the artist, and on November 10, he posted his fifteenth song in what he calls his Kuki Land series.

Looking beyond the horror and brutality, I tried to find some logic in the hate and anger that Tapta and a section of the Meiteis were spewing. Why were they calling the Kuki-Zo tribes 'outsiders' and 'infiltrators'? How could you be at war with your fellow citizens?

Identities Weaponized

According to Binalakshmi Nepram, the founder and director of Manipur Women Gun Survivors Network and Control Arms Foundation of India, co-founder of the Global Alliance of Indigenous Peoples, Gender Justice and Peace and convenor of the Northeast India Women Initiative for Peace, 'identities ha[ve] been weaponized' and Manipur is facing 'an existential threat'. This is what she told Karan Thapar in an interview on June 15, 2023. When Thapar asked her for a response to the demand of the Kuki-Zo for a separate administration, she first asked him to take his question back and then went on to speak emotionally about how Manipur's identity was based on the unity and integrity of the entire state because the Hills and the Valley had been inseparable parts of a whole for centuries.

A few days earlier, on June 6, 2023, Thapar had sat

down with Pramot Singh, the convenor of Meitei Leepun, an organization accused by Kuki groups of inciting violence. It has been said that Meitei Leepun is patronized by Chief Minister N. Biren Singh and has a close link with the Rashtriya Swayamsevak Sangh, BJP's ideological fountainhead.–Pramot Singh had posted on Facebook, on April 28, shortly before the mayhem started in May: 'This is the right time…let's annihilate our traditional rival on the hills and live peacefully'. He asserted in his interview to Thapar, contrary to Nepram, that the Kukis are 'outsiders'. The Kukis 'are not part of the family', he said, adding that they are 'not indigenous to Manipur'. He described them as 'tenants' in Manipur and claimed that 'the majority of Kukis are illegal'. Thapar, however, points out that he did not have any facts to back the claim. He summarizes his interview with Singh thus:[13]

'Pramot Singh explains he "worships" Biren Singh because the Manipur chief minister "understands the Meitei problems with the Kukis and is standing up for Meitei rights". He accepts that the Meitei Leepun is involved in giving gun training to people who have gun licences. Singh says Meitei Leepun has no official connection with the RSS or other Hindutva groups but says that he is personally a member of the ABVP [Akhil Bharatiya Vidyarthi Parishad] and heavily influenced by it. He says Meitei Leepun has no relationship with the Arambai Tenggol—another Meitei organization that is accused of involvement in the violence by the Kukis—and, he adds, when he's tried to meet them they have refused…'

After the admission Pramot Singh made in the interview about gun training by Meitei Leepun, the national Kuki student body, Kuki Students' Organisation, filed a complaint against him. The police, in the FIR they registered, booked Singh under Sections 120B, 153A, 504, 505, 506 and 34 of the Indian Penal Code (IPC)—i.e. for criminal conspiracy, promoting enmity between groups on grounds of religion, race, place of birth, residence, language, etc., act pre-judicial to maintenance of harmony, intentional insult with intent to provoke breach of peace, public mischief and punishment for criminal intimidation.[14]

But what was this Meitei identity which some among that group were out to kill for?

Pan-Mongoloid Movement

For most of India, Manipur is synonymous with Vaishnavism and the Raas Leela, which is recognized as one of the classical dance forms of our country along with Kathak, Bharatnatyam, Odissi, etc. We have all seen the elegant dance, with women wearing their colourful costume, the cylindrical *potloi kumin* skirt beautifully embroidered with mirrors, silver and gold thread and a matching blouse made with velvet. The liquid, graceful movements of dancers in that costume makes them look like celestial beings floating in space. Miniature dolls wearing this stunning costume are eagerly bought by tourists visiting Manipur for the first time.

It was during the reign of King Bhagyachandra (1749–1798) that the first performance of the Manipuri Raas Leela took place at the Shri Shri Govindajee temple at Imphal, the biggest temple in Manipur. The dome of the temple was originally covered by gold leaf and the floor was made of pure marble. These were of course looted by the British and auctioned when they occupied the Kangla Fort in 1891.

Meitei identity movements, however, are based on a clear rejection of the *Hindu* culture and religion, which they say was brought by the Aryans and which was the cause of the alienation of the Meiteis from the people living in the hills.

Meitei nationalism began as a pan-Mongoloid movement against what is referred to in history as the Aryan invasion. In an essay on the 'Politics of Indigenous Theatre' in Manipur, dramaturg and theatre scholar, Rustom Bharucha, has traced the origin of the Meitei identity movement from revival of the pre-Hindu religion to the birth of the militant organization, People's Liberation Army. I quote his succinct summary below:

'The chief proponent of this early movement was [early twentieth-century Meitei religious leader] Naoria Phullo... [who] resuscitated the past by reaffirming the worship of Sanamahee in opposition to the Radha-Krishna cult. He also resisted the imposition of the Bengali script and initiated the revival of the Meithei script, stimulating valuable questions of language that remain unanswered even today.

'In the late 60s and early 70s, Phullo's ideas were radicalized. If the cultural impetus of the revivalist movement involved a conscious rejection of Hindu values...the political goal of the movement was nothing less than the establishment of an "autonomous Meithei State". Along with the Meithei State Committee, there was a burgeoning of many groups of like-minded Meitheis with varying degrees of militancy. Most prominently, there was the United Liberation Front that emerged (or so it is believed) from the Pan-Mongoloid Movement, which attempted to link all peoples of Mongolian descent living in eastern India and the tribal regions surrounding the Burmese border. The Front, in turn, organized the Revolutionary Government of Manipur, advocated the "liberation" of Manipur from "Indian occupation".

'Along with this overtly revolutionary activity, there was a cultural counterpoint provided by the Pan Manipuri Youth League (PANMYL) that was formed as a "non-political organization" in 1969. Ethnic identity provided the foundation for the social programmes of PANMYL, which advocated "Meithei-tribal-ethnic oneness" and cultural solidarity. PANMYL became a force to reckon with through its monthly publication *Lamyanba* (Pioneer) and the English weekly *Resistance*.

'Both are now defunct as the work of defining cultural activity and revolutionary consciousness has been taken over since 1978 by more militant organizations like the People's Liberation Army (PLA).'[15]

I remember attending the first conference of the Naga People's Movement for Human Rights held in Ukhrul in 1985. Activists from all over India had come to it, but the only person invited from the Meitei community was R.K. Thounaojam Tarun Kumar, the Editor of *Resistance*. (The prefix 'RK' generally stands for Rajkumar, and implies association with the royal family.)

Several years later, I made a considerable effort to photocopy all the back issues of *Resistance* from the Manipur state archives. In the pages of the weekly, there was an attempt to construct a history of Manipur which included all the communities and tribes (excluding the 'mayang' which included the Nepalis and Marwaris who had lived in Manipur for at least a century if not more).

However, in the course of my work in the human rights movement (mainly representing Nagas), I found that Naga and Meitei human rights activists seldom, if ever, worked together. For instance, when I was in Manipur in connection with the human rights violations committed against Nagas in Senapati district by the Indian security forces, although many aided the effort in an individual capacity, there was no attempt to co-ordinate between the Meitei-dominated Civil Liberties and Human Rights Organization (CLAHRO) and the Naga People's Movement for Human Rights (NPMHR).

Later, a Zomi human rights organization too was formed. I still remember how, when they first contacted me, they asked me whether I would be willing to take up a case on behalf of the Kukis, since I usually represented the Nagas. I told them I took up cases depending who contacted me![16]

The human rights movement was rooted in identity politics. Today, when the idea of a pan-Mongoloid movement is sought to be resurrected in Manipur, it does not resonate with the tribal peoples of Manipur as it once did at the time when the movement had begun. In part, this is because of the rise of armed insurgent groups, each purporting to represent their own separate identity.

The armed resistance to the Indian state is thus divided along ethnic lines. But often these armed groups co-operate with each other in the jungles of Myanmar or Bangladesh.

The Meitei Identity

On September 25, 1978, Nameirakpam Bisheswar Singh, trained in guerrilla warfare in China, formed the People's Liberation Army to work for the independence of Manipur through armed struggle. The original aim was to organize a revolutionary front covering the entire Northeast which could unite all ethnic groups, including the Meiteis, Nagas and Kukis. According to the South Asia Terrorism Portal, the 'PLA, though a Meitei outfit, claims itself to be a trans-tribal organization seeking to lead the non-Meiteis as well'. The SATP also says that 'PLA recruits were trained in guerrilla warfare by the then united National Socialist Council of Nagaland (NSCN) at its headquarters in Challam, beyond the Somrah Tract, in north Myanmar during the eighties'.[17]

The organization was later banned and Bisheswar arrested. The latter penned his thoughts on Meitei identity in a pamphlet titled *The Last Expression On My Death Bed* (Imphal: Pax Publications, 1986). His views represent the kind of reasoning that has led to the Meiteis demanding Scheduled Tribe status. Here's an excerpt from the pamphlet, written in English, which I reproduce exactly as it was published:

The Meiteis are Vaishnavite Hindus since the Meitei King, Pamheiba, in Meitei name but Garibniwas in Hindu name. In fact, they are a Hindu from hand to foot. Not only in religion but in culture, the Meitei since then becomes a full Hindu, indeed a staunch and devoted Hindu. They even believe [*sic*] that theirs is a real home of the Hindus, themselves being a real and pure Hindu for which reason they feel proud, and claim that they are not Meitei by caste but a Hindu by caste. To them there is nothing left for their being a Hindu.

Why, then do the younger generations of the Meiteis discard Hinduism. No, they do not discard it. Our younger generations advocate the cult of Meitei-ism (Meitei religion). They speak of cultural imperialism of Hinduism which is indeed a foreign object to them. They have branded Hinduism as Mayangism. They call Hindu religion a Mayang religion. They consider the Hindu way of life as a Mayang way of life, Hindu culture as Mayang culture. They allege that the role of Hinduism has reduced them to a slave of the Mayangs. They cannot feel they are Indians at the bottom of their hearts. Instead, they feel that they are being colonised. And, the way to their colonisation, according to their apprehension, is nothing but Hinduism. That is why Hinduism becomes to-day the target for them. Even the Hindu God and Goddesses are Mayangs in the eye of them. Even Hindu deities are their enemies.

In short, to them everything Mayang (Indian) is an enemy, to speak the truth. They always call the Hindu Meiteis the voice of Mayangs or Indians. They drop their Indian names in favour of their ancient Meitei names.

Bishweswar does not sound very coherent. But this incoherence also reflects the incoherence of identity politics, which is a mixture of race and religion, and mixed and ill-informed facts. He complains that the conversion of Meiteis to Vaishnavism (Hinduism) meant that they had integrated with the mainstream Indians who are Hindus. He is unaware of the many movements of Hindus against the Indian state. He goes on to say that the Meitei youth were rejecting everything Hindu.

Further on, he speaks of his real grievance: that Meiteis were a minority twice over—a Hindu minority in the midst of Christians in the Northeast and a non-tribal minority among the tribals. And then he proposes a solution whereby Meiteis could consider being a part of the Indian Union to save the Meitei identity from being submerged in the Indian/Hindu/ mayang identity:

> The Meeteis can be saved either by joining the mainstream of their tribal brothers in the North-East by reducing to and declaring themselves to be tribals or by deliberately granting them, for their being Hindu Minority a special status in the Indian Constitution as Muslim minority in Kasmir [*sic*], or by upgrading the tribals to the stage of non tribals with the closure of the Indian dividing policy to rule the North-East in the form of a colony.

Obviously, Bishweswar was ill-informed about the status of the Muslims in Kashmir. However, what is disturbing is that he does not acknowledge anywhere the discrimination against the tribal people within Manipur and how Meitei domination was resented by them. Also, even if Meiteis did return to their old religion, the tribals were not giving up theirs, Christianity. Nor were the Meitei Christians and Meitei Muslims going back to Sanamahism.

The Meiteis are in fact not a homogeneous group. For instance, there are the Loi, a distinct group among the Meitei who worship the god Koubru, said to reside in Mount Koubru in Kangpokpi district. They have traditionally made their living through occupations such as distillation of liquor, rearing of pigs, silkworms and pottery-making. They are included in the list of Scheduled Castes.

Within the broad community of Meiteis are included the Meitei Muslims as well as the Meiteis who did not convert to Hinduism, who assert their pre-Hindu identity and follow their ancient Sanamahi religion. According to the 2011 Census, while 83.38 per cent of Meiteis practise Vaishnavism, around 16 per cent follow the traditional Sanamahi religion. Roughly 8 per cent are Muslims; Christians within the Meitei community form a little over 1 per cent.

Kangleipak

Before Manipur joined the Indian Union, it was a kingdom. There is some debate around the origin of the word 'Meitei' but it is accepted that to begin with the Meiteis were divided into seven clans, each ruling a part of the Valley. Then the Ningthouja clan emerged as the most powerful in the first century AD and unified the other clans, establishing a kingdom with Kangla as its capital.

The Meiteis have their chronicles, which record the history of the kings from ancient times to the present. The most famous chronicle is the *Cheitharol Kumbaba*, which tells the story of seventy-eight kings, beginning with the first Meitei king, Nongda Lairen Pakhangba, who is believed to have ascended the throne in AD 33. Historically, the kingdom was called Kangleipak, which means, literally, 'dry land'.

The British defeated the Kingdom of Manipur on April 27, 1891, a day which the Meiteis commemorate as the Dark Day. It was the day that the British flag was hoisted in Kangla Fort.

While its days as an independent kingdom were over, the King continued to rule the princely state under the British Raj till 1949, when Manipur joined the Indian Union. According to the Meitei militants, this accession was illegal and the King was forced to sign the accession agreement.

The symbol of the ancient Kingdom of Kangleipak is of course the Kangla Fort situated right in the middle of Imphal. Kangla is thus the most important historical and spiritual site of Meitei culture and civilization. There were once as many as 360 sacred places within the fort: places for worship of the ancient gods.

Sanamahism is a well-developed religion with its own gods and goddesses, priests and priestesses, rites and rituals. It has extensive scriptures written in sacred books called *puyas*. The script used in them is also an ancient one called Meitei Mayek, which has eighteen alphabets, each representing a part of the body. This religion is still alive in Manipur.

When I first went to Imphal, the signboards were in the Bengali script, introduced by Hindu missionaries after the King converted to Vaishnavism in the eighteenth century.

The Meitei had a long language movement, like many other groups in the country, which ended with the recognition of the Meitei language (under the name 'Manipuri') by the Indian Union. It was included in the list of official languages—the

Eighth Schedule—by the 71st Amendment to the Constitution in 1992.

There was also the affiliate demand for the Bengali script to be replaced with the ancient Meitei Mayek. By the late 1990s, the signboards were in the old script. In 2006, the script was introduced in the schools and it is replacing the Bengali script even at the college level now. Newspapers too decided, in December 2022, to switch to the old script early in the following year. The 'seven vernacular morning newspapers, nine evening papers and four periodicals will have to exclusively use Meetei Mayek or Manipuri script, replacing the Bengali script which has been in use in this tiny hill State since the early parts of the 18th century', *The Hindu* reported. 'The All Manipur Working Journalists Union and the Editors Guild, Manipur came to an understanding with the script activists of the Meetei Erol Eyek Loinasilol Apunba Lup (MEELAL) a year ago, agreeing to replace the Bengali script in their newspapers from January 15, 2023, an extension from the previous deadline in February 2022'.[18] The violence in Manipur, however, led to a further extension of the deadline.

Lai Haraoba

While Manipur's Raas Leela is justly famous, Lai Haraoba is less so. The latter is a religious festival of ritual dance and music, which is much more sombre than that of the Raas Leela and has its roots in ancient Meitei culture. It is performed by Sanamahi priestesses and priests, who are called *maibis* and *maibas*, respectively. Lai Haraoba means 'merry making of the gods' in Meiteilon, i.e. the Manipuri language. This festival celebrates the contribution of the gods or spirits in creating the universe including plants, animals and human beings.

The Lai Haraoba goes on for ten days, with the songs sung to the accompaniment of the *pena*, a bowed, mono-stringed lute. *Numit Kappa* is among the hymns that are sung during the festival.

I have stayed up all night watching the maibis perform this slow, ritual dance which depicts the cycle of life. One can genuinely feel transported to a primeval world listening to the ancient songs and the haunting music even if one does not fully understand the language. At one moment they'll play music that sounds like the mad torrent of a hill stream striking the boulders along its banks, and then at another, they will appear to imitate, through dance, light-footed goats jumping about on rocky hill slopes. Maibis mimic the sound of spinning and weaving, depicting Creation itself as the same act performed on a magnificently grand scale. According to their belief, it was Leismbi, the God of Handicrafts, who taught the Meiteis how to weave.

Conversion to Hinduism

The first Meitei king to convert to Hinduism was Charairongba (1697–1709), around 1707, by a Gaudiya Vaishnava guru from Bengal, Gopal Das. But it was during the reign of his son, Pamheiba, popularly known by the title given by the Muslims, Garibniwaz (1709–1748), that the ancient Meitei culture was sought to be suppressed and even destroyed under the influence of Shanta Das Goswami, the missionary who followed Gopal Das.

The old chronicle, *Cheitharol Kumbaba*, records the opposition to conversion to Hinduism:

> Oh King! How can we discard our own so very ancient language and tradition? And how can we adopt an alien

tongue and faith? This way, all our own language, tradition, culture and religion will soon vanish; and in its place an alien counterpart will take over and submerge the entire Manipur firmament into permanent gloom. All your subjects are against it because ultimately the monarchy will suffer too great a humiliation. Please reconsider it.[19]

Shanta Das encouraged the King to be more aggressive, who 'became much more spirited and endowed with greater valour, prowess and inspiration…[realized] his aggrandizement policy and wartime pursuits to achieve Greater Manipur'. He was more influenced by Lord Rama than the Bhakti-inspired worship of Krishna, notes Professor Sairem Nilbir, noted scholar and author of many books on Manipuri culture.[20]

With the zeal of the newly converted, the King prohibited the eating of beef, pork and chicken. He imposed the Bengali script, and even destroyed the temples of the ancient religion, not sparing even the image of Lainingthou Sanamahi himself, the supreme god in the Sanamahi faith. Hindu rituals such as cremation were introduced and Brahmans came to be accorded both patronage and prestige.

The Meiteis still remember and commemorate every year the day the King committed the most egregious outrage against their ancient culture by burning the sacred puyas, or scriptures—October 17, 1732, though some historians claim that this happened on January 23, 1729. They call it the Puya Mei Thaba Commemoration Day.

It was during Garibniwaz's reign that the name of the kingdom was changed to Manipur. One book, published in 1965, identified it with the 'Manipur' mentioned in the *Mahabharata.* It went so far as to contend that this was the kingdom ruled by Babruvahana, the son of the Pandava prince Arjun and Chitrangada.

In the very first chapter of his *A Short History of Manipur*, Jhaljit Singh writes that Manipur has always been a part of India and that the 'first reference to Manipur is [in the] Adi Parva on the occasion of Arjuna going from Hiranyavindu to see the eastern region. After seeing the Mahendra mountains, he proceeded slowly along the coast, reached Manipur and married Chitrangada, the princess of that Kingdom. She was of the complexion of a madhuka flower, i.e. mahua flower. A mahua flower is of golden colour. Chitrangada was of golden complexion. This suggests that she might be of Mongoloid descent'.[21]

The author, Rajkumar Jhaljit Singh (1924–2021), a member of the royal family, was among the early journalists of Manipur, and editor of one of the oldest local newspapers, *Anouba Matam*. He wrote several books on various aspects of Manipuri literature, poetry and culture. He was also awarded a Padma Shri for his contributions to these fields. But his history of Manipur caused so much controversy that his family members themselves withdrew the book from circulation.

Influence of Wars

Meitei identity has been deeply influenced by the wars between Manipur and Burma. As one book on Manipur states: 'In retrospect, the Manipuri-Burmese relation had been found to be belligerent for nearly five centuries and a half, since the 13th century. Both the countries have evolved their own versions of history. Manipuri victory over Burma has [an] important place in Manipuri history...'[22]

The Meiteis have well-developed martial arts such as the Thang Ta (*thang* means sword and *ta* is a spear), and Sarit Sarak, unarmed combat. The British banned these martial arts after the Anglo-Manipur War of 1891, but the Meiteis continued to practise them secretly. The popularity of these ancient martial art forms has been increasing in recent years. One can easily find videos on YouTube of children performing Thang Ta at the Chainarol Sindamshang Temple, learning under a well-known guru in Manipur.

It was with the experience of war that the Meiteis developed their famous Manipur pony, which emerged from cross-breeding the Arabian horse with the Mongolian horse. This pony is the star of the famous Sagol Kangjei, or Manipuri polo, invented according to legend by Marjing, the God of War, who is also the God of horses, polo and sports. A 120-feet-tall statue of a polo player riding a pony at Marjing Polo Complex in the Imphal East district was unveiled by the Union Home Minister on January 6, 2023.

This equestrian animal is celebrated by the Meiteis, for it was riding the Manipuri pony that their cavalries defeated the Burmese, with the help, of course, of their unique weapon, the *arambai.* Here is a description of the use of this weapon by Colonel James Johnstone, political agent to the Manipur Kingdom appointed by the British government in 1877:

> The cavalry used the regular Manipuri saddle protecting the legs, and were armed with spears and two quivers of darts. These darts in a retreat were grasped by a loop and swung round in a peculiar way, when the shaft formed of peacock feathers with an iron head suddenly became detached, and flying with great force inflicted a fatal wound wherever it struck. A skilful man could throw them with great precision.[23]

The All Manipur Arambai Association, established in the year 2005, has been regularly showcasing the art of arambai during the Manipur Tourism Festival, renamed in 2010 the Sangai Festival.

The field of battle has great significance in Meitei culture; the kingdom has been at war over many centuries. The early section of *The Chainarol* (The Way of the Warrior), an ancient Meitei puya, is believed to have been composed as early as the first century AD, not long after the ascension of the Ningthouja dynasty.

This sacred text has recently been translated into English and contains the following verse:

> Haya He He He Leeklai O!
> Yeepungthou Nongthourel Pumapa O!
> O All Pervasive Spirit Primordial,
> Thou Lord of all, and Progenitor Sole!
> Of times olden when thy noble vassals
> Matchless in might and dauntless in battles,
> In games of war grim well they were adept
> Safe the borders of their homeland they kept.[24]

The tribal people living in the Hills do not share this history, culture or religion. A revealing incident took place on my first visit to Manipur in 1982. I was a part of the first women's fact-finding team which went there to study the impact of the Armed Forces (Special Powers) Act. Our delegation was led by Pramila Dandavate, the prominent member of parliament.

We took a flight from Delhi to Imphal and drove straight to Ukhrul, the then headquarters of the East district which was soon after renamed Ukhrul (the headquarters of the district is Ukhrul town). On arrival, and in her first speech in Ukhrul, the home of the Tangkhul Nagas, Dandavate said she was happy to be in the home of Arjun and Chitrangada.

Our Tangkhul Naga translator looked puzzled. He had no idea who the two people she was referring to were, but not wanting to embarrass the visitors, or offend them, he translated it, finding 'Chitrangada' a tongue twister.

The Nagas certainly do not trace their origins to the *Mahabharata*; nor do the other tribal communities living in the hills of Manipur.

However, the Meiteis argue that it was because of their conversion to Hinduism that a division between the Hills and Valley came about. With the conversion came the caste system, the idea of ritual purity and pollution, and the tribals became the 'untouchables'.

The tribals, when they go to buy daily provisions at a shop owned by a Meitei, are expected to stick their hands out so the shopkeeper can drop the change without having to touch them. My husband, a Tangkhul Naga from Manipur, recounted a similar experience with the vegetable seller from his time as a little boy growing up in Imphal. Mischievous as little boys often are, he would touch her hand, leaving her to shout after him, '*Mange, mange.*' Mange means unclean, or ritually polluted. She had been polluted and had to purify herself by bathing!

Meitei nationalists cite this as the reason they wish to discard their Hinduism or Vaishnavism and embrace their older religion which has no notion of purity and pollution and which regards people living in the Hills and the Valley as equal.

The Debate Over the Merger Agreement

The princely state of Manipur ceded to the Indian Union by the Merger Agreement signed on September 21, 1949, in Shillong by the Governor-General of India and the Maharaja of Manipur. What comprised the territory of the state, however, is hotly debated. Meitei nationalists maintain that the Kangleipak

Kingdom included the people of the Hills. The tribal people, on the other hand, assert that it was confined to the Valley. Given the centrality of this question to the relationship between the people of the Hills and those living in the Valley, it is no wonder that it is also among the most contentious.

In November 2022, a history of Manipur written by an officer of the Central Reserve Police Force, late Brigadier Sushil Kumar Sharma, was banned. The book, based on Brig Sharma's PhD thesis, is titled *The Complexity Called Manipur: Roots, Perceptions and Reality*. The Manipur government had objected to the book because, according to them, it contained 'grossly misleading and scandalous' content.

An order issued by the Principal Secretary (Home) specifically pointed to a claim made in the chapter 'Merger of Manipur with the Indian Union': 'The total area which the Manipur merger agreement covered was this territory of 700 square miles or 26,500 Paris/hectares. Not even a single inch of hill areas was covered under this agreement'. This implied that the areas inhabited by Naga, Kuki and other tribes had not been part of the agreement. The order stated that the history of the 'Merger Agreement' was a very sensitive and emotional topic for the people of the state, and therefore that the facts presented may amount to a breach of peace and public tranquillity and maintenance of harmony between various communities residing in the state, thus making it a threat to national security and integrity.[25]

History does record that the boundary of the Manipur Kingdom, for short intervals, extended from the Barak river (now in Assam) to Chindwin (now in Myanmar). Under weaker rulers, the Kingdom got restricted to just the Valley. But in this debate over the boundary of an ancient kingdom, what is not taken into account is that the pre-modern and modern ways of demarcating political units are very different. In the past there was no notion of precisely determined borders and absolute sovereignty of a kingdom over a piece of land.[26]

In 2000, a pamphlet titled 'Territorial Rights of Outer Manipur Tribals', brought out by the All Tribal Students' Union of Manipur (ATSUM) had made a similar case. Under the heading 'The Chiefs are Lords of the Soil', the pamphlet states:

> [The tribal chiefs] were lords of the soil within the territory they occupied, ruled and governed. They collected taxes and levies from their subjects independently. So, the Merger agreement signed by the Manipuri Maharaja could not and did not cover the territory occupied by the tribal Chiefs and their subjects, because the Maharaja of Manipur was not a tribal representative who had authority to act on their behalf, and the tribals were not his subjects.

This view seems to be corroborated by historians writing about the relationship between the Hills and Valley. An essay titled 'Economic History of Manipur During the British Raj' by H.D. Sharma and A.B. Sharma, editors of a well-known compendium on the history of Manipur, notes:

> Under both the native systems and the British innovation, the hills were controlled from the plains only from the geographical point of view. Before the coming of the British, the Meitei kings ruling from the valley failed to evolve a lasting systematic set up of hill administration. They failed to put the Hill tribes under their administrative subservience permanently. Particularly, before 1824 the relations between the Raja and the remote hill tribes were confined to collection of tributes and reprisals for raid[s] and aggression by the tribes. Till then the tribal communities in the hills were... [merely a] 'source of profit' and until 1891 as much tribute

as possible [was] extracted from the hills while not a single rupee spent for their benefit. Even after 1891 there was no proper administration of the hill tribes and no adequate provision made for them in the budget. The expenditure on them was only a quarter of the amount they paid in taxes.[27]

The Manipur government set up a fifteen-member committee on September 16, 2022—for verifying the accuracy of books on the history, culture, tradition and geography of the state— to control the debate on just such matters that are deemed controversial. Authors writing on these subjects are now required to submit their manuscripts to the Director of Higher Education and the University of Manipur for verification and approval.

Meitei Demand for Scheduled Tribe Status

In a way, the violence in Manipur started over the Meitei demand to be recognized as a Scheduled Tribe, a demand strongly opposed by the tribals of Manipur. This may seem like a fairly uncomplicated issue, but it has become so controversial and volatile that the Office of the Registrar-General of India (RGI) declined to make public its position on whether the Meitei community in Manipur could be categorized as a Scheduled Tribe as per the criteria currently in use. The office of the RGI said that disclosing this information would 'prejudicially affect the sovereignty and integrity of India, the security, strategic, scientific or economic interests of the state, relation with foreign state or lead to incitement of an offence'.[28]

The Meiteis have been demanding to be included in the list of Scheduled Tribes for a long time, from 1981,[29] in fact. One report, discussed below, claims that this demand has been considered and rejected twice since 1982, although this claim, like so many others about Manipur's history, is debated. The Scheduled Tribe Demand Committee of Manipur Valley (STDCMV), the foremost organization leading this agitation today, was formed in January 2012. In November of that year, representatives of the Committee met Governor Gurbachan Jagat and put forward their demand once again. According to contemporary accounts, the Governor assured them of assistance towards the realization of the demand. 'Since Meetei/Meiteis, with Mongoloid physical features, are the foremost settlers of Manipur and sections of them practis[e] animism though some are absorbed in Hinduism, there is no reason that the community should not be included in the ST list of the Constitution,' they argued.[30]

Meitei identity movements had the effect of counter mobilization by the tribals, who felt threatened by the dominant community's actions. As far back as 2010, Sekholal Kom, an assistant professor of political science at Moreh College, Manipur, wrote on this mobilization and counter-mobilization: '[T]he Meitei identity mobilization in the process seems to have excluded other communities from the Hills... The result has been cycles of mobilization and counter-mobilization, which eventually turn into conflictual politics posing serious deterrence to governance. Of late, the growing identity mobilization of the Meiteis [has induced] fear in the minds of the minority tribals who are numerically insignificant and politically less dominant. In short, much of the politics centres on the question of preserving one's own identity.'[31]

From the start, the tribal people in Manipur, led by the ATSUM, opposed the demand on the ground that inclusion of the Meiteis into the list of Scheduled Tribes would only result in greater Meitei dominance, both political and economic. To begin with, the tribals demanded greater autonomy under the

Sixth Schedule of the Indian Constitution, which pertains to the administration of tribal areas in the Northeast. The Centre was inclined to accept the demand but the state government scuttled it. In a letter to the then Chief Minister Okram Ibobi Singh, Deputy Prime Minister L.K. Advani wrote on April 7, 2003:

> The Government of India has been receiving representations for extension of the provision of the Sixth Schedule constituted under the Manipur Hill Areas (District Councils) Act, 1971. These Councils are functioning in Chandel, Churachandpur, Sadar Hills, Senapati, Tamenglong and Ukhrul districts of Manipur.
>
> Government of Manipur has recommended to the Home Affairs on 7.4.2001 that the state Government had no objection to the extension of Sixth Schedule provisions in the Hill Areas of Manipur with 'certain local adjustments and amendments'. The Ministry had sought details from the State Government regarding local adjustments and amendments to be made. The State Govt had reported in April 2002 that the matter was [under] active consideration of the State Cabinet and the Manipur Hill Areas Committee of the Manipur Legislative Assembly. However, the details of the local adjustments and amendments to be made, while conferring Sixth Schedule status to the Councils, are yet to be received from the state government.

Tribal alienation from the Meitei-dominated governance only grew after that, and by 2003, the ATSUM had put forward the demand that the tribal areas of Manipur be declared a Union territory. The demand was made in a memorandum submitted to the chairman of the National Commission for Scheduled Castes and Scheduled Tribes vide Memo PSD/ATSUM/98-1 dated April 28, 2003. The memorandum is a testament to the anguish and anger of the tribals of Manipur:

> No human expression could cover the misery, plight, hardship and sufferings of the tribals under the maladministration of Manipur State. The Manipur people (Valley people) are very much advanced and developed [compared to] the tribal people. Taking undue advantage [of] it they constantly... deceive, misguide and harass innocent tribals under various forms for their [benefit] and interests.

In June 2022, the tribals reacted sharply against Chief Minister Biren Singh for allegedly saying that 'land belongs to Mother Nature and not to any particular community'.[32] The tribal organizations asserted that land is the identity for tribal communities and that they had a sacred connection with it.

The Scheduled Tribe Demand Committee of Manipur (STDCM)—the 'Valley' was dropped from the name of the Committee in September 2013[33]—has persisted with their campaign. They argue that before the merger agreement with the Indian Union in 1949, the British had designated the Meiteis as a 'tribe amongst tribes'. According to them, they were merely asking for a restoration of that status.

The tribals, on the other hand, argue that it was the Meiteis themselves who had refused to be included in the list of Scheduled Tribes post-Independence since they considered themselves superior to the tribals. However, the Meiteis point out that only some Hindu Meiteis refused ST status and that those practising the Sanamahi religion were not asked. This view is reflected in an article by L.B. Singh, a retired captain of the Indian Navy and frequent contributor to news websites on this subject, in *The Sangai Express*:

'The Meithei (Meetei/Meitei) was classified as a "Hill Tribe" in the census conducted by the British from 1891 to 1931. However, the Meiteis were excluded from the list of STs promulgated on 20 September 1951, but the Nagas and the Kukis were included. The reason for the exclusion was based on the statement of a few prominent citizens of Manipur, who highlighted only the ceremonials and rituals related to Hinduism but failed to bring out the ceremonials and rituals related to the indigenous worship of Sanamahi, Leimarel Sidabi, Umang Lai (Forest Gods), etc.'[34]

In 2015, the Manipur government introduced three bills: the Manipur Land Revenue and Land Reforms (Seventh) Amendment Bill, 2015; the Protection of Manipur People Bill, 2015; and the Manipur Shops and Establishments Act (Second) Amendment Bill, 2015. The Bills ostensibly aimed to protect the rights of 'indigenous' people, by defining who 'Manipur people' were. They sought to restrict who could buy land in the state and the people an employer within the state could employ. These pieces of legislation came after a long-standing demand of the non-tribal Meiteis in the Imphal Valley for introducing an Inner-Line Permit[35] system—whereby only Indian citizens are allowed entry into a protected area, for a limited period, and only with an official travel document issued by a competent authority—which they felt was necessary to regulate the entry of 'non-Manipuris' into the state. The tribals had not participated in this agitation, though they were not expressly opposed to it.

The then Congress government claimed that the three Bills—which were all passed in the course of a single day—were drawn up after a thorough consultation with all MLAs, including tribal representatives. Not only did the tribal groups in Manipur deny the government's claim, they jointly opposed the Bills and demanded their withdrawal. They argued that if the Meiteis were recognized as 'indigenous' people under the Bills, it would amount to giving them ST status. They felt that the Bills would only strengthen Meitei economic and political dominance and control in Manipur, and also that they would lead to encroachment of tribal areas by non-tribals, mainly the Meiteis. They insisted, moreover, that the Hills were not even receiving their just share of development funds, including funds for tribal welfare, which were diverted to the Valley.

In the protests against the Bills, nine people from Kuki-Zo communities, including an 11-year-old boy, died. The Kukis in Churachandpur refused to bury their dead for 632 days.

President Pranab Mukherjee denied his assent to the Bills and asked the state legislature to reconsider them.

A new government came to power in Manipur in 2017 led by the BJP. The chief minister, N. Biren Singh, made it clear that his government would not support the passage of Citizenship (Amendment) Bill, 2016—a key agenda of the Narendra Modi government—unless there was a provision for protecting the indigenous people of the Northeast. Singh also stressed that his government would want the President's assent to Manipur People's (Protection) Bill, 2018, which his government had introduced.

Finally, the central government conceded that the changes to India's citizenship law would not be applicable to regions in the Northeast protected by the Inner-Line Permit and Sixth Schedule provisions. (The ILP was extended to Manipur vide a Presidential order No. SO 4433(E) dated December 11, 2019, and came to effect on January 1, 2020.)

*

To be clear, the controversy over who should or should not be included in the list of Scheduled Tribes is part of a wider national and political issue. The Narendra Modi-led government at the Centre has been trying to change the criterion for the inclusion of a community in the list of Scheduled Tribes ever since it came to power in 2014.

The Constitution does not define the criteria for recognition as a Scheduled Tribe and hence it was the definition contained in the 1931 Census which was used in the initial years after Independence. As per that census, Schedule Tribes are termed as 'backward tribes' living in the 'Excluded' and 'Partially Excluded' areas. The first time provision was made for the representation of the 'backward tribes' in provincial assemblies was in 1935 through the Government of India Act.

In 1965, an Advisory Committee on the Revision of the Lists of Scheduled Castes and Scheduled Tribes was constituted, chaired by B.N. Lokur, at the time law secretary to the central government. The Lokur Committee's five criteria for recognition of a community under the ST list are indications of primitive traits, a distinctive culture, geographical isolation, shyness of contact with the community at large and backwardness.

The criteria were described by an internal government task force formed in February 2014 as being 'obsolete', 'condescending', 'dogmatic' and 'rigid'. The task force, led by then Tribal Affairs Secretary Hrusikesh Panda also said that the procedure being followed was 'cumbersome' and 'defeat[ed] the Constitutional agenda for affirmative action and inclusion'. It concluded that these criteria and procedure were resulting in the exclusion of or delays in the inclusion of nearly forty communities across the country.

The first Modi-led government, within days of taking charge in 2014, moved a draft note to change the procedure and the criteria, based on the report of the task force.[36] However, little action seems to have been taken at the time, and since then, Arjun Munda, tribal affairs minister in the second Modi-led government, has insisted in parliament that the criteria set out by the Lokur Committee were appropriate and that tribal societies do not change.[37]

Yet it is feared that the government may try to exclude Christians from the Scheduled Tribe category. This has a direct bearing on the tribals in Manipur who are largely Christian. In December 2021, the central board of trustees of the Vishwa Hindu Parishad (VHP) passed a resolution demanding that the central government make necessary amendments to the Constitution to 'exclude tribals who converted to other religions' from the list of tribes. Alok Kumar, working president of the VHP, said in a statement: 'According to the Constitution of India, people who convert to Christianity and Islam should not be eligible to get reservation and other benefits given to the Scheduled Tribes. But, even after getting converted, they are availing both types of benefits.'[38] In February 2023, *The Meghalayan* reported that another RSS-backed organization, Janajati Dharma-Sanskriti Suraksha Manch (JDSSM), had demanded the withdrawal of Christians from the ST list.[39]

Indigenous People

The Manipur government had been dragging its feet on the inclusion of the Meitei community in the ST list for ten years. Then, in March 2023, the single judge bench of the Manipur High Court directed the government to consider the request of the community's inclusion within four weeks, and to send a recommendation to the Union government for its consideration. The directive of the High Court came after hearing a petition filed by the Meetei (Meitei) Tribe Union (MTU), asking for restoration of their status as tribals, which they said they had lost after the Merger Agreement. It is interesting that it was not the STDCM which had gone to court but the newly formed MTU.

The Meiteis maintain that they needed constitutional safeguards if they are to be prevented from becoming a minority. Given the influx of migrants, which the People's Protection Bill, 2018 was brought in to check, they argue, they face possible extinction. What is more, they feel that the lack of ST status deprives them from buying land in the Hill areas and confines them to the relatively small area of the Valley. Non-tribal communities, including the Meiteis, are prevented from buying land in tribal areas, through Section 158 of Manipur Land Revenue and Land Reforms Act, 1960 under Article 371C of Indian Constitution.[40]

We may note that, while the Scheduled Tribes are entitled to various welfare schemes and have reservations in jobs and educational institutions, Meiteis already have job reservations under the SC (Scheduled Caste), OBC (Other Backward Classes), and EBC (Economically Backward Classes) categories.

The Scheduled Tribes Demand Committee, however, was at pains to emphasize that their demand was 'not about reservation in jobs, educational institutions and tax relief and is more about protecting the ancestral lands, culture and identity of the Meitei people threatened consistently by illegal immigrants from Myanmar and outside the state'.

The High Court order of March 27, 2023, became public soon after and the ATSUM announced that it would organize protest rallies in all the hill districts of Manipur against the demand. This was the Tribal Solidarity March of May 3, 2023. It was a peaceful rally, not very different from previous protests by the organization on this issue.

The High Court had directed the state government to submit its recommendations to the central tribal affairs ministry. Obviously, the High Court has no power to confer ST status on a community; that decision has to ultimately be taken by the Union ministry, acting on the recommendations of the state, and requires the approval of the Registrar General of India and the National Commission for Scheduled Tribes. It is only then, when the Union cabinet is satisfied with the merit of a particular case, that a bill is introduced in the parliament and the process initiated to amend the Constitution.

The tribal student leaders were well aware of this, that the court order would not immediately lead to the Meiteis being included in the ST category. The ATSUM could not have imagined that at the end of their peaceful protests there would be such an eruption of violence.

*

On October 14, 2023, *The Hindu* made a shocking revelation, six months into the case being heard in the Manipur High Court. It reported that a 'proposal on the inclusion of the Meitei community in the Scheduled Tribes list has been examined and rejected twice over the last four decades, according to the documents seen by *The Hindu*: once, in 1982, by the Office of the Registrar General of India; and again, in 2001, by the Government of Manipur. The Union and Manipur Governments have not made this information public during the ongoing ethnic conflict in the State, nor presented these records in the Manipur High Court case on the Meitei petition for inclusion'. Immediately, the report in *The Hindu* was challenged by three Meitei researchers.[41]

The documents had been accessed under the Right to Information Act, 2005. The records showed:

> ...that the Office of RGI had looked into the Meiteis' inclusion in the ST list on a request from the Ministry of Home Affairs in 1982. [The RGI] found that, based

on 'available information', the Meitei community 'does not appear to possess tribal characteristics', and said it was not in favour of inclusion. It noted that historically, the term had been used to describe the 'non tribal population in the Manipur Valley'.

Almost twenty years later, when the erstwhile Ministry of Social Justice was revising the SC/ST list of States and Union Territories, it had sought recommendations from the Manipur Government. In response, the tribal development department of Manipur on January 3, 2001, told the Centre that it agreed with the 1982 opinion of the Office of the RGI on the status of Meiteis.

The Manipur Government, then headed by Chief Minister W. Nipamacha Singh, had said that the Meitei community was the 'dominant group in Manipur' and need not be included in the ST list. It noted that Meitei people were Hindus and 'assumed the status of Kshatriya caste in the ladder of Hindu Castes', adding that they had already been listed as other Backward Classes.

The controversy continued on the pages of the local press. On the streets, the violence did.

CHAPTER THREE

I Realize How Much You Hate Me

'Who am I? I am a Zo/Kuki if I go by my indigenous identity. I am an Indian, if I go by my nationality, and I am a Manipuri if I go by domicile. This is the only state I have known: this has been home always.'
—'Today, I realize how much you hate me',
an op-ed article on *EastMojo* from May 4, 2023,
by Sangmuan Hangsing, a Kuki

I got to make haste
I got no time to waste
I had left home in a hurry

Now I got to return quickly
My home might disappear before I reach there
My wife, my children—my family might disappear
My whole village might disappear,
…become just like an unclaimed, incinerated corpse
—'Matam Leite' by Laishram Samarendra (1925–2016)

From the first day of the violence in Manipur, churches were a prime target of the mobs, many of them led by the Arambai Tenggol, the militant Meitei organization. Many reporters, especially outside Manipur, thus described the violence as a communal clash between the Hindu Meiteis and the Christian Kuki-Zo. However, the first attacks were on Meitei churches and the Meitei Christian community living in Churachandpur, the Kuki-Zo-dominated hill district; and Meitei churches in the Valley were attacked by Arambai Tenggol.

Further, the attack on Kuki-Zo churches led by Arambai Tenggol cannot be described as attacks by Hindu Meiteis since the organization has rejected the Hindu identity and in fact aims to revive the Sanamahi religion.

Churches had never before been attacked on this scale during past conflicts.[42] But then, past conflicts had involved Nagas and Kukis, both of whom were Christian; or the Thadou Kuki and Paite communities, which too are Christians.[43] This was the first time there was violence which involved Meiteis, who were either Hindus or Sanamahi, and the Kuki-Zo. The Naga churches were left standing since they were not party to this violence.

On May 3 and 4, for example, a church was destroyed in Imphal's Sangaiprou. The St Paul's Parish Church caters to a parish which includes people of all ethnic communities of Manipur—Meiteis, Kabui, Tangkhul, Paite, among others. The violence witnessed at this church started on May 3, at around 8.30 pm, when the church was attacked by a mob which began smashing and destroying the church and everything inside it. It was burnt to ashes in the intervening period of May 3 and 4.

Then the mob also attacked the Pastoral Training Centre, a regional training centre which conducts a two-year diploma course for lay catechists, which was located in the same campus as the church. The centre had forty-six inmates (four priests and thirty-seven trainees, among other staff). The mob forced its way into the premises and sought the identity of the inmates. Those in charge tried to reason with the mob, explaining to them that there were no Kukis among them. But the mob would not be satisfied without visiting each room. Not finding anyone from the Kuki-Zo community there, they set the building on fire anyway.[44]

In a petition filed before the Supreme Court (WP [Civil] 540 of 2023) on June 3, 2023, Manipur Tribal Forum, Delhi, a recently formed body of tribal activists, claimed that there were videos showing the Arambai Tenggol leading the mob in the attacks on the Kuki-Zo community. The Forum described Arambai Tenggol in its petition as an organization created with the objective of eradicating the Kuki-Zo tribals who have settled mostly in the southern districts of Manipur.

The petition mentions videos which point to the involvement of this organization. I too had seen some of these in the early days of the violence and they left me deeply shocked. In one of these, shot at night, little is discernible other than women with their *inaphis*, or shawls, blowing around as they run after a vehicle. They look like zombies, but it is not the image which strikes one but the voices. Here are transcripts shared by the MTF in their petition which show how this was a premeditated attack on specific groups:

> Lady 1: 'Now the Arambai are also here at Lamphel... We are heading to Langol. We've destroyed a church and a house—we burnt it down. I could not make a video of that. It's exploding—look at that!'
>
> Lady 1: 'If it is a Hao [tribal] make sure to beat them up... hit them on the head. Let the vehicle go but do check if they are Meitei or Hao.'
>
> Person 3: 'We are only after Kuki. Only Kuki.'

Arambai Tenggol

No one seems to know the exact date on which Arambai Tenggol was formed but its members are recognizable by their black T-shirts with the red emblem of dart-throwing warriors riding ponies. By all accounts, they emerged in Manipur in the early 2020s. They have adopted a religious and nationalist rhetoric, invoking the ancient Meitei religion of Sanamahism and the historical Meitei kingdom of Kangleipak. The organization claims to be involved in preserving and promoting Meitei culture, but it is a far cry from the Meitei cavalry of old. This new cavalry of sorts rides on motorcycles, not on Manipur ponies. And they do not carry poisoned darts but sophisticated weapons.

According to reports, the Arambai Tenggol were in the forefront of the attacks on the Kuki-Zo community, confirming what had been alleged in the Manipur Tribal Forum's petition mentioned above. But how did they learn to use the sophisticated weapons they are alleged to wield?

The commander-in-chief of the organization is a man called Korounganba Khuman who proudly posts pictures of himself on social media holding deadly assault rifles and firearms. He and other Arambai Tenggol members have been seen with such weapons as an AKM, the Benelli M2 shotgun and the WP4523 1911 .45 Auto pistol, along with military body armour and gear.

The organization has inducted Meitei insurgents into its ranks. According to the Indigenous Tribal Leaders' Forum, surrendered cadres from several Meitei militant groups, often referred to as the VBIG, or Valley-Based Insurgent Groups, most of which are banned—such as the Kanglei Yawol Kanna Lup (KYKL) formed in 1994, the People's Liberation Army

(PLA) and the United National Liberation Front (UNLF)—have joined the Arambai Tenggol.

On May 28, 2023, there was a clash between Arambai Tenggol militants and the 37 Assam Rifles column at the Sugnu-Serou area of Manipur. It was reported in *India Today NE* that 'the surrendered VBIG militants have now joined forces under the banner of Arambai Tenggol. What was once believed to be a peaceful transition has taken a violent turn as these militants, armed with weapons allegedly provided by state Meitei commandos, engage in a confrontation with the 37 Assam Rifles'.[45]

The chairman of Arambai Tenggol is Leishemba Sanajaoba, the titular King of Manipur and member of the Rajya Sabha who was elected on a BJP ticket in 2020. According to a report, *Analysis of Criminal and Financial Details of Newly Elected MPs of Rajya Sabha, June, 2020*, conducted by the Association for Democratic Reforms (ADR), Sanajaoba was found to be the poorest among the sixty-two MPs that were analysed. His assets totalled to Rs 5,48,594, as opposed to, say, Alla Ayodhya Rama Reddy, the MP from Andhra Pradesh, with total assets amounting to Rs 25,77,75,79,180. Nor was Sanajaoba found to have any cognizable offences registered against him.

However, six major socio-cultural organizations of the state strongly opposed his bid for election and subsequently derecognized him as the King of Manipur for mixing the institution of monarchy and politics. These include the All Manipur United Club Organisation (AMUCO), International Peace and Social Upliftment (IFSA), United Peoples' Front (UPF), Heritage Council (HERICOUN), Committee of Civil Societies Kangleipak (CCSK) and the League of Indigenous Peoples' Upliftment (LIPUL). They compared him to Pamheiba, or Garibniwaz, the illustrious king who made Hinduism the state religion, but who is not always remembered very fondly.[46]

More worryingly, though, there are photographs and videos of members of the Arambai Tenggol taking oath on September 25, 2022, at the residence of Leishemba Sanajaoba, the oath-taking ceremony being led by Korounganba Khuman.

In the last week of May 2023, the organization announced its temporary dissolution. They insisted that claims about the women's wing of Arambai Tenggol organizing mobs that stormed the residences of the politicians were rumours. They denied any involvement in any such activity and clarified that they did not even have a women's wing.

The organization appealed to all not to use their name in protests against the state and central governments. Their press release stated: '[At] such a critical juncture when taking a united stand is of utmost importance, certain individuals with [a] vested interest are attempting to drive a wedge among us. It is clear that attempts are made to permanently eradicate the organization from Manipur...' They prohibited their members from using the name of the organization while it remained dissolved, but indicated that they will make a return when the situation demanded it.[47]

The organization was back in action in the first week of October when they attacked the house of Babloo Loitongbam, an internationally known human rights activist, after he gave an interview to *Newsclick*[48] in which he was critical of the Meitei Leepun and the Arambai Tenggol, accusing them of fanning violence against Kukis. Loitongbam had been demanding the resignation of Chief Minister N. Biren Singh.

Loitongbam had said in the interview that these two organizations 'have articulation [*sic*] like the Rashtriya Swayamsevak Sangh'. 'Not a single church stands in the valley now,' he claimed.

The United Nations Human Rights Office urged Indian authorities to ensure his protection and that of his family after members of Meitei Leepun and Arambai Tenggol attacked his home.

Sanajaoba is not the only BJP leader who is a patron of the Arambai Tenggol. There were others, too, like Lourembam Rameshwor,[49] MLA from Keirao, Leishangthem Susindro, from Khurai, who is also a minister in the state assembly. Even the chief minister, N. Biren Singh, is known to be a patron of the organization. Singh did not act against Meitei radical and supremacist groups like the Arambai Tenggol and Meitei Leepun who carried out attacks on Kuki villages.[50]

*

Nongthombam Biren Singh (b. 1951) was a professional footballer who played for the Border Security Force from 1979 to 1984 in Jalandhar. When he returned to Manipur, he sold off a two-acre plot inherited from his father and started a vernacular newspaper called *Naharolgi Thoudan*, of which he was the editor till 2001.

Biren Singh entered the political arena in 2002, when he joined the Democratic Revolutionary Peoples Party. He was elected to the state assembly in 2002 from Heingang in the Imphal East district, and retained his seat in 2007, contesting on a Congress ticket after joining the party in 2004 (the year the DRPP merged with the INC). He held several cabinet portfolios under the Congress government. He won his third consecutive assembly election in 2012.

In 2016, however, Biren Singh quit the Congress and joined the BJP. The following year, he was sworn in as chief minister after his party formed a coalition government in the state. He was the first BJP chief minister in Manipur.

He became the chief minister once again after the 2022 elections, this time with a comfortable majority of thirty-seven BJP seats as opposed to just twenty-one in 2017. Despite this, Biren Singh showed a tendency for being intolerant of criticism. At least two bloggers in the state, Kishore Chandra Wangkhem and R.K. Echanthoibi, were arrested and detained for posts critical of his government.

Biren Singh is the ex-officio chairman of the Shri Shri Govindajee Temple Board, and, since 2021, the president of the Lainingthou Sanamahi Temple Board, the first incumbent chief minister of Manipur to hold that post.

In August 2022, the Manipur assembly unanimously resolved to reaffirm the resolution, passed originally on August 1, 2003, to recommend to the government of India that the Sanamahi religion be recorded in the census report and also allotted a separate code number in the Census 2021 (postponed due to the Covid pandemic). Members of the community have been urging Biren Singh for some time to push for including it in the list of minority religions defined by the National Commission for Minorities (NCM) Act, 1992. Reportedly, the latter has received such depositions positively.[51]

*

As per the 2011 Census, Sanamahi followers form roughly 7.78 per cent of the total with a total population of 2,22,315. Hindus, with a population of 11,81,876, made up 41.39 per cent. The latter formed the largest population in the state followed by Christians, which were 41.29 per cent of the total with a population of 11,79,043. The third largest population was that of Muslims, who constitute 8.4 per cent of the population with 2,39,836 adherents.

While the Hindu population's share declined from roughly 62 per cent in 1961, that of the Christian population rose from 19 per cent in the same year. In 1901, it was recorded as 0.02 of the population. In the Hills, which comprise roughly 90 per cent of the state's land area, of course, Christians formed the overwhelming majority. Of the nine districts in Manipur, five districts had a Christian majority. The small but significant portion of the non-ST Christians, numbering between one to three lakhs, are mainly Meiteis.

Evangelization

The established churches in Northeast India have often warned people of the dangers of sects and cults, such as the Church of Almighty God. The Church of Almighty God (*Quannengshen* in Chinese) is a secretive, theologically aberrant religious movement that started in 1991 in China, where it has been banned. The cult was established by Zhao Weishan, a former physics teacher from Henan province in central China. They hold that Jesus Christ has returned to earth in the form of Zhao's wife, Yang Xiangbin. Zhao and Yang fled to the US in 2000 where they were given asylum.

This group has been working in the Northeast for some time now, including in Nagaland and Manipur. In fact, it was claimed by the Bible Society of India (BSI) Dimapur Auxiliary in October 2022 that the Church of Almighty God has been 'using the name of [the BSI] in order to penetrate the Churches and educational institutions'.

Zelhou Keyho, general secretary of the Nagaland Baptist Church Council has warned against the cult, calling it violent and fundamentalist. W. Konghar, general secretary of the Manipur Baptist Convention, says a similar cult based in South

Korea was found to be active in the state from 2019.[52]

Around the first week of August 2023, a video of a Christian missionary, Daniel Stephen Courney, streaming live from Manipur surfaced on social media. Originally from New York, USA, Courney was apparently a combat medic in the US Army and was allegedly put in the psychiatric ward because of his 'preaching' activities. He had been deported once before, in 2018, convicted for his rabid preaching, but was found streaming from Manipur once again in 2023.[53] He claimed that Christians were being attacked in Manipur.

I refer to these sects and cults only to explain how Northeast India has been fertile ground for such cults and sects. Added to this are the proselytizing activities of the more traditional churches. I have myself been witness to the aggressive manner in which they try to convert people.

Some evangelists had tried to convert me when I was there in 1988. I was staying for some time in the Manipur Baptist Convention church compound. As I've mentioned in a previous chapter, I was there to represent the Poumai Nagas who had suffered human rights violations at the hands personnel of the Assam Rifles. What irked me was the refusal of the members of the church to acknowledge my actions as an act of solidarity as an Indian, as someone who wished to speak out against the wrongs committed by the Indian armed forces. They saw me only as an agent of their God come to help them. And their duty was to convert me! The evangelizing forced me to shift to Langol.

I also noticed the divide between the Baptists and the Catholics. Naga villages had even passed resolutions to the effect that only one denomination be allowed in each village. When I asked my Naga Baptist friends whether they approved, they laughed it away. Worse, I was told I was speaking on behalf of the Catholics since my husband was one. But I had not got married in a church, and I was then, as now, speaking as a human rights advocate.

One incident of such aggressive evangelizing came to light about one and a half months before the violence began in Manipur:

On March 26, 2023, Pastor Takhellambam Ramananda was preaching during a gospel outreach programme of the Sagang Baptist Church. He made highly offensive references to the traditional Meitei religion, even spitting on the stage as he spoke. A video clip of his speech went viral on social media and he was duly detained by the Imphal Police when they were notified. He was later released, apparently upon the intervention of a local MLA.[54]

Arambai Tenggol members assembled in the front courtyard of Ramananda's home, on April 3, 2023, demanding an apology. But they were quickly dispersed by the police and any untoward incident was avoided.[55]

But Leishemba Sanajaoba, the titular king and Rajya Sabha MP, lashed out viciously against the 'uncouth man' who had dared to speak thus of the Meiteis. 'If he does not apologize,' wrote Sanajaoba in a Facebook post, 'I swear in the name of Ebudhou Pakhangba that I would skin him alive. I do not care whether I remain an MP or not.'[56]

Ramananda later apologized to the Meitei community and to Sanajaoba personally.[57]

Vandalizing and Burning of Churches

Notably, the state had carried out church demolitions in Imphal in the early part of the year. On April 11, 2023, three churches in the Tribal Colony, Imphal were demolished as they were, according to the government, constructed on government land without any approval or permission from the district administration. The three churches were: the Evangelical Baptist Convention Church, the Holy Spirit Catholic Church, the Evangelical Lutheran Church Manipur; one of them had been built as long back as 1974.[58] At the same time, a notice was given to the Mantripukhri Masjid in Imphal claiming that it was an illegal structure. The Manipur Muslim Welfare Organization (MMWO) protested. They argued that the mosque was one of the oldest in Manipur, with a history of over 105 years, and had been in existence before Manipur merged into India.[59]

From May, when the violence started, churches began to be systematically destroyed, mostly by mobs led by the Arambai Tenggol. The situation quickly escalated. Archbishop Dominic Lumon of Imphal came out with the following statement on June 15, 2023:

'Each of the over 200 Kuki villages attacked had either one or multiple churches, depending on the number of Christian denominations… About 249 churches belonging to the Meitei Christians have been destroyed. All these destructions [*sic*] took place with precision within 36 hours of the start of violence.'[60]

In a letter to *The Indian Express*,[61] the archbishop wrote, 'The wonder is, in the midst of the fight between the Kukis and the Meiteis, why did the Meitei mob burn down and destroy 249 churches located in the Meitei heartland? How is it that there was almost a natural attack on the church in the Meitei localities itself and how did the mob know where the churches were located if not previously planned?'

At a meeting organized by Meitei Christians in Delhi in July, one of the speakers was Pastor Nabachandra Maibram, a

Meitei Christian living in Kuki-Zo-dominated Churachandpur. The Pastor was visiting his daughter in Bengaluru when the clashes began on May 3. Maibram's home and those of around 127 Meiteis from his congregation were burnt down; his sons had moved with their families to relief camps in the Meitei-dominated Imphal Valley.

While Archbishop Lumon's letter suggested that there was a religious angle to the violence, incidents such as the latter indicate that the conflict was not necessarily religious. As we shall see, the violence was likely more of an ethnic clash.

Meitei Christians

The Meitei Christian Churches Council, Manipur (MCCCM) went to great lengths to assert that the ethnic violence in Manipur was not a case of a dominant community attacking the Christian minority, insisting that the conflict was instead between 'Manipuris and illegal immigrants'.

In the writ petition (540 of 2023) filed by Manipur Tribal Forum, Delhi before the Supreme Court, they listed the Kuki-Zo villages that had been attacked, the list of churches vandalized or destroyed, along with testimonies of individual victims. The MCCCM appealed to the MTF to remove the names of Meitei churches in their petition.

In a press statement on June 11, 2023, Senjam Kakanti, the MCCCM secretary general, said:

'It has come to our attention that the Kukis have included 70 of the 251 Meetei Churches that were burnt and dismantled during the communal clashes [between the] two communities [with] the list of Kuki churches... We strongly condemn this attempt to align the Meitei churches with the Kukis in the aforementioned writ petition. We appeal to the petitioner of the writ petition Manipuri Tribal Forum Delhi to remove the names of the Meitei churches from the petition.'[62]

The MCCCM filed another petition (WP [Civil] 875 of 2023) before the Supreme Court to highlight the fact that the state and the Centre did nothing to prevent the destruction of the churches belonging to the Meitei Christians. They claimed that '240–247 churches stand vandalized, looted and burnt down in the violence which started on 03.05.2023 and church property including furniture, valuable and parish church register and title documents either looted or deliberately burnt'. For this reason, they could not produce documentary evidence to substantiate their assertion. They requested police protection to congregate and hold prayers.[63]

The MCCCM also tried to organize a public meeting at Delhi's Jantar Mantar to publicize their stand in the conflict. The venue of their meeting was shifted to the Constitution Club of India at the last hour after they were denied permission to organize at Jantar Mantar. The meeting was finally held on July 15, 2023, organized jointly with the Meitei Heritage Society.

The testimonies of the Meitei Christians exposed the tension between ethnicity and religion, especially felt by this community. The speakers wished to emphasize that although they were Christian, they stood firmly with their fellow Meiteis on the issue of the integrity and unity of Manipur and that they did not support the demand of the Kuki-Zo for a separate administration, even though the latter were Christian.

One of the best known faces among the Meitei Christians has been Philem Rohan Singh, a member of the Ministry of Reconciliation—an independent church. He is known for his bicycle and motorcycle expeditions across India for numerous social causes. In 2018, he cycled from Delhi to Imphal. He has taken up the cause of Burmese refugees, the Pulwama martyrs and also worked to bring attention to the water crisis in Kerala.[64]

In an *India Today* podcast with Pragya Gulati on July 13, Rohan explained how the Meitei Christians have been targeted by both his own people, the Meiteis, and also by Kukis, with whom he shares his faith. Singh's co-religionists from the Kuki community, he says, now liken him to Christ's disciple Judas who betrayed him to the Jewish clergy.

According to Rohan, the violence in Manipur could not be called communal or anti-Christian. He pointed to the destruction of churches and Meitei Christian homes, including that of a Meitei pastor (referring to Pastor Nabachandra Maibram), in Churachandpur. He added that the Meitei mob too (he carefully avoided mentioning the Arambai Tenggol or Meitei Leepun) attacked Meitei churches, accusing the Meitei Christians of siding with the Kukis since they worshipped the same god, a revealing accusation, since it showed the primary battle lines to be drawn along the ethnic divide. Rohan talked about how the Nagas were not touched, as also churches belonging to other communities not party to the conflict.

Meitei Christians were a 'minority of a minority', lamented Rohan, looked upon with suspicion by both sides in the conflict. He flies two flags on his electric motorcycle—the Indian Tricolour and the Salai Taret, which represents the seven clans of ancient Kangleipak.

In August 2023, Meiteis alleged that Kukis burnt down 393 Meitei temples and places of worship. The claim was made by the Working Committee on Protection of Meitei Temples formed under Umanglai Kanba Apunba Lup (UKAL).[65] Rohan too had mentioned the vandalization of temples. Some fact-checking done by *The Quint* showed that non-Manipuri Hindus in Kuki areas, however, were not attacked: 'Allegations about Kukis who are predominantly Christians, attacking Hindu temples in tribal-dominated areas were circulated in social media since May 3. However, on May 9, the Bihari Society, the Bengali Society and the Marwari Society of Manipur issued a joint statement that non-Manipuri Hindus were not attacked or harmed in the Kuki areas.'[66]

Claims and counter-claims have been made in heated exchanges between those who saw the violence in Manipur primarily as a clash between two ethnic communities and those who saw it as religious or communal violence. While there is no denying the ethnic nature of the conflict, we also cannot turn a blind eye to the strong element of communal hatred, as illustrated by the incident in which a Meitei mob burnt alive two Meitei women and a child of seven.

Joshua Hangshing's Story

Joshua Hangshing was a mason by profession. He lived in a small, predominantly Kuki village called Kangchup, some fifteen kilometres from Imphal. The village has a water treatment plant which is the source of water for the Imphal Valley. Joshua lived here with his wife and three children—his daughter, a class eight student, the elder son, a class ten student, and a younger one barely eight years old.

On May 4, a day after the Tribal Solidarity March, violence had broken out. Joshua had heard that Kukis were being attacked and he decided to shift his family to the 22 Assam Rifles camp where they had opened a relief facility. He felt safe under the protection of the security forces. And for a month their little family did manage to survive. There were several other families there too.

The camp 'stood in the middle' of several Kuki and Meitei villages. Both sides had their bunkers in each, incessantly firing at each other. On June 4, there was a firing incident and a bullet hit the iron rods in the window from where a splinter ricocheted to hit Joshua's seven-year-old son, Tongsing, in the head. Another bullet splinter hit Tongsing's mother Meena Hangshing's hand.

It was about four in the evening and Joshua was outside the shelter fetching water. This is how he describes what happened:

'The moment when my son saw me, he yelled, "Papa, Papa," from the window, and he went silent. Then, my wife, Meena called me, "Papa, come and see what happened to our son." I rushed to the room and I saw my son covered with blood from his head and crying in pain. I was so shocked that I went into semi-consciousness state [*sic*] and all my body got numb... I suspect my son was hit on his head by a splinter when Meitei terrorists fired using a sniper rifle.'

The Assam Rifles company commander informed the Imphal West superintendent of police and an ambulance was duly sent with three commando vehicles to escort it.

Joshua wanted them to take his son to an army hospital at Leimakhong but the police decided to take the child to the hospital at the Regional Institute of Medical Sciences, Imphal. Joshua felt uneasy when he learnt that the Assam Rifles were not going to escort the ambulance. But then he reasoned that his family should be safe because his wife, Meena, was a Meitei and so was the female relative accompanying his wife. He did not dare accompany his wife and son in the ambulance himself, because he was a Kuki and the ambulance had to pass through Meitei-dominated areas.

An Assam Rifles escort did finally accompany the

ambulance for around two kilometres, after which the Meira Paibis did not allow them to go any further. The Meira Paibis are the legendary 'torch bearers' of Manipur. In the 1970s, they stepped up to fight drug trafficking and abuse. Later, as insurgency grew in the state, they began rescuing innocent young men from the security forces, saving many from torture. This time, however, they were found to be part of the mobs attacking the Kuki-Zo community.

From that point on its journey, the ambulance was under the protection of only the police: the Imphal West superintendent himself and around ten Manipur police commandos spread across three vehicles.

Barely ten kilometres from where the Assam Rifles retreated, a massive mob of some 2,000 people waylaid the convoy. This happened in Imphal's Iroisemba area, a locality which falls under the Lamphel police station, around five kilometres from Imphal city. The ambulance was set ablaze and the three members of Joshua's family were burnt alive; only charred remains and a few bones were what was left of them.

The dead were identified as Tongsing Hangshing, 7, his mother Meena Hangshing, 45, a Meitei Christian, and their relative Lydia Lourembam, 37, also a Meitei Christian.

Joshua was not informed until two days later. And even then, it was not the police who told him, but his father-in-law who had read the news in the local paper. Joshua could not even go to the hospital to recover the charred remains of his wife and child. It was just too dangerous for a Kuki to go to a Meitei-dominated area.

One of the most shocking things about this story is the coverage it got; or rather did not get. On June 5, 'the top story across [*Sangai Express*, *Imphal Free Press* and *People's Chronicle*—Manipur's most widely read English papers] was an attack by "Kuki militants" on security forces, leading to one death and two injuries... [T]he story of a mob burning alive a seven-year-old child and his mother did not make it to the three newspapers'. Such instances only 'lend credence to the apprehensions expressed by tribal journalists about the bias of the Imphal-based media'.[67]

Hindutva Campaign and Solidarity

Despite having largely rejected Hinduism and embraced Sanamahism, their ancient religion, Meitei extremist groups have welcomed the support they have got from Hindutva forces. For instance, at a Meitei rally at Jantar Mantar in the first week of August, a member of the Akhil Bharat Hindu Mahasabha gave an impassioned speech assuring his Meitei audience that they should not feel alone in their struggle; they should know that 1.25 crore Hindus were behind them!

One journalist pointed out how the 'Hindutva campaign targeting Kukis for their Christian faith is leading to global perception of the Manipur situation as a religious conflict, diverting focus from the real issues'.[68] One reason why the violence in Manipur began to be perceived mainly as persecution of Christian tribals has been the 'overzealous online campaign by Hindutva activists vilifying Kukis for their Christian identity'.

'Soon after the beginning of the conflict on May 3,' writes independent journalist Snigdhendu Bhattacharya in *Outlook*, 'started a flood of social media posts targeting Kukis as "Christian terrorists". While tweets from handles belonging to Meiteis mostly blamed "Kuki terrorists" or "Kuki militants" or "Kuki drug mafias" and "Kuki narco terrorists", the profiles belonging to Hindutva activists, operated mostly by people outside Manipur, started vilifying "Kuki Christian terrorists".

'A look at how social media campaigns peddled different narratives reveal that the handles operated by Kukis initially described it as an attack on tribals, and blamed Meiteis, but did not refer to them as "Meitei Hindus". However, the emergence of the "Save Meitei Hindus" or "Save Hindus in Manipur" campaigns coincided with their strategy of highlighting the Christian identity of the Kukis.

'Visuals of the burning and destruction of churches added fuel to the campaign on religious lines, and so did the visuals of attacks on temples, though the latter were fewer in number...

'Multiple Hindutva handles...highlighted the conflict as an attack on Hindus soon after the violence broke out, trying to implicate Christian missionaries for the mayhem. They started popularizing the hashtag #justiceforManipuriHindus...

'However, most pro-Meitei handles did not refer to the religious identity of either side for most of May. This started changing ahead of the June 4 "peace rally" by Meiteis at New Delhi's Jantar Mantar, an event for the success of which the Hindutva camp visibly made significant efforts.'

At least one pro-Kuki handle on Twitter observed that '[t]he Sanamahi fanatics have now attempted to [present] the situation as a religious clash in order to gain sympathy from the Hindu population'.

International Condemnations

The burning of churches had repercussions both within India as well as internationally. In neighbouring Mizoram, Chief Minister Zoramthanga said he would not share the stage with the Prime Minister during the state assembly elections scheduled for November even though his party, the Mizo

National Front, was a member of the BJP-led North East Democratic Alliance and the National Democratic Alliance. He told the BBC that 'when the people of Manipur [Meiteis] burned hundreds of churches in Manipur, [Mizos] were totally against that kind of idea. To have sympathy with the BJP at this time will be a big minus point for my party'.[69]

Interestingly enough, some sympathizers of the BJP, too, admitted that the conflict was not religious. For instance, Jaydeep Mazumdar, associate editor of *Swarajya*, wrote that '[a] number of Christian bodies, as well as leftists and "wokes", have been trying to portray the conflict between Meiteis and Kukis in Manipur as a Hindu-Christian strife'. The reason for doing so, according to him, was that they wished to get 'the West to denounce India and the Narendra Modi government'.[70]

He may have been referring to the remarks made by the American Ambassador Eric Garcetti, speaking at a news conference in Kolkata in the first week of June. The Ambassador said that the United States had 'human concerns' about the violence in Manipur and was 'ready, willing, able to assist in any way if asked'. He did hastily add that he recognized that Manipur was an internal matter of India.

A week after the US Ambassador's remarks, the European Union passed a resolution 'strongly condemn[ing] the acts of violence, loss of life and destruction of property in Manipur' and 'denounc[ing] in the strongest terms nationalistic rhetoric deployed by leading members of the BJP'. It called on India to 'take all necessary measures and make the utmost effort to promptly halt the ongoing ethnic and religious violence, to protect all religious minorities, such as Manipur's Christian community, and to pre-empt any further escalation'.

The resolution was passed on the day Prime Minister Narendra Modi landed in France on an official visit. The five parliamentary factions that authored the resolution were the left Greens-European Free Alliance, the centre-right European People's Party (EPP), the centre-left Progressive Alliance of Socialists and Democrats (S&D), the liberal Renew group and the right-wing European Conservatives and Reformists (ECR) group. Together they account for around 80 per cent of the lawmakers in the 705-member European Parliament.[71]

Fiona Bruce, Britain's special ambassador for religious freedom and MP, asked in the UK parliament what the Church of England could do to help those in Manipur who were suffering. She also accused the BBC of not accurately reporting on the Manipur violence.[72]

While indeed there were people in the West like Bruce who appeared to stress 'the apparent role of religion in fuelling these attacks', the US-based Foundation for India and Indian Diaspora Studies (FIIDS) argued that 'the violence has historical baggage, inter tribes distrust, fear of economic impacts, drugs and insurgency as factors. However, it is important to note that, although religious polarization exists among the tribes, we did not find evidence of religious violence. Instead, it is based on an ethnic divide and historical distrust and rivalry between the tribes'.[73]

Perhaps not many noticed that in Israel too there was concern over the destruction of two synagogues and a Torah in Manipur. A report published in the *Israel Times* on May 5, 2023 states:

'Members of a small group tracing their heritage to the ancient Israelites and seeking to move to Israel found themselves caught up in violent ethnic clashes in northeastern India this week, when at least one member of the community was killed, 10 more went missing, and over 200 homes were torched in the state of Manipur.

'A father of four from the 5,000-person-strong Bnei Menashe community is known to be dead and 10 others are unaccounted for...'[74]

The Bnei Menashe are believed to be the descendants of the Menashe tribe, one of the ten lost tribes of Israel. They are from the Kuki-Zo community and many have already left for Israel. It is in fact reported that 206 Kukis are part of the Israel Defense Forces (IDF) and were recalled as reservists to take part in the conflict that broke out in Gaza in October 2023.

The *Israel Times*, quoted above, did not mention the fact that more than 200 churches had been destroyed too.[75]

The World Kuki-Zo Intellectual Council (WKZIC) wrote to the General Secretary of the United Nations on June 29, 2023, and Prime Minister of Israel, Benjamin Netanyahu, on June 30, seeking urgent intervention in favour of their demand for a Kuki state carved out of the hill areas in Manipur.

In a memorandum submitted to Prime Minister Netanyahu they asked for his 'personal intervention' to help with the grant of 'Kuki statehood under Article No 3 of the Indian Constitution for self-governance free from the control and discrimination in all aspects by the majority community or... [the integration of] all Kuki-Chin territories of Chin State (Myanmar/Burma), Chittagong Hill Tracts (CHT), Bangladesh and Mizoram (India) and Kuki Hills in outer Manipur respectively, to be merged with one of the more friendly countr[ies] in Southeast Asia'.[76]

The Manipur government banned the organization in November 2023.[77]

Few condemnations by the international community mentioned the demolition of Hindu temples and the desecration of sacred Sanamahi sites. While the concern expressed may still be justified, one cannot forget that the international community has its own political agenda when it makes a statement condemning human rights violations in any particular country.

The Ministry of External Affairs' response was that Manipur was an internal matter and that foreign countries had no business commenting on the events there. But international condemnations were made, in part, because the Indian government, including the Prime Minister, maintained a steady silence while Manipur burned. The pleas and demands for the resignation of the Chief Minister fell on deaf ears even as India's top security experts were claiming that the state government was complicit in the violence, an aspect of the tragedy we will deal with in later chapters.

CHAPTER FOUR

Who Is the Outsider?

My dream and only hope for my people born and unborn
That one day in Manipur the new sunrise equally shines
    on all people
[...]
To peaceful coexistence where all people feel home safe
    and secure
To the day when our freedom fighters are honoured as
    National heroes
To the sanity [which makes us] see one another as
    neighbours; not as foreigners
To the days where people are helping instead of hurting
And...all hearts [are filled] with humility and humanity as
    one Manipur

—'My Dream for a Future Manipur' by
Shongminthang Haokip, April 2021

Don't kill me, I'm an ordinary man, I'm not an enemy of man,
I don't think evil of man, I'm not a bad man.
He was also born in this land, I was also born in this land,
You and I are one;
Don't get me wrong.

—'Don't Kill Me, I Was Born in This Land'
(from *Illusionary Country*, 1999)
by Thangjam Ibopishak Singh (b. 1948), a Meitei poet

The violence in Manipur began on May 3, 2023 and it continues even as this book goes to the press, six months later. By this time, nearly all the Kuki-Zo families in the Valley, even those who had built their homes there, had been compelled to leave. Some found themselves in relief camps, others moved in with relatives living in the Hills and some flew out of Manipur.

Ten families (numbering twenty-four men, women and children) remained in Imphal, defiant and courageous, until they were driven away on the night of September 2. They had decided to stay in their homes in the New Lambulane locality. Among these people was 78-year-old Reverend S. Prim Vaiphei.

New Lambulane is merely 1.5 kilometres away from the chief minister's residence and even closer to the Manipur police headquarters. The neighbourhood has produced several distinguished Kuki-Zo officers for the Indian Administrative as well as Police Services, among other central services, including former Goa Chief Secretary T. Kipgen, whose son S. Kipgen was India's ambassador to Ukraine from 2002 to 2005.

Rev Vaiphei's son, Samuel S. Vaiphei, too, is an officer in the Indian Revenue Service. He had passed his civil services examination in 2012. At a felicitation ceremony organized for him at their New Lambulane home by the All Manipur Christian Organisation (AMCO), the general secretary of AMCO, Fr T.S. Dominic is said to have exhorted 'Samuel to no longer see [individuals] as Kuki, Naga or Meitei but as people created in the image of God'.[78]

I met Rev Vaiphei several times when I had stayed in the Manipur Baptist Convention church compound. I remember him for his enormous dignity and the warmth with which he had welcomed me into his home. He never made me feel like a 'mayang'. I know he would have stood strong and dignified as he faced the brutes who had knocked at his door that night.

The state government said he was not safe in his own home despite the round-the-clock security to protect the locality from mob attacks. Once, in the last week August, some unidentified men had managed to enter the locality and torch three abandoned houses. A mob followed some time after but was prevented from entering the neighbourhood and dispersed by security forces with tear gas.

Rev Vaiphei had been living in the colony since 1983. Speaking to *Times of India*, here's how he explained his refusal to move out of his home:

'Being a clergyman, I believe in God. I believe God will protect me. I am not an enemy of Meiteis. I believe that Meiteis are my brothers and so are the Kukis and Nagas. But there are some black sheep that create trouble for society. Why should I be scared of these black sheep?'

On the intervening night of September 1 and 2, a team of uniformed armed forces personnel claiming to be acting under the direction of the Home Department forcibly evicted the ten families. They were not given time to pack their belongings, and quite literally herded into the waiting Casper bulletproof vehicles. Many of them were woken up from sleep and pulled by the arms into the vehicles in the clothes they were wearing. Rev Vaiphei was not given time to even pick up his precious Bible.

They were taken to an Assam Rifles camp twenty-seven kilometres away in Motbung, in Kangpokpi district, which is home to the Kuki-Zo community. Rev Vaiphei protested in a press statement:

'We express our strong displeasure at this high-handed abduction-like forcible evacuation executed against our will. We regret that a country like India is unwilling to ensure the life and security of its citizens at the place of their residences, succumbing to the intimidation of chaotic forces trying to destroy the society and the state.'

The Kuki Inpi Manipur, the apex body of the Kuki tribes, called the eviction of these ten families a 'total separation of the Kukis and the Meiteis'. To them, it justifies the Kuki demand for a separate administration, which they say India ought to constitutionally recognize.

Manipur Muslims the Peace Makers

During the four months when Rev Prim Vaiphei and the other families had decided to stay on in Imphal, unable to venture out, they had had to rely on their Muslim (Meitei Pangal) neighbours to bring them supplies.

This was not the only case of the Pangal community arranging for food, shelter, clothes and other relief materials to the victims. They had in fact helped both members of the Kuki-Zo communities as well as the Meiteis, sometimes risking their lives to save the families of friends and neighbours. Some Muslims were indeed attacked and they sustained injuries in the process. However, none lost their lives.

On May 4, when some 3,000 Kuki-Zo sought shelter in the Muslim-dominated area of Hatta Golapati in Imphal, Meitei Muslims bravely opened their doors to them. The women cooked food and the men guarded them till the Assam Rifles came to the rescue of the Kukis.[79]

Kuki-Zo People Are Not 'Outsiders'

Fifteen-year-old Ngamgouhou Mate was staying in his uncle's home in Khonsai Veg, a Kuki-dominated locality in Imphal

East. On May 4, 2023, when he heard a mob approaching, the young man quickly took his football boots and his academic certificates, stuffing them into a bag before running towards a nearby school which had been turned into a relief camp. But they were not safe there either. Columns of the Indian Army too had been deployed recently in Imphal East. They took the people to a Naga settlement just in time; the school was burnt down.

Ngamgouhou later saw photos of his uncle's home. It had been burnt down as was his scooty, which he used to ride to Imphal's Classic Football Academy. Remarkably, the young man continued to practise and on September 10, 2023, captained India to victory at the U-16 South Asian Football Federation (SAFF) Cup tournament in Bhutan, defeating Bangladesh in the final.

Just after they won the match, Ngamgouhou rushed to phone his parents, living in a relief camp which too had been attacked when fresh violence broke out. Fortunately, they had fled to safety. But the family could not get together to celebrate.

Mate now stays in Siliguri and continues to play with Meitei teammates but they do not discuss the events in Manipur. They just ask each other formally if they have eaten; they have become strangers.

*

It is difficult to have 'objective' or unbiased accounts of the conflict. Each community has its own narrative rooted in its own perception of its past. As one reporter observed: 'It is said that there are always two sides to every story and the truth lies somewhere in between. But in Manipur, the truth lies not only somewhere in between, but it is unfailingly wrapped in several layers of conflicting interpretations.'

However, there is one objective fact which is undeniable, and that is that the Kuki-Zo people living in Manipur are not foreigners, nor are they outsiders or infiltrators or encroachers—they are citizens of India.

The Kuki-Zo have always asserted their loyalty to the Indian Union. Even in the midst of the violence, they waved Indian flags and sang the Indian national anthem. The Thadou Kukis in particular have been well represented in politics and the bureaucracy. Outer Manipur, the tribal Lok Sabha constituency of Manipur, has elected seventeen members of parliament since 1952 and an overwhelming fourteen of these have been either Thadou or Tangkhul Naga. The Thadou tribe is also disproportionately represented in the bureaucracy. The first ever person to ever qualify for the IAS from Manipur was a Thadou—K. Kipgen—in 1956. Similarly, the first tribal IPS officer from Manipur (1965), T. Misao, was a Thadou. Thadous dominate the intellectual discourse as well. Many scholars quoted in media reports or writing in international publications on the current conflict, like T. Haokip from JNU, H. Sitlhou from the University of Hyderabad and M. Sitlhou, are all Thadou.[80]

The Census of 1901 recorded the population of Manipur at 2,84,488, of which, the Kukis accounted for 41,262. This amounted to 14.5 per cent of the state's total population in 1901. According to the 2011 Census, the population of the Kuki-Zo was 4,48,214 to the state's total of 28,55,794. In other words, they were 16 per cent of the population in Manipur.

In 110 years, therefore, the growth rate of the Kuki population has been less than 2 per cent.[81] Clearly, their numbers have not expanded in a manner that can give credence to concerns about any influx from across the border.

The Kuki-Zo community organized several meetings at

Delhi's Jantar Mantar as violence raged in Manipur. On May 29, several speakers emphasized that they were Indian citizens, not foreigners. They reminded the audience of their ancestors' role in the freedom struggle. 'We are not illegal immigrants,' they declared.

At another rally, the former MP from Manipur, Kim Gangte, who had once been a member of the BJP, asked rhetorically, 'Am I [a] refugee?' She asked why she was being called a refugee in her own state. She said her forefathers had fought for freedom in the Anglo-Kuki War of 1917–19 and later for Manipur. She said her people were nationalists and that they 'stand for this country'. Then she asked, her voice betraying anger and anguish, 'Why can't the Prime Minister open his mouth?'

Much before the violence erupted on May 3, Manipur's state government had begun labelling the entire community of Kuki-Zo tribals as 'illegal immigrants' and 'foreigners' without any reliable data or evidence. This despite the fact that the decadal census from 1901 to 2011, as noted above, has not shown any unusual growth of the non-Naga tribal population.

It has been alleged that there has been a higher decadal growth rate of the population in the Hills compared to the Valley in Manipur. The 2011 Census raised suspicions that people were illegally migrating from neighbouring countries like Myanmar, Nepal and Bangladesh. However, as late as 2018, N. Biren Singh, speaking at the India Today Regional Conclave, had claimed that, unlike Kashmir, there were no insurgents from outside. Seven or eight Rohingyas had been caught, he said, but otherwise there were no illegal migrants in Manipur.[82]

There was no mention of poppy cultivation in the Hills, drug trafficking or infiltrators. He said Naga, Kuki and Meitei were living together peacefully. The Prime Minister had assured him at the time that the unity and integrity of Manipur would not be affected. (The latter presumably said so in the context of the Indo-Naga peace talks whereby the Naga insurgents wanted the integration of Naga-inhabited areas, which included parts of Manipur, under one administration.)

And yet, in 2023, the Kukis were being openly portrayed as 'outsiders'.

When the Manipur government claims that there are illegal migrants coming in from Myanmar, there appears to be a deliberate attempt to conflate an illegal migrant with a political refugee. After the military coup in Myanmar in February 2021, followed by widespread repression under the military junta, many citizens took shelter in India, mainly Manipur and Mizoram. We will discuss the issue of refugees in the chapter on Myanmar. I mention it here to emphasize that this scare of the outsider is sought to be built up in support of the largely Meitei demand for a National Register of Citizens (NRC).

Created in 2003 by an amendment to the Citizenship Act, 1955, the NRC, as the name suggests, is envisaged as a means to document legal citizens of the country and identify the illegal ones. If past experience is anything to go by, the implementation of the NRC in Assam, for example, there is a legitimate fear that many people will not have the required documents to prove their citizenship—including a great many Indians, to be clear, especially tribals living in the Hills—and may find themselves being categorized as 'doubtful citizens' and detained, often in appalling conditions.[83] Although there were many Hindus and tribals who were declared to be 'doubtful' in Assam, the bulk of people who stand to have their citizenship revoked are Muslim. The Kuki-Zo fear the same eventuality for themselves if the NRC is implemented in Manipur; as do the Nepalis living in Manipur since before Manipur joined the Indian Union.

Refugees Are Not Illegal Migrants

I have some first-hand knowledge of the refugee situation because I have been handling cases of Burmese refugees since 1990, after they first crossed into India following the military crackdown on the national uprising of August 8, 1988. I was then in Imphal representing the Nagas who had been victims of the brutal counter-insurgency operation codenamed Bluebird, after Naga insurgents had raided an Assam Rifles post and walked away with a large cache of arms and ammunition in July 1987.

It was my Naga and Meitei friends who virtually compelled me to take up the case of the Burmese refugees. I had been deeply impressed by the sense of the solidarity that the Meiteis felt, knowing of their long history of wars with Burma. I helped these people—who were from various parts in Myanmar—get their refugee status affirmed by the United Nations High Commission for Refugees (UNHCR). Many of them were resettled in different parts of the West. I am in touch with many of them even now.

While in exile, some of them started a media house called Mizzima. The person behind Mizzima was Soe Myint, the student activist who, in 1990, hijacked a Thai Airlines plane from Bangkok and diverted it to Kolkata to press for an end to military rule in Myanmar. I had got him acquitted and he had returned to Yangon in 2012, when Daw Aung San Suu Kyi and her party were involved in restoring democracy in that beleaguered country.

He returned to India several times after 2012, and our government had given him, along with other Mizzima team members, gratis visas. In an effort to boost India's ties with Myanmar, the Prasar Bharati had even signed a memorandum of understanding with Mizzima in August 2018, the first such agreement with a private media company.[84] According to the MoU, Mizzima was to broadcast one hour of content from India, including Hindi movies, which he subtitled in Burmese, or interviews with Indian authors, etc.

Exactly one year before the February coup, in February 2020, I had hosted a team from Mizzima which included Soe Myint and Sithu Aung, the cameraman. I had organized for them to visit old Buddhist caves. They then drove to Ratnagiri where the last Burmese King had spent his last years in exile.

On the very first day after the February 2021 coup, Mizzima, along with other media houses in Myanmar, was banned. Soe Myint had already evacuated the journalists and they had moved to safe houses from where they continued reporting. Sithu Aung decided to come to India where he felt he would be safe. After all, just a few weeks before the coup, he had been given a gratis visa on a visit to the country.

Sithu Aung had got onto an express bus on the first day of the coup and landed at the border and crossed over. Contrary to what he had expected, he found that the Indians were not willing to accept him as a refugee and he was being treated as an illegal migrant. This was in stark contrast to the friendly reception they got when they had visited me the previous year. Sithu Aung had left behind his wife, and he had lost two close family members to Covid. Now, he was stuck in Moreh, the border town between Manipur and Tamu in Myanmar, with the virus taking its toll.

I felt angry that Mizzima, which had all along promoted

Indo-Burmese friendship through its broadcasts, was now being treated so badly, its members considered illegal migrants and threats to the security of India. I looked at Mizzima (not only Soe Myint) as a friend of India. My husband, Sebastian, and I were in Goa, where we lived at the time. We decided that we should try to rescue Sithu and his colleagues. It was the second wave of Covid and we knew we were vulnerable, both because of our age and the state of our health.

On April 11, 2021, we took a flight from Goa to Kolkata and from there to Imphal and left for Moreh the same day in Sebastian's sister's car. We had on a previous occasion travelled across the border and had lunch in Tamu thanks to the Free Movement Regime (FMR) between India and Myanmar, under which every member of the hill tribes, who was either a citizen of India or of Myanmar and who was a resident of any area within sixteen kilometres on the either side of the Indo-Myanmar Border (IMB), could go across with a border pass (with a one-year validity) issued by a competent authority and stay for up to two weeks per visit. But this time the border was closed and the Friendship Bridge at Moreh had been barricaded.

In Moreh, we were joined by a young lawyer, Khalter Khampa. Khampa was from the Anal Naga community. We met Sithu Aung, his colleague Pau Khan Thawn and his family; there were three small children among them. I asked Khampa to get the affidavits of Sithu Aung and Thawn notarized at the court. I had wanted to file the case in their names and argue as their lawyer.

After an hour or so, Khampa came back looking rather scared. He said he could not get the affidavits notarized because the other lawyers advised him not to, since Burmese refugees would likely be arrested and deported. They were treating the refugees as 'illegal migrants', they told him.

This is when I was made aware of the Government of India's stand on treating refugees as illegal migrants. The Government of India's Ministry of Home Affairs had issued an advisory No. 19/2/2020-NE: II dated March 10, 2021, to the chief secretaries of Mizoram, Nagaland, Arunachal Pradesh and Manipur. Paragraphs 2, 3, 4 and 5 of the advisory read thus:

… MHA has already issued an Advisory dated 25.02.21 to the Chief Secretaries of Mizoram, Nagaland, Manipur and Arunachal Pradesh and also to Border Guarding Force (BGF) along IMB (Assam Rifles) to stay alert and take appropriate action to prevent the possible influx into Indian territory.

Now, it has been reported that illegal influx from Myanmar has started. Attention is invited to MHA letter No. 24013/29/Misc/2017-CSR III (1) dated 08.08.2017 addressed to the Chief Secretaries of all state Governments and Union Territories (UT) Administrations wherein instructions were issued to sensitize all law enforcement and intelligence agencies for taking prompt steps in identifying the illegal migrants and initiate the deportation process expeditiously and without delay.

Foreigner's Division MHA had also issued instructions to Chief Secretaries vide letter No. 25022/63/2017-F. IV dated 28.02.2018 advising them to sensitize the law enforcement and intelligence agencies for taking appropriate prompt steps for identifying illegal migrants, their restrictions to specific locations as per provisions of law, capturing their biographic and biometric particulars cancellation of fake Indian documents and legal proceedings including initiation of deportation proceedings as per provision of law.

Further, it is reiterated that state governments and UT administrations have no power to grant 'refugee' status to any foreigner and India is not a signatory to the UN Refugee Convention of 1951 and its 1967 Protocol.

Since I could not get signed affidavits by Sithu and party without putting them at risk of being arrested as illegal migrants, I filed a writ petition before the Manipur High Court as a petitioner-in-person. I argued that refugees were a totally different category from migrants, and that even though India was not a signatory to the 1951 UN Convention, the Indian Constitution guaranteed all foreigners living inside India certain basic rights.[85] Besides, India was a signatory to the UN Declaration of Human Rights and other conventions which inter alia protect refugees. For example, Article 14 of the Declaration states: 'Everyone has the right to seek and to enjoy in other countries asylum from persecution'.

The courts in India have held that asylum seekers are entitled to the right to equality before the law and protection against arbitrary action, under Article 14 of the Constitution, and the right to life. The Supreme Court and the High Courts have often protected refugees from deportation to their country of origin where their lives would be in danger.

The first hearing of our petition was to be held in the open court, but by then Covid cases had reached an alarming level, and the hearing was conducted online. The hotel where we were staying had been requisitioned for quarantine purposes and we had to shift to another.

The High Court granted my interim prayer of allowing me to get the Burmese refugees from Moreh to Imphal. The court ordered that we were to be escorted by the police. And so, we drove back to Moreh and brought the refugees to our hotel.

At the time, we were told by the police that they did not feel confident of escorting us safely. Instead, they requisitioned a vehicle of the Manipur Commandos to accompany us. The police personnel informed us that there was danger that the Assam Rifles may try to detain the refugees and deport them, in violation of the High Court order. Having worked in Manipur before, we were not too alarmed though it did seem odd. There has always been a tension between the local police and the central forces, which are seen as 'outsiders'. Fortunately, we returned to Imphal without incident.

Finally, the Manipur High Court granted my prayer and the seven refugees were able to fly to Delhi where they were given protection by the UNHCR. In the course of our final arguments, the central government counsel had said that I should have been arrested for meeting illegal migrants and not reporting them to the police. I thought it was an absurd argument and I did not bother to reply. I had no idea that it was something much more serious.[86]

And so, I went back to Goa.

A year later, well beyond the period for appeal, there was a news item in the *Hindustan Times* which alleged I had brought seven Rohingyas to Delhi and not produced them before the police station, and that they had gone missing. The police came with a summons to Goa. The central government had challenged the Manipur High Court judgement; the case is still pending.

The *Hindustan Times* had reported:

'The Supreme Court on Monday stayed a 2021 order of the Manipur high court that allowed seven members of the Rohingya community—including four journalists—a "safe passage" to Delhi to seek refugee status from the United Nations High Commission for Refugees (UNHCR).

'The order came on a petition filed by the Centre, which said that the seven persons were "untraceable", and responsibility for their going missing ought to be fixed on human rights activist and lawyer Nandita Haksar, who moved a petition on their behalf before the high court and took personal responsibility that their presence would be marked at Parliament Street police station on their arrival in the Capital.

'Taking serious view of the matter, a bench of justices A.M. Khanwilkar and A.S. Oka issued notice to Haksar and stayed the May 3, 2021 HC order "provided the same has not been acted upon by the concerned authority so far". Posting the matter to May 6, the bench said, "We are informed that the persons concerned are not traceable. In that case, the writ petitioner (Haksar) has to take responsibility of producing them before the authorities concerned."'[87]

I wondered where the national daily had got their facts. The seven Burmese refugees I had brought to Delhi were Mizzima journalists and their family, including two women and three children. I had ensured that they were produced before the police station and handed over to the protection of the UNHCR. And none of them were Rohingyas! One was a Buddhist and the rest were Chin or Christian. In any case, even if they had been Rohingyas who wanted to take refuge in India, should they not have been given humanitarian assistance?

The government notice of 2017 mentioned in the advisory quoted earlier was meant for Rohingyas but by March 2021 encompassed all refugees. And now, by some strange machinations, our own citizens belonging to the Kuki-Zo community are being called illegal migrants!

This was my first glimpse into how refugees from Myanmar were made out to be illegal migrants or infiltrators. What was even more disturbing was that, when the Mizzima team presented themselves at the police station in Delhi, the police had told them and N.D. Pancholi, the lawyer accompanying them, that the UNHCR identity card was no protection, and if they—the police—wanted, these people could be deported.

But what was heart-warming was that even as the Manipur government turned to deporting refugees after the 2021 coup in Myanmar, many individuals, Meitei, Naga and Kuki-Zo offered humanitarian assistance to them. The people were extremely sympathetic to the refugees. It was due to pressure from the people that the state government allowed them access to health facilities in Imphal. However, under pressure from the Centre, they soon began treating the refugees as illegal migrants, confining those who had arrived to the border, with the threat of the Assam Rifles pushing them back looming over their heads. As a result, the refugees had to go into hiding and it fell on the shoulders of the Kuki-Zo communities, who were the majority living in the border areas, and some Meiteis, to provide them with food and shelter and to protect them from deportation.

Mizoram Chief Minister Zoramthanga, on the other hand, refused to acquiesce to the Centre's orders. He wrote to the Prime Minister in March 2021, a month after the coup in Myanmar, stating that it was impossible for his state to follow the directions of the Ministry of Home Affairs and push back the refugees from Myanmar:

'Mizoram shares a 510-km-long border with Myanmar, and every day terrified Myanmar citizens are struggling to cross over to Mizoram in search of shelter and protection. Myanmar areas bordering Mizoram are inhibited by Chin communities, who are ethnically our Mizo brethren with whom we have been having close contacts throughout all these years even before India became Independent. Therefore, Mizoram cannot turn a blind eye to this humanitarian crisis unfolding in front of us in our backyard.'[88]

Mizoram has an estimated 40,000 refugees from Myanmar

living in some sixty camps. This act of solidarity would make them vulnerable to accusations that they were harbouring 'illegal migrants'.

More recently, in September 2023, the Manipur government agreed to provide basic shelter to the refugees from Myanmar but said they would register the individuals and collect biometric data, as required by the directive sent by the central government in June. One of the Burmese refugees I spoke to told me they had no objection as long as the data was not shared with the military junta back home. The Mizoram government, however, which had at first agreed to carry out a similar biometric survey, later announced that it would not. Mizoram cabinet minister Lalruatkima stated: 'Collecting the biometric data of Myanmar refugees would amount to discrimination against people who are of our blood and kindred brothers and sisters.' [89]

(There is as yet no reliable figure for the number of refugees from Myanmar. In this book, we are concerned with the refugees from Myanmar in Manipur and Mizoram, and those are overwhelmingly Chins who are Christians. Some idea of the figure can be formed through humanitarian crisis reports published by ReliefWeb, a New York-based humanitarian information portal founded in 1996.[90])

Sexual Assault in Time of War

Pramot Singh of the Meitei Leepun has consistently maintained that the violence in Manipur 'is all about illegal immigration in Manipur' and 'external aggression against India' by armed Kuki groups from Myanmar. According to him, armed Kuki groups in India, Myanmar and Bangladesh share a common vision of carving out their own homeland. When Singh was asked by an *India Today* correspondent for his opinion on the viral video of two Vaiphei (Kuki) women who were stripped, paraded naked and sexually assaulted, this is what he had to say:

'Meiteis always respect women. As a Meitei, I'm ashamed that this happened in Manipur. I, along with all the people of the state, condemn this. At the same time, this is a war. So many rumours are floating everywhere. People kept saying that Meitei women were also paraded naked. So, these incidents could also be emotional reactions to such narratives. This is by no means a justification of that heinous crime. However, we should also examine why the video was leaked just a day before [the] Parliament session. Those who leaked it with [an] ulterior motive should be given exemplary punishment.'[91]

From the first day of the violence in Manipur, women from the Kuki-Zo communities were targets of sexual assault and at least two were murdered.

In one incident on May 4, two young women at a girls' hostel of a nursing institute in Imphal's Porompat were brutally assaulted. The two women from the Kuki-Zo community are identified in a *Scroll* report about the incident as simply the 19-year-old and the 20-year-old.

A mob—comprising both men and women—arrived at the hostel in the afternoon that day and started clanging the gates. They finally managed to enter even as the students watched from the windows. Two women, who were part of the mob, went into the hostel demanding the identification cards of all students.

The hostel had a mix of women from the Meitei, Naga and Kuki communities. The 19-year-old woman told the reporter that there were eight from the Kuki-Zo community—six of them had managed to hide in one part of the hostel, 'but my senior and I were not able to do so'. The 20-year-old said she tried telling the woman checking the identity cards that she was Naga. The woman reassured her: 'That's okay—we are looking only for Kuki girls.' But when they forced their identity cards out of them, they discovered both were Kuki. They were caught, beaten and 'left to die' by the side of the road outside their hostel. Eventually, a police car picked them up and took them to a hospital.

Both young women later filed complaints with the police. The 20-year-old wrote in her complaint: 'Some radical mobs belonging to the Meitei community armed with sophisticated weapons…chanting anti-tribal slogans…barged into my hostel room and dragged me onto the road… I was harassed, abused, tortured and beaten.' The 19-year-old claimed that the mob accused her of being an 'illegal immigrant from another country'.[92]

Two young Kuki women, who worked at a car wash in Imphal, were murdered in another incident that occurred a day after that. Their grieving fathers recounted their painful experience in an article published in *The Wire* on May 29, 2023:

> Our nightmare began on May 5, when one of the mothers of the girls received a call from her phone at around 5 pm that day. On the other end of her phone was a woman, screaming, and asking in Manipuri, 'Do you want your daughter alive or dead?' Before her mother could react, the woman cut the phone. We dialled and dialled our daughter's number thereafter but it went unanswered and soon went dead.
>
> It was nearly night time and we didn't know what to do. We waited in trepidation and got to know next morning from two co-workers belonging to the Naga community

that they were both killed at their workplace by a mob the previous evening itself. The mob included women too.

According to the co-workers, the owner was not present at that time. The mob gagged them first and then dragged them to a room. Seven-eight people from the mob including women entered the room and locked it. They were inside the room for some time which has made us suspect that our daughters might have been sexually abused too, though we can't say it for sure yet. They were killed by the mob inside that room. One of the co-workers made a video of the mob attack at the car wash; we have a copy of it.

After the news of their death reached us, we tried contacting the owner but he would not pick up our phone. It was his responsibility to protect his workers no matter which community they belonged to. He didn't, forcing us to ask, was he involved in it too? Only a proper investigation of the matter will bring things to light.

Based on what evidence we have, both of us have filed an FIR each at the Saikul police station...

However, we have an immediate issue at hand. Since May 5 night, the bodies of our daughters have been lying at the morgue of the government-run Jawaharlal Institute of Medical Sciences at Imphal. With the violence continuing in areas that are on the way to Imphal from our district, we are scared to venture out. We know of no Kuki person residing in Imphal at the moment. We, therefore, request the state authorities through this article of ours in *The Wire* to hand us over the bodies of our daughters and allow us to see them one last time.

It is not easy for parents to mourn the loss of their children but if we get their bodies, we can breathe with some relief that we have succeeded in giving them a decent burial at the least. The fight to get them justice will continue.[93]

B Phainom Village

A Meitei mob came to B Phainom village, Kangpokpi district directly to the north of Imphal, on the night of May 3, 2023, but they were repelled by the villagers.

The mob returned the next day, on May 4. The FIR filed at the Saikul police station stated that the mob comprised of some 800–1,000 armed individuals, suspected to be members of Meitei youth organizations like the Meitei Leepun and Arambai Tenggol, but also other groups such as Kangleipak Kanba Lup (KKL), World Meitei Council (WMC), and the Scheduled Tribe Demand Committee of Manipur (STDCM).

The FIR stated that the 'violent mob vandalized all the houses, burnt them to the ground, and looted all moveable properties, including cash, furniture, electronic items, utensils, clothes, grains, and cattle'.

Some of the villagers did manage to flee and hide in the forest nearby. These included a 56-year-old man, his 21-year-old daughter and 19-year-old son, and two other women, aged 42 and 52. They were later rescued by a police team on their way back to their station.

However, they were blocked on the way by a mob. The policemen instead of driving them to safety, allegedly drove towards the mob instead. The 56-year-old man was killed on the spot. As per the FIR, the three women were 'physically forced to remove their clothes and were stripped naked in front of the mob'.

One of the women, the sister of the 56-year-old man, said, 'They [the mob] lined us up, but not together, on the same road… When they caught us, my brother's daughter had already collapsed unconscious. So, her brother carried her along and ran. The Meiteis chased him. They circled him. My granddaughter and I managed to get away. The Meiteis beat my brother to death...'[94]

After the report filed on May 18 with the police, a complaint was sent to the National Commission for Women, but no action appears to have been taken. A video of the incident appeared two months later in July attracting national and international attention. (It began to be claimed in a WhatsApp message circulated at the time that this horrific act was revenge for the alleged rape of a Meitei nurse by Kukis. This was fact-checked by *The Quint* which found that the image being shared was of a woman murdered in Mathura in 2022.[95])

It was only after the video went viral that the Prime Minster broke his silence on Manipur. It was the first time that he spoke about the violence, and it was on July 20, 2023, for only thirty-six seconds, while speaking to the media. While he condemned the act of sexual assault, he said nothing about the context. He pointed out that such attacks also happen in states run by the Congress, carefully avoiding a statement on the situation in Manipur.

Many civil society organizations and women's groups across the country made similar statements on the sexual assault and violence against women—but most times without discussing the context. The context clearly was that one community, the Kuki-Zo, had become the target of hate and malicious assault in Manipur.

*

None of this is to say that the Meitei community did not suffer. As we have seen, Meitei Christians were targets of both Kuki and Meitei Hindu/Sanamahi groups. As early as the third week of May, already 7,472 Meiteis had migrated from the hill districts to the Imphal Valley while 5,200 Kukis had left Imphal and surrounding areas of the Valley. This was reported by the Coordinating Committee on Manipur Integrity (COCOMI), an organization working with all stakeholders to restore peace in the state.[96]

Meiteis in Churachandpur and Moreh, now living in relief camps, were the ones particularly affected. The condition in the relief camps was dismal; all of them were overcrowded and experiencing food shortages. A September 2023 report, for instance, mentioned 'a relief camp in Naorem Birahari College [which housed] more than 300 people. The government provid[ed] them with 400 grams of food daily, which was clearly insufficient'.[97]

Many Meitei villages were attacked and burnt and there have been cases of alleged rape of Meitei women also. There are reports of such incidents from the very start of the violence, like that of the heinous gangrape of a 37-year-old Meitei woman in Churachandpur on May 3.[98]

*

According to the Meiteis, the violence was started by the Kukis. Whether or not that is indeed the case, it does not explain the extent and nature of violence, nor the length of time it went on for.

Senior analyst with the International Crisis Group, Praveen Donthi explains that the overwhelming evidence points to the fact that 'the Meiteis appear to have been the more aggressive side. As Manipur's largest community, they enjoy immense social, political and economic advantages, not least dominating the state government, and therefore its police force, which gives them an upper hand in the conflict'.[99]

The majority of digital media outlets in Imphal, the state capital, are owned and controlled by the Meiteis. If the following on YouTube—which has undeniably become the source for news for many of us—is anything to go by, Imphal-based digital broadcast media houses are the largest in the state. At the start of November 2023, TOM TV had 776,000 subscribers, Impact TV had 704,000, ISTV LIVE, 494,000, Elite TV, 210,000, and MAMI TV NETWORK had 174,000. For regional channels, hosting much of their content in the local language, these figures are quite large.

There are documented instances of clear bias in reporting displayed by some of these channels.[100] Similar arguments can be made against Imphal-based dailies as well, as we saw in the coverage of Joshua Hangshing's story in the previous chapter. One can certainly point to honourable exceptions where Meitei reporters have risked their lives doing stories which challenge mainstream narratives, but on the whole, the media has reflected the views of the dominant Meitei community. And there are few who seem to be ready to question it.

Fluidity of Tribal Identities

The term Kuki is an exonym and is fairly new and there is no dispute about that. The earliest written reference to Kuki is from 1777, in the British record of an attack on colonial subjects in Chittagong (in present-day Bangladesh) by Kuki tribesmen. It finds no mention either in Burmese records or in the royal chronicles of Manipur's Ningthouja dynasty. It is believed that the word could be of Bengali origin, to refer to hill people who undertook jhum, or shifting cultivation.

What is more, the definition of the Kuki people is rather dynamic and continues to change even now. The 1931 census records two groups of Kuki tribes—the Old Kuki and New Kuki. The Old Kukis migrated to different parts of Northeast India, especially to Manipur, at various times in the past. The Hmar, Kom and kindred tribes, for example, were already well settled in the fourteenth century. According to the Gazetteer of Manipur, 1886, there were approximately 8,000 'Old Kukis' who traditionally lived in the state. Over time, many of the Old Kukis opted to identify and align themselves with the Naga group of tribes. However, as we shall see below, some like the Kom, once part of the Old Kuki grouping, have opted to stand on their own.

The Gazetteer states that there were about 17,000 'New Kukis' who migrated to Manipur from the Lushai Hills (present-day Mizoram) during the early nineteenth century. The New Kukis were in fact settled at strategic locations by the British, who used them as mercenaries, or as a buffer to protect the Manipur valley from raids by Naga tribes. In an effort to neutralize the threat they posed, the British established Kuki settlements next to Naga villages or in places where the Naga tribe predominated. And so, while there is rivalry among tribes, the Hills also have a mixed population.

But to give a sense of the lack of clarity about the Kuki-Zo identity, the British classified the Anals as Kukis, yet during the first census after Independence, in 1950, the Anals classified themselves as Naga; and at one time, they united with the Moyon, Monsang and Lamkang and called themselves Pakan. Even the names of the sub-tribes are fluid. The tribe that call themselves Paite in Manipur, for example, call themselves Zomi in Myanmar, and identify themselves as Mizos in Mizoram.

Before the reorganization of the Scheduled Tribes of Manipur in 1956, the tribes were classified under three somewhat broad and amorphous groups as an interim arrangement: Any

Naga tribes; Any Kuki tribes; and Any Mizo (Lushai) tribes.

However, with the completion of necessary surveys in Manipur in 1956 (see the Scheduled Castes and Scheduled Tribes Orders (Amendment) Act, 1956), the umbrella terms were deleted and 29 tribes were listed individually, each on the basis of their respective distinct language/dialect, culture and identity. 'Any Mizo (Lushai) tribes' remained unchanged in the list though.

In 2003, the term 'any Kuki tribes' was re-inserted into the list.

There has been steadfast opposition in Manipur to the inclusion of the term 'Kuki' as a tribe. In a memorandum submitted in July 2021, for example, the Thadou Inpi, the apex body of the Thadou Kukis, objected to a recommendation to that effect by the state government. They argued that Kuki was a generic term to refer to a number of different tribes, like the word Naga.

The larger ethnic group, too, has been called by various names. Some use the term Zo people, others prefer to label them Chin-Kuki-Mizo (CKM). The total population of this group is said to be between nine and ten million and is spread across Mizoram, Manipur, Assam, Tripura, Nagaland, Meghalaya, Bangladesh and Myanmar. The Chins, referred to as such in Myanmar, were recognized in the 1947 Constitution of the Union of Burma as among the four founding groups of the nation, along with the Kachin, Shan and Burma. In India, the group has its own state—Mizoram.

The fluidity of identities can be cause for controversy. The numerically smaller tribes are especially vulnerable and under pressure to join one or the other larger conglomerations.

For instance, amid the renewed Kuki demand for a separate administration within Manipur, the Aimol Tribe

Union Manipur (ATUM) in August 2023 expressed concern and dissatisfaction with one of its own leaders, R.T. Akhel Aimol, for maintaining ties with the Kuki Inpi. They didn't want the Aimol tribe to be seen as part of the Kuki group. Their president, S. Munthuireng, emphasized that the Aimol tribe was an indigenous tribal group specific to Manipur. He even pointed to the centuries-old royal chronicle of Manipur, the *Cheitharol Kumbaba*, as a source which confirmed the tribe's distinct identity.[101] In November 2015, the Aimols had launched a protest against the erection of a Naga monolith in Chandel declaring them to be a Naga tribe. Such monoliths hold immense cultural significance among the Nagas. The Aimols had declared then that they were neither Naga nor Kuki. Interestingly, at the time, the president of the ATUM, which had led the protest, was R.T. Akhel Aimol.[102]

Then there was the controversy over the identity of the Kom tribe. The Kom Union Manipur (KUM) publicly distanced itself from the crisis which unfolded in 2023, and appealed to all to not associate the Kom people, who are Christians by faith, with either side. It was being said at the time that M.C. Mary Kom, the famous boxer and ex-Rajya Sabha member, had lobbied central government leaders and stationed troops of the Sikh Regiment of the Indian Army at Kangathei, a Kom village, and that she had made the troops open fire at Meitei villages. KUM advisor Voyes Kom called this a baseless rumour. Mary Kom herself submitted a memorandum to Union Home Minister Amit Shah in this regard. She was unequivocal in her memorandum that the Koms, a small indigenous tribe of Manipur, 'are neither Nagas nor Kukis. This has been our position for generations'.

Estimates place the number of Koms at 20,000; the 2011 Census recorded their population at 14,000. But they are scattered in five districts in central and south and south-east Manipur—Churachandpur, Chandel, Kangpokpi, Imphal East and Imphal West. Here is how the president of the KUM, Serto Chungjahao Kom, described their predicament: 'We are the most victimized. When gunfights take place between the valley and the hills, we at the foothills become human shields… We live in the periphery between the hills and the valley. These days they call it the buffer zone.'

The tribe was caught in the Naga–Kuki crossfire in 1992 and suffered for almost a year with both the Nagas and Kukis claiming Koms as part of their ethnic group. And now they are caught between the Meiteis and Kukis.

A story came out in September 2023 of the murder of an Indian Army soldier in Tarung, Imphal West. Serto Thangthang Kom had retired from the Assam Regiment in 2018 and joined the Defence Service Corps in 2019. He was deployed at the Leimakhong Military Station and was at home on leave when he was killed. He was playing with his seven-year-old son in their porch when three people came and abducted him in a white car. The next day, his body was found by the side of the road.[103]

Eleven Kom villages had to be evacuated amid the violence. The people were left with little choice but to move in with their relatives, since they could not even go to relief camps, suspected as they were by both the Meiteis and Kukis.

*

The classification of tribes is not a straightforward affair. Sometimes these have been made in pursuance of a policy of divide and rule on the part of the ruling dispensation. Once, smaller tribes were coming together to form larger tribes, but they appear to be breaking up into smaller entities to assert their separate identity and demand access to various quotas in welfare schemes.

Smaller tribes and communities within the Kuki group have tried to bind themselves together under one umbrella term when it comes to uniting for a cause. They seem to have arrived at a recent consensus that they would like to be called 'Kuki-Zo', as was noted in the Prelude. 'Kuki' effectively refers to Thadou Kukis, politically the most dominant, and the Zo are the smaller non-Naga tribes or communities such as the Vaiphei, the Paites, the Hmars, etc.

Whatever the classification, it is essential to recognize that the Kuki-Zo are Indian citizens and the refugees from Myanmar are not. Controversies over the classification must not lead to conclusions about any of these tribes or communities being outsiders or infiltrators. The concluding section of this chapter was only meant to give a glimpse into the complex problem of classification of tribes into various categories. Whether or not the influx of refugees from Myanmar is a threat to Manipur's demography will be discussed in chapter eight.

CHAPTER FIVE

The Power of the Poppy

Never ever underestimate
The Power of Poppy
Poppy plays politics of the third kind
Politics of disharmony, hatred, separation and balkanization
Poppy addicts [*sic*] and destroys youths
Poppy makes them do what they should never do
Either you kill Poppy or Poppy will kill you
[…]
Never ever underestimate
The Power of Poppy
Poppy makes the rich richer and the poor poorer
Poppy pauperizes people
Poppy corrupts and Poppy power corrupts absolutely
Poppy makes politicians blind to people's plight
Kill Poppy or Poppy destroys future generations.
　—poem by Rajendra Kshetri, webcasted on September 10,
　　　　　　　　　　　　　　　2023, *The Sangai Express*

My home is a gun
pressed against both temples
a knock on a night that has not ended
a torch lit long after the theft

a sonnet about body counts
undoubtedly raped
definitely abandoned
in a tryst with destiny.
                —'My Invented Land' by Robin S. Ngangom

I remember the day, sometime in the late 1980s, the jail superintendent in Imphal told me that he had got results from tests done on prisoners and found that several were HIV-positive. He was worried how the men would deal with the news; they would be stigmatized and face isolation. I remember asking him to which community the men belonged and he said they were from all—Naga, Kuki, Meitei and Pangal.

That was my first encounter with the deadly disease and its connection with drug abuse. I did not fully understand the consequences of the growing drug menace but it did fill me with an unspoken dread.

I had seen the Meira Paibis, the women torch bearers, pick up people selling drugs and hand them to the police or to the courts directly. In court I saw heart-rending scenes of frustrated parents handing over their sons to the police to cure them of their addiction. Once, I heard a stream of expletives emanating from a police van. The voice was of a man who was obviously angry. I asked an advocate what had happened who said it was a young man who was angry with his father for handing him to the police and refusing to take him out on bail. I turned around to see the diminutive father, standing at a little distance from the van, looking alone, but very dignified, with sorrow etched on every line on his face.

After the Indo-Naga ceasefire, there was a time when parents used to hand over their sons to Naga insurgents to cure them of their addiction. In one case, some ten to fifteen young Nagas had been rounded up by the insurgents and taken deep into the forest. There the boys were made to dig their graves and then blindfolded. They were sure they would be shot dead. And the insurgents did indeed fire, but in the air. According to the parents, this was the best cure to make their sons quit using drugs.

I used to read reports of militants shooting drug addicts in the leg and sometimes women too for violating their codes. In September 2006, three banned Meitei militant groups, United National Liberation Front (UNLF), the Kanglei Yawol Kanna Lup (KYKL) and the People's Revolutionary Party of Kangleipak (PREPAK), gave a joint statement announcing a ban on the sale and consumption of heroin, opium, Spasmo Provyvon (SP) tablets and chewing tobacco products. The statement warned: 'Drug traffickers would face capital punishment without any trial and anyone found guilty of selling liquor would get a bullet in the leg.' They did make good on their threat.[104]

In 2002, militants of the KYKL had warned of the death penalty to local women in Manipur who did not adhere to a traditional dress code, and wore trousers or saris in public. They were expected to wear the *phanek*, a traditional sarong.[105] They had previously shot people in the leg for using unfair means during examinations. At least three Manipur University officials had been 'punished' for allegedly tampering with some students' marks.

In this background, it is difficult to believe that the militants were involved in narcoterrorism. It is entirely possible that they used drug money to buy arms while at the same time protecting their people from drugs. I have no way of knowing.

I was deeply shocked by the drastic measures taken by family members of drug addicts and wondered why there weren't better ways of dealing with this social problem. I knew there was a proliferation of NGOs running rehabilitation centres and other programmes for people dealing with addiction. There was a lot of international funding but it was obviously not being put to very good use. The government had scarcely any effective schemes. It was not until June 2022 that the Anouba Mangal De-addiction Centre at Sunusiphai, Bishnupur district was inaugurated. It was the very first state-run de-addiction centre directly run by the Social Welfare Department, Government of Manipur.

Heroin enters into the picture in Northeast India around the early eighties. Within two decades, there were over a lakh addicts in the Northeast and 6,871 HIV-positive cases. Manipur came in third among all states in India, with nearly 8 per cent of the country's total HIV-positive cases. Three-fourths of the people with HIV got it from intravenous drug use, and they passed it on to their sexual partners and children.[106]

Recent investigations by *Tehelka* in 2023 into drug addiction revealed that 'a substantial number of state government employees, including engineers, contractors, clerks, and worryingly teachers—who are entrusted with the responsibility of spreading awareness against drug abuse—are also falling victim to heroin addiction. Sources indicated that approximately 10–15 government employees sought treatment [in just one] drug rehabilitation centre in Imphal', adding that precise figures for other rehab centres in Imphal could not be obtained.[107]

All these years, I had not heard the word narcoterrorism associated with the growing problem of drug addiction. There is a big difference between drug trafficking and narcoterrorism. The Wikipedia page on narcoterrorism defines it as 'the attempts of narcotics traffickers to influence the policies of a government or a society through violence and intimidation, and to hinder the enforcement of anti-drug laws by the systematic threat or use of such violence'. As with most definitions of terrorism, it typically only refers to non-state actors. Manipur had seen drug trafficking, and more recently, manufacturing, but government policy seemed to be countering this trend to some extent. In any case, there were no allegations that government policies were being decided by the drug mafia.[108]

Sometime in 2002–03, a young Naga woman from Myanmar working in a call centre came to me in tears. She said her sister had been arrested with some quantity of heroin. I do not remember how much but it was a big haul. The sister had been booked on a flight to Nigeria and was apprehended under the Narcotic Drugs and Psychotropic Substances Act, 1985; she was lodged in Tihar Jail. The woman had heard that I had taken up cases of Burmese refugees and told her sister to contact me. I said that as a human rights lawyer I did not take up cases of drug trafficking.

Later, I heard from some Naga friends in Canada that this young lady had been there as well although no one suspected her to be a drug trafficker. In 2012, I had gone to Moreh, where I discovered that the young lady had escaped and was now in Tamu. Would I like to meet her? I was asked. I said no, I would not. But I was curious about how she had managed to escape Tihar Jail. An escape such as hers was not very likely to have been successful without the assistance of the jail authorities. And the jail authorities would not risk helping her unless there were some powerful forces behind her. This was my first glimpse into the world of drug trafficking.

But even before poppy cultivation had started, ganja or cannabis grew wild in the hill areas. Of course, people resorted to cultivating the crop largely to meet living expenses. One study conducted in Ukhrul district in 2014 showed that '[i] ndebtedness was a common feature among the ganja cultivators, and it was found that about 66% of the respondents were in debt. In fact, the debt was passed on from one generation to the other. About 12% of the respondents engaged in ganja cultivation to pay off family debts. It was found that only a few respondents resorted to ganja cultivation for purchasing assets like land, house and consumer durables (6%)… Nearly half of the respondents cultivated ganja to meet the educational expenses of their children and siblings. The study found that more than 70% of the households had one or more members of the household going to college'.[109]

As many as one-third of the respondents' parents were reported to have cultivated ganja in this Ukhrul study, an indication of how widespread the practice was. However, I do not remember any one community being singled out and blamed for the traffic in ganja. There have been reports for several years that ganja is going to be legalized in Manipur as it has been in Uttarakhand and in several cities in India such as Pushkar in Rajasthan.

In August 2022, R.K. Nimai, a former IAS officer, commenting on a cannabis plantation near Andro in *Frontier Manipur*, wrote: '[An] MOU was signed between [National Botanical Research Institute, Lucknow] and [the Manipur State Medicinal Plants Board] on 14.12.2020 for collaborative work in terms of taking up of cost effective activities on Medicinal and Aromatic plants in Manipur. Indica Neutraceuticals have reportedly been granted licence to deal in bulk medicinal plant products by the State Ayurvedic Drugs Licensing Authority who is the Director of AYUSH, Govt of Manipur. The surprising element is that Indica Neutraceuticals was a company registered only on July 19, 2020 and had not furnished any return to the registering authority as per the latter's website.'[110] Such reports raise concerns about the drive to legalize the drug.

In any case, it is not ganja that has been at the centre of controversy in Manipur but the poppy. The poppy plant, *Papaver somniferum*, produces opium, whose derivatives include morphine, codeine, heroin, and oxycodone. The website of the museum of the US Drug Enforcement Administration informs us, 'The term "narcotic" refers to opium, opium derivatives, and their semi-synthetic substitutes. Narcotics are used therapeutically to treat pain, suppress cough, alleviate diarrhoea, and induce anaesthesia. However, they are some of the most addictive substances known to humans and when misused as drugs they are often smoked, sniffed, or injected.' The poppy is supposed to have been cultivated in Mesopotamia. The earliest reference to opium use is in 3,400 BC. It was used for medical purposes in India too. India lies sandwiched between the two major poppy cultivating regions in the world. One of them is the 'Golden Crescent', which includes parts of Afghanistan, Iran and Pakistan. The cultivation and trafficking in drugs in Manipur can be traced to the rise of the 'Golden Triangle'.

The Golden Triangle

The infamous Golden Triangle is a region comprising eastern Myanmar, and north-western Laos and Thailand. Official records from the Narcotics Control Bureau show that the crude product of poppy grown in Manipur is smuggled out to the triangle through the porous border with Myanmar, which itself accounts for a massive share of global poppy cultivation, estimated to be about 65 per cent in 1998.[111] The fertile soil and availability of cheap labour in the remote hilly areas of

Manipur favour poppy cultivation here as well.

Thounaojam Naresh Singh and Nongmaithem Kishorchand Singh trace the origins of the Golden Triangle in their paper in the *European Chemical Bulletin* titled 'The Poppy Menace in Manipur: Causes, Consequences and Responses'.[112]

The origins of the Golden Triangle—the term itself was invented by the Central Intelligence Agency (CIA)—lead us back to the 1950s and the West's policy of containment of communism. In 1949, the Chinese Communist Revolution culminated in the defeat of the Kuomintang party (KMT) led by Chiang Kai-shek—the West-backed antagonist in the Chinese Civil War (1945–49)—and the establishment of the People's Republic of China (PRC). While most of the KMT forces retreated to Taiwan (then called Formosa), a small part made a base in the Shan state of north-eastern Burma and later moved to the Thai-Burma border. With the support of the USA, the KMT continued their fight against Communist China, trying several times to invade the Chinese province of Yunnan, but suffering defeat each time.

The authors of the paper write:

'Despite receiving financial assistance from the CIA, the KMT sought more sources of funding to enable them [to] expand their operations against the communists and bolster their local bases. As a result, given the anarchy and access to vast tracts of uninhabited terrain where they were stationed, they entered the illegal opium trade. The KMT secured and transported the opium, which was primarily cultivated by the indigenous populace, to syndicates in Thailand, where it was later processed into heroin and exported to other nations. Thus the opium economy of the Golden Triangle developed in full swing.

'On 22 April 1953, U. Nu (independent Burma's first

prime minister) brought up issue in the UN General Assembly to adopt a resolution calling for the KMT party to give up its weapons and leave the nation.'

But the KMT brought in reinforcements.

'General Tuan Shi-wen,' they note, 'a renowned KMT commander, in mid-1960s [said] in an interview: "Necessity knows no law. That is why we deal with opium. We have to continue to fight the evil of communism. To fight, you must have an army. An army must have guns. To buy guns, you must have money. And in these mountains? The only money is opium."

'The Golden Triangle's Burmese region saw a 10–20 fold increase in opium output by the mid-1950s, reaching an annual yield of 300–600 tonnes.'

The presence of the KMT all but destroyed the rice-based economy of the tribal village of the Shan state. With the demand for opium growing, many farmers abandoned their paddy farms and moved to the hills, taking up the cultivation of poppy. New developments took place in the following decade:

'... [O]nly opium was traded in the Golden Triangle until the middle of the 1960s, but because of the conflict and the chaos in the frontier regions, private armies led by regional warlords were able to establish their own fiefdoms where their soldiers guarded a novel development: the establishment of laboratories where raw opium was refined into morphine and, later, heroin. Expert chemists from Hong Kong and Taiwan were brought in, and the trade in this brand-new, pricey, and extremely deadly medicine for Southeast Asia generated massive profits... The first heroin refineries in Southeast Asia were built in the middle of the 1960s in the hills of Ban Hauay Xay, Laos, which is located across the Mekong River from Chiang Khong, Thailand. Later, other refineries were built along the Thai-Burma border. The economic policies of Gen Ne Win also contributed to the enlargement in drug production that occurred in the mid and late 1960s.'

At the time, the KMT's illegal business was not called narcoterrorism, but it fits the definition.

Narcoterrorism in Manipur?

The term 'narcoterrorism' was coined by a former President of Peru in 1983 when describing terrorist attacks against his nation's anti-narcotics police. It has become a subject of controversy, largely due to its use in discussing violent opposition to the US government's so-called War on Drugs. In June 2011, the Global Commission on Drug Policy, a global panel of world leaders and intellectuals that aims to encourage 'informed, science-based discussion about humane and effective ways' of dealing with the drug menace, released a critical report on the War on Drugs, declaring: 'The global war on drugs has failed, with devastating consequences for individuals and societies around the world.' According to Human Rights Watch, in the United States, the War on Drugs has caused disproportionately high arrest rates of African Americans. Many others have claimed that President Nixon used the war on drugs to criminalize and disrupt Black and hippie communities and their leaders.

In case of Manipur, especially after the violence which began in May 2023, the target of the attacks has been Kukis, who have been repeatedly called narcoterrorists and blamed for encouraging poppy cultivation. However, every study as well senior law enforcement officers have pointed out that all communities in Manipur are involved in this dangerous trade. The major grievance of the Kuki-Zo community is that they have been collectively been accused of narcoterrorism, which they feel is grossly unfair and unjust. This is the reason why some members of the legislative assembly from the Kuki-Zo community withdrew their support to the Biren Singh government and from the BJP more generally.

The Kuki People's Alliance (KPA), which supported the BJP, had two MLAs in the Manipur assembly. The KPA was formed by former Indian Foreign Service officer Tongmang Haokip and Wilson L. Hangshing on January 2022. They withdrew support to the Biren Singh government in August 2023. As Haokip said on August 7, 2023: 'The situation now has changed because the present government is anti-Kuki people. Even the CM himself has openly denounced the Kukis as a terrorist group, narco-terrorists and outsider[s] or foreigner[s] and also poppy cultivators and drug smugglers and whatnot... In this situation, we have no way out other than withdrawing our support from the present government...'[113]

Government figures clearly show that all communities are involved in the illicit trade, even though the cultivators are largely the tribals. According to one report, 'of the 2,518 people arrested under the NDPS Act between 2017 and 2023, only 873 were from the Kuki-Chin community, while 1,083 were Meitei Muslims (Pangals), 381 were Meiteis, with 181 from other communities. [It was found that] the Kuki-Chin community cultivated poppy in 13,121.8 acres of land and the Naga community only 2,340 acres. Interestingly, state data indicates that the extent of land used to grow the poppy plant...has increased more than three times from 1,853 acres to 6,742.8 acres [in this period]'.[114]

We need to examine the facts carefully in order to understand the difference between those who cultivate poppy compelled by poverty and lack of development and those who actually control the cultivation and the trade in this deadly business. There are those who are the members of the drug cartels and then there are those who are mere pawns in the larger operation.

The War on Drugs in Manipur

During 2017–19, Manipur police destroyed poppy cultivation over an area of 2,858 acres. The seizure of drugs like WY (World is Yours) tablets, SP capsules, methamphetamine, poppy derivatives like opium, heroin and brown sugar, and other contraband substances, the value of which runs in crores, became a fixture on the front pages of the local dailies. (It is believed that sometimes even officials and politicians have resorted to drug trafficking.) But the trafficking and manufacture of drugs continues despite the war on drugs launched by the government of Manipur, which was backed by the Centre.

Why is it that the destruction of hundreds of poppy fields in the hills of Ukhrul, Senapati, Kangpokpi, Kamjong, Churachandpur and Tengnoupal districts has not solved the problem?

Civil society organizations have been critical of the war on drugs, raising many vital questions, especially pointing out how the state government 'had conspicuously omitted addressing cannabis plantations in the hills of Manipur', focusing instead primarily on the destruction of poppy plantations. There has been no reported destruction of ganja or cannabis plantations in Manipur under this campaign, a fact that can be easily verified.

In September 2023, the government constituted an Anti-Narcotics Task Force (ANTF) in response to a communication from the NCB. 'The government's decision to exclude cannabis eradication from the ANTF's purview,' wrote one concerned citizen, 'raises questions about the comprehensiveness of its approach to addressing the drug problem in Manipur. While opium poppy cultivation is undoubtedly a serious concern, it should not overshadow the need to address the cannabis issue effectively.'[115]

Addressing the broader question of the legitimacy of the war on drugs in Manipur, another informed resident of the state writes in *Frontier Manipur*: 'As sporadic and intermittent violence continues to ravage Manipur, the government's response has been nothing short of dismal. Rather than taking proactive measures to counter these menacing elements, there [are] mounting questions over alleged collusion between government officials and the very drug cartels plaguing the state. If the allegation is true, it would be a total betrayal of the people's trust and a testament to the dark depths of corruption.'[116]

It became clear during the first phase of the war against drugs in 2018 that the drug lords likely had state protection. Civil society groups working in the field, such as the Coalition Against Drugs and Alcohol (CADA), say that drug smuggling in the state is growing despite frequent seizures because the real perpetrators and kingpins of drug smuggling rackets are never tracked down. Others have gone so far as to argue that the so-called war against drugs in the state is indeed a big farce. They claim that there are reports that the government agencies destroyed poppy fields *after* the harvest to make a show before the public and asserted that none of the plantation owners were actually arrested.

For instance, on June 20, 2018, a team of the Narcotics and Affairs of Border, led by Additional Superintendent of Police

Thounaojam Brinda, arrested a man named Lhukhosei Zou and seized 4.595 kg of heroin, 280,200 WY tablets, Rs 57.18 lakh in cash, another Rs 95,000 in demonetized currency notes and several other incriminating articles.

Brinda returned her gallantry award because she claimed she was pressurized to release Zou, who was ultimately let out on bail and acquitted. According to an affidavit she filed, the vice-president of BJP Manipur Pradesh, Chief Minister Biren Singh, an associate of his named Olish and some high-ranking police officers had been working to let off Lhukhosei Zou, who belongs to the Kuki-Zo group of tribes. It was during the Congress government that Lhukhosei Zou was elected as the chairman of the Chandel Autonomous District Council. Zou and all the elected members of Chandel ADC joined the BJP after the BJP-led government was formed in the state.

Babloo Loitongbam, the Imphal-based activist, filed a petition before the Supreme Court against the acquittal of the alleged drug lord. The Supreme Court on March 27, 2022, slammed the state government for not pursuing the case against Zou who had been acquitted in 2020 by a special court.[117]

What is more, the CADA reports that the BJP scheme of giving alternative crops, such as lemongrass and cardamom, to farmers to discourage poppy cultivation has been shelved and so the gap between policy announcement and its implementation is obvious.

But how is this poppy cultivation being linked to the violence taking place in Manipur?

Biren Singh's 'war on drugs' undoubtedly widened ethnic fault lines in the state, but not necessarily for the reasons cited by many Meitei academics.

Addressing a press conference a few days after the violence started in Manipur, a senior professor at the Jawaharlal Nehru

University from the Meitei community claimed that the violence was a part of a 'well-planned conspiracy' by the Kuki drug mafia. He said: 'The BJP government (in Manipur) took strict action against the drug mafia. This is why the drug mafia became active in this incident and they have a big role in this Manipur violence.' He also alleged that '[t]he Kuki community fears that if the Meiteis in Manipur are given ST status, then the Kukis will be at risk of being denied jobs. This is another reason for the violence'.[118]

A journalist from *Scroll*, who has been covering the Northeast for many years, reported that in Meitei-dominated Imphal he was told over and over again that '[i]n the hills, they are cutting down all the forests and planting poppy. And because our chief minister asked them not to, they are raising hell now'. For instance, Kuhraijam Athouba, spokesperson of the COCOMI, told him that 'What is happening is simple. It is a classic case of narco-terrorism'.[119]

The Meiteis allege, writes Arunabh Saikia, '[that] the violence is the culmination of a long-drawn conspiracy by Kuki groups, both overground and underground, to thwart Chief Minister Biren Singh and his "war on drugs"... According to proponents of the theory, this has had an impact on the financing of the Kuki militant groups who rely on "narco-money" for their operations... But there seemed to be a wide-ranging consensus among officials in Manipur's security establishment that poppy was a potent funding source for militants of all shades', and not only the Kuki-Zo insurgents.

The Kuki-Zo community have criticized Biren Singh's war on drugs 'as having "selectively target[ed]" the community. The crackdown became particularly contentious when the government threatened to "derecognize" villages found guilty of harbouring poppy plantations. With distrust already running high, Kuki groups saw it as a 'ploy to "steal ancestral lands" of the community'.

This fear appeared to be confirmed when the Chief Minister said in March 2023: 'These people [the Kukis] are encroaching everywhere, whether reserved forests, protected forests, doing poppy plantations and drugs business.'[120]

But the facts clearly show that although the Kuki-Zo may be involved in the cultivation, the big profits that are reaped are not taken by the villagers. Those who do often belong to the security forces, or the political leadership (across parties and ethnicities).

Binalakshmi Nepram, founder of the Manipur Women Gun Survivors Network, writes: 'In February 2013, a public relations officer of the Indian Army was caught with 24 crore worth of narcotic drugs... Others nabbed included members of a private airline and a family member of a former home minister of Manipur. Which begs the questions: Why was one of India's premier private airlines' first ever flight scheduled from Delhi to Imphal, capital of Manipur? Whose bags are not checked while boarding a flight in India? Not just some members of the armed forces, the police and politicians too have often been indicted in India's narcotics industry.'

She claims that she 'found "some armed groups" being set up in the region to protect the drug trade in the Northeast. These groups were supported by political parties who later lobbied in elections, forcing people at gun point to vote'. She remarks that the 'story of small wars and insurgencies in Northeast India is also a story of guns and drugs'.[121]

More recently, an article in *Frontier Manipur* focused on the serious allegations being made that the Assam Rifles is affording protection to Kuki militants involved in drug trafficking. 'This claim finds support in an FIR filed by the

Manipur Police,' the report says, 'which alleges that the AR assisted Kuki militants in evading arrest by providing them safe passage through their checkpoints. There are also allegations that the AR facilitates the movement of drugs through its checkpoints. This is made possible by the AR's substantial presence in Manipur, which shares a border with Myanmar... Another serious accusation is that the AR is accepting bribes from Kuki militants in exchange for protection and collaboration in drug-related activities.'[122]

The Assam Rifles is directly under the Union Ministry of Home Affairs, and so, the allegation is that the ministry has turned a blind eye to the involvement of this force in drug trafficking.

How will the people ever know the truth? When a celebrated police officer who took on the drug mafia was silenced, who else will dare expose these nefarious activities?

Thounaojam Brinda has claimed that she was the first to have used the word narcoterrorism in the context of Manipur. Whether or not that is accurate, given her experience as a senior police official—she has been described as 'a nightmare for Manipur's drug cartel'—she speaks with authority. She asserts that no single community can be blamed for poppy cultivation. 'The poppy cartel in Manipur can be divided into four distinct groups. First, there is the top-level group that reaps the maximum share of profits. Second, there are the financiers. Third, there are the militants, commonly referred to as narco-terrorists. Last, there are the farmers, who are the poorest among these groups,' she explains in an interview to *The Week*.[123]

Biren Singh, she says, 'isn't fighting against drugs, he is rather a part of it. He is a part of the drug cartel. He is protecting them, he is their patron'.[124] She said this clearly to

Tamal Saha of *News The Truth*, an online English news portal, and repeated this in her interview to Karan Thapar for *The Wire*. According to her, it is the drug mafia which is behind the violence in Manipur; it is they who are interested in the ethnic conflict.

In the first week of October, members of Meitei extremist organizations, Arambai Tenggol and Meitei Leepun, arrived at Brinda's home and accused her of being against Meiteis and supporting the Kukis. An FIR too was filed against her for defaming the Meitei community. The protesters who arrived at her residence said she had to apologize for accusing the organizations for taking part in the violence. Even while surrounded by the goons bullying her she held her own, and though she finally apologized she said the investigations by the CBI and NIA would reveal the truth.[125]

One journalist writing about drug trafficking in *Frontier Manipur* says:

'Those who are well versed with the concept of [the] Narco-State know that governments can be directly or indirectly controlled by [the] drug mafia. "We all know what all institutions can drug money reach today. Important Northeastern states are under [the] complete grip and control [of] illegal drugs traders [playing a] pivotal role in proliferation of the same in South Asia. These states are not controlled by New Delhi as it appears to be. Being funded and part of international drug syndicate, these states are controlled by China and hence its leaders are indirectly picked by China, although apparently they seem to be chosen by New Delhi. We know how drug money is funding the so-called representatives of the people in one way or the other. And who knows how they can influence people's representatives both at the state and national levels in India," says an analyst who does not want to be identified. The same person has also closely observed the unfolding of illegal drug trade in the state of Manipur and ha[s] opined that facts and circumstances can be twisted to protect the primary accused or ring leaders in many drug related cases. If views expressed by the analyst [are] proven true, the present and future political economy of Northeast or even India can be severely damaged [to the] no point of return… [We must] ponder on the question—where does India's national security stand in relation to illegal drugs and the overarching influence of China in South or South East Asia?'[126]

Chinese nationals, but not necessarily the Chinese government, have been known to be involved in illegal operations in Myanmar. In arrests carried out in September 2023 by the United Wa State Army, one of Myanmar's largest and most powerful ethnic minority militias, more than 1,200 Chinese nationals allegedly involved in criminal online scam operations were repatriated.[127] Chinese nationals have been similarly found to be involved in the drug trade in Myanmar too. What cannot be said with any degree of certainty is whether and to what extent the Chinese state or Chinese businessmen are able to influence people's representatives in India, as claimed by the unnamed analyst mentioned in the report quoted above.

But if allegations about collusion between state officials and central forces and drug cartels are indeed true, then the violence in Manipur is a symptom of things to come. The rhetoric of identity politics will ensure in future, as it has till now, that the different ethnic communities do not come together to fight their real enemies. They will instead remain stuck in this diabolical political quagmire with a leadership increasingly indifferent to their plight.

Poverty and Poppies

While identity politics drives the various narratives on the causes of the violence,[128] what is missing in most of these accounts is the link between poverty and poppy cultivation. It is almost impossible to find any thoughtful reporting on the deeper problems facing the people across the ethnic divide. Nor have community leaders properly addressed the problem of the growing poverty and impoverishment in the state. They seem content to articulate demands for homelands based on their respective ethnic or religious identities.

Scattered across the media, both local and national, we do come across reports of how the lack of economic development in Manipur has affected people in both the Hills and the Valley. But rarely does anyone delve into the underlying causes of growing impoverishment in agriculture and the increasing number of poor people in the state. In fact, Manipur is ranked the third poorest state in India with 36.89 per cent of its people living below the poverty line,[129] behind Chhattisgarh (39.93 per cent) and Jharkhand (36.96 per cent). Urban poverty is the highest in Manipur.

Several writers have pointed out that there has not been a policy for development in Manipur from the time it joined the Indian Union. In the 1970s, the Centre set up the North East Council, a statutory authority charged with the duty to ensure balanced development of the region. Yet agriculture and industry have been neglected and 'central agencies such as the North East Council and the Ministry of Development of North Eastern Region have failed to fulfil their roles as catalysts for development. Manipur is now a dependent state that serves as a captive market for products from the rest of India. Bolstered by the huge inflow of central funds for infrastructural development, its economy is a purely monetary phenomenon, which in reality has no leg to stand on'.[130]

One report notes that 'Manipur's economy is largely based on the agriculture sector, with 52.8% of its workforce engaged as cultivators and agricultural labourers. Despite the agrarian sector occupying a major share in the workforce, surveys suggest that not much has been done to improve the sector'.[131] Agriculture in the state remains largely rainfed due to the lack of irrigation facilities. What is worse, the irrigation projects that do exist have proved counterproductive as they have destroyed local ecologies.

In fact, many of the developmental projects have adversely affected agricultural growth. For instance, one of the first projects of the North East Council in Manipur was the cement factory at Hundung, in Ukhrul district. This was where the best wet paddy fields in the entire district were located. To set up the cement factory, on January 6, 1981, the government of Manipur brought out a notification announcing that the compensation for villagers who would lose their land would be 0.04 paise per square foot for second-grade land and 0.06 paise for first-grade land. The villagers challenged this notification, but they lost the case at the lower level because, they said, they could not afford to pay a bribe to the judge.

In 1990, the case was still pending and the villagers asked me to help them. I filed a public interest litigation on their behalf that year. The focus of that petition was the effect of the Nungshangkong Mini Hydro Electricity project; the water had been diverted to the cement factory, thus converting the prized wet paddy fields into dry fields.

The *wet* paddy fields provide more than just rice. In them, the cultivators have fishponds and their fertility allows for inter-cropping of maize, beans, soya beans, etc. Thus, the yield of the wet paddy field is 80 per cent higher than a dry paddy field. Apart from higher yields compared to a dry field, a wet paddy field is also a source of fish, frogs and a variety of insects which are eaten and are a cheap source of protein. People cannot buy meat which is expensive, so the deprivation of these sources of protein has a very adverse effect on their diet.

This is just one example of how development projects have led to the impoverishment of the people. There are eight major, medium and multipurpose irrigation projects but, as noted above, they have led to more grief and sorrow than to progress or prosperity.

One report from 2018 notes that, at the very outset, the Thoubal Multipurpose Project, or the Mapithel Dam, saw over a thirty-year delay leading to a revision of the cost several times. 'Tumukhong is the immediate downstream village,' the report goes on, 'hardly around 600 metres away from the main reservoir. [P]ost construction of the dam, the Thoubal River's riverbed has shrunk and the village is transformed into a dry barren [land]. Small-scale sand mining from the riverbed constituted the economic domain of the village [which subsisted on] farming, fishing, harvesting of local forest resources, etc. Loss of livelihood in [the] absence of alternative arrangements is the concern of the villagers. The once flourishing vegetables around the village riverbanks [have disappeared and a weary appearance has become an] inherent feature of the village'.[132]

The tragedy is repeated in Tamenglong district where there has been massive deforestation and soil erosion and dumping at several places along Tamenglong–Tousem to Haflong double-lane road construction, which could lead to climate change effects in the region. The official report from the forest division of Tamenglong district records the destruction of at least 431.656 hectares of forest land. This is in addition to the many natural rivers, streams and rivulets that have been destroyed, which has led to several villages facing drinking water problems, apart from affecting local wet fields as well.[133]

It is reported that 'these irrigation projects are viewed as failures and the Manipur farmers feel that they are not only a curse to the farmers, but they also limit paddy as a mono-crop. In 2022, the harvest of rice—the staple food of the state—amounted up to 98% of the total food-grain production... Earlier, one *sangam* (1/4th of a hectare) would yield approximately 30 bags of rice, but in 2022, yields declined drastically to about six to ten bags per *sangam*'.

The people living in the hills and closer to the international borders are much poorer. In a study by the North Eastern Hill University, professor of economics Utpal Kumar De came to the conclusion: 'The district-wise analysis results [are] in line with our expectations that the poorer districts of Senapati, Churachandpur, and Chandel record higher levels of deprivation than the richer districts of Imphal-West and Imphal-East. However, it is to be noted here that STs [were] the most deprived category in 2011–12 and [were] replaced by OBC in 2015–16.'[134]

In August 2021, the then Congress MLA from Ukhrul, Alfred Kan-Ngam Arthur, tried to raise the issue of discrimination against the Hills when it came to development expenditure in the state assembly:

'Speaker Sir...as per the response from the Tribal Affairs and Hills department...[funding] for development activities in the year 2017–18 was Rs 108 crore; in 2018–19, it was Rs 150 crore; in 2019–20, it was Rs 120 crore, and [for] 2020–21, it was Rs 41 crore.

'Speaker Sir...as per this Finance Department report, Rs 5,000 crore [was allotted] in 2017–18, Rs 4,900 crore in

2018–19 [for the Valley. However, the] actual expenditure in 2019–20 is 5,000 crores, and in 2020–21, it is 7,000 crores…

'[Speaker] Sir…the actual expenditure…is 7,000, 6,000, 5,000 crores [for the Valley] and you are allocating 100 crores for development of hills… [Manipur's] budget is very beautiful, but when the expenditure is not done, Speaker, sir, how will the Hills grow?'[135]

Analysing the figures presented by Arthur, social activist Janghaolun Haokip, writing in the *Frontier Manipur*, pointed out: '[I]n the fiscal year 2020–2021, the total budget allocation for Manipur was 7,000 crores out of which 6,959 crores were sanctioned for the valley and just 41 crores were sanctioned for the hills. Moreover from the fiscal year 2017 [to] 2021, out of the total budget allocation of 21,900 crores for Manipur, only 419 crores were allocated for the Hills while a staggering 21,481 crores were used in the valley. This is grossly unjustified considering that the valley only covers 10 per cent while the Hills cover 90 per cent of the total geographical area of Manipur.'[136]

These figures are further buttressed by the analysis presented by Raile Rocky Ziipao in his book *Infrastructure of Injustice: State and Politics in Manipur and Northeast India* (2020). The economic divide between the Hills and Valley is enforced by the legislative structure, he argues. The unicameral legislature of the state 'at present…comprises 60 members who are directly elected from single-seat constituencies, of which 40 are in the Imphal Valley and 20 in the surrounding hill districts. So the MLAs from the Hill Districts can never really challenge the policies or laws which discriminate against their constituencies'.

But to see this discrimination only in terms of identity politics gives an incorrect picture of the causes of the injustice.

First of all, the Minister of Tribal Affairs at the time when Arthur presented the figures in the assembly was a not a Meitei. It was Vungzagin Valte, the same man who was beaten by Meitei goons and left to die in May 2023. Valte did not reply to the Naga MLA, and the government later denied the accuracy of the figures.

This is not to say that the development projects in the Valley, say, the state's capital, Imphal, or even townships in the Hills, have always been received positively. For instance, the Smart City Imphal project. On June 25, 2015, Prime Minister Narendra Modi launched the Smart Cities Mission. His cabinet approved Rs 98,000 crores for the development of 100 smart cities under this project, and the rejuvenation of 500 others. Imphal was among the chosen cities. Several Smart City-related projects promoted in Imphal included flyovers, underground passes and footbridges, and the introduction of smart cycles. Activists have pointed out that Smart City projects promote the marginalization of poor and vulnerable communities by citing the example of traditional diesel and petrol rickshaw drivers who were being pushed out of business due to unilateral decisions to introduce and promote e-rickshaws in Imphal. This had even led to a three-day protest in 2020 by the impacted drivers, bringing the entire city to a halt.[137]

On November 19 and 20, 2014, the Thadou Students' Association (TSA) had protested against the acquisition of 3,000 acres of land at Haolenphai of Moreh, to set up International Township, a 'smart city'.[138] As part of the protest, TSA imposed a 48-hours *bandh* on national highways within Manipur, and also staged a mass peaceful protest at Jantar Mantar in Delhi on November 22. (The Kuki-Zo got control of the Moreh town after a bloody conflict with the Nagas in 1993 and with the Tamils in early 1995. The clash was largely over control over the profitable trade that flourished there, mostly illegal, including that of drugs. In the 2023 violence, too, the clashes in Moreh between Kukis and Meiteis have been some of the most violent.)

In 2023, a report by *India Today NE* in March said: 'Imphal East district administration has served eviction notices to over 167 households residing along the eastern bank of Imphal River in the Sanjenthong to Minuthong stretch for expansion project under Imphal smart city mission.' According to a joint action committee formed to oppose the drive, the 'evictions of residents from their homes and businesses would cause significant hardship and disrupt their way of life. Many of these residents [we]re already struggling to make ends meet...'[139]

It has been nearly a decade since the Manipur Conservation of Paddy and Wetland Act, 2014 was passed but the government is yet to furnish the rules for administering the Act. With rapid urbanization, the size of cultivable fields is also being reduced, increasing the stress on farmers.

Then there was the planned ecotourism project around Loktak Lake. Located on the border with Myanmar, the Loktak is the largest natural freshwater lake in India, and a sight to behold. It is formed by the meandering drainage of the Manipur, Imphal and Nambul rivers in the valleys south of Imphal. More than 1,500 fishermen and women live in houses built on the floating *phumdis* (heterogeneous masses of vegetation, soil and organic matter at various stages of decomposition).

According to reports, '[i]n November 2020, the Government of Manipur invited tenders for a Mega Ecotourism project which [would] span over 82 hectares of the Loktak lake [wetlands]. Neighbouring the Keibul Lamjao National Park, the mega eco-tourism project propose[d] to build jetties, a resort, and a golf course. This "world-class tourist destination" [was to] share its space with about 200 aquatic plant species and 400 faunal species, including the endemic and endangered brow-antlered Sangai deer and over 60 species of birds, most of which are migratory'.[140]

Many activists and artists ran campaigns to save the Lake and other wetlands. Finally, in February 2022, the Manipur High Court stayed all development projects around the Loktak Lake. A press release on the order by the All Loktak Lake Areas Fishers Union, Manipur noted that the Lake was a Ramsar site—a wetland site designated to be of international significance under the Ramsar Convention signed in 1971 in Ramsar, Iran under the auspices of UNESCO.

The impacts of climate change are being felt globally, with Manipur currently facing its own share. A 2021 study by the New Delhi-based Council on Energy, Environment and Water ranks Manipur as the sixth most vulnerable state to climate change in India, with the Imphal East district ranked the ninth most vulnerable. With the drastic changes in the rainfall pattern in the state over the past few years, crop yields too have come down.

Increasing poverty and lack of employment opportunities have led to thousands of youth from Manipur, especially from the hill areas, leaving their villages and moving to cities and towns in search of work. This generation, of which David Theik of Langza in Churachandpur was a part, are really the first generation of migrant workers from Manipur.

A 2019 study published in the *Economic & Political Weekly* used a probability-based sampling technique (surveying sixty households from three hill districts in Manipur—Kangpokpi, Churachandpur and Tengnoupal—that engage in poppy cultivation for opium). In-depth interviews were conducted with thirty opium farmers. Narratives from the field revealed that 'poverty, food insecurity, and material needs are the drivers of illegal opium production in Manipur'.[141]

'The total area under poppy cultivation in different hill districts in Manipur,' says the author, 'can roughly be estimated to be 6,000 acres by 2017–18... During January and February 2018, personnel from the [Narcotics and Affairs of Border], along with the help of other security agencies, destroyed poppy plants that were illegally cultivated across more than 600 acres of land in seven districts, namely Ukhrul, Kamjong, Churachandpur, Senapati, Kangpokpi, Tengnoupal, and Chandel. This joint team managed to destroy approximately 6,000 kg of opium, with a net worth of over Rs 45 crore... The price of 1 kg of opium in the local market usually ranges from Rs 50,000–70,000. During the off season, the price of opium can go as high as Rs 1,50,000. Compared to other crops, it is a significant return for an area of one acre. To the marginalized rural people, nothing is more appealing than poppy cultivation. Unlike rice, cereals, and vegetables, the returns on poppy plantation are significantly higher...

'Deprived of any form of development and living in conditions of abject poverty, villagers in interior areas of Manipur cultivate poppy for opium production. For many households, opium production provides off-farming season employment, as the opium harvest takes place later. During the harvest season, an individual can earn between Rs 300 to Rs 400 a day, which is a decent amount of money in rural Manipur. According to a village chief, "In the past three years, [poppy cultivation] comes as a substitute owing to the irregularities on the part of the government in providing bare minimum employment under the Mahatma Gandhi National Rural Employment Guarantee Act to job cardholders." For many people, including women and children, poppy cultivation has become an income generator during the farming off season... Poppy cultivation also has certain advantages over other crops: it can be cultivated almost everywhere and is a relatively high-value product that has an assured market.

'This expanding illicit economy in interior areas of Manipur has made many communities dependent on the income derived from poppy farming.'

Many of the farmers surveyed for the report explicitly stated that food insecurity was among the reasons for them cultivating poppy.[142]

The Narcotic Drugs and Psychotropic Substances Act, 1985 lists poppy as a contraband substance. But decades of neglect of the people by the state government and lack of an effective development policy by the Centre has led to poppy cultivation being seen as a viable economic activity, to say nothing about the growing influence of the drug mafia, which no authority seems truly interested in wanting to dismantle.

CHAPTER SIX

Failure of a Double Engine Government

The leader said: 'You can be whatever you would like to be. We are not concerned about this or that. We will kill you now. Our mission is to kill men.'

I ask: 'In what manner will you kill me? Will you cut me with a knife? Will you shoot me? Will you club me to death?'

'We will shoot you.'

'With which gun will you shoot me, then? Made in India, or made in another country?'

'Foreign made. All of them made in Germany, made in Russia, or made in China. We don't use guns made in India. Let alone good guns, India cannot even make plastic flowers…'

'Whatever it may be, if you must shoot me please shoot me with a gun made in India. I don't want to die from a foreign bullet. You see, I love India very much.'

'That can never be. Your wish cannot be granted. Don't ever mention Bharat to us.'

Saying this, they left without killing me; as if they didn't do anything at all. Being fastidious about death I escaped with my life.

—'I Want to Be Killed by an Indian Bullet'
by Thangjam Ibopishak Singh
(translated into English by Robin S. Ngangom)

'Prime Minister Narendra Modi on…August 10 finally broke his silence on the floor of the parliament about the ongoing violence in Manipur while replying to the no-confidence motion moved against his government,' reported *The Wire*. 'However, in his speech that lasted around two hours and twenty minutes, the Prime Minister spoke about Manipur for barely ten minutes in which he said that his government is working towards peace.'[143]

Two months later, he found time to visit Ahmedabad on November 19 to watch the cricket world cup. He hadn't found time to visit Manipur though, where the violence raged on and the state was under a prolonged internet shutdown.

Chief Minister N. Biren Singh announced on October 19, 2023, that Manipur was 90 per cent normal and peace would return to the state soon. But as this book goes to press, Manipur is far from normal and even the internet services have not been restored entirely. It is now seven months since the violence began.

The Times of India reported that, by August 2023, 'the reinforcements sent by the Centre…from the CRPF, SSB, ITBP and BSF add to the 9,000 personnel, or 124 companies of central armed police forces already deployed in the troubled state since the violence began on May 3. Around 10,000 soldiers have also been on the ground for more than two months, assisting in area domination, sanitation and other law and order exercises'.[144]

The allegations and counter-allegations continue, but we are no nearer to the truth as to who was responsible for the violence, and why.

There is so far no official explanation of the causes of the violence. The central government has set up a commission of enquiry headed by the former chief justice of the Gauhati High

Court Justice Ajai Lamba, retired IAS officer Himanshu Shekhar and retired IPS officer Aloka Prabhakar. The commission was set up on June 4, mandated to probe the causes and the spread of violence and rioting targeting members of different communities.

The probe will look into the sequence of events leading up to the violence that began on May 3, and see whether there were any lapses on the part of the various authorities.

The problem is: is it enough to simply look at the 'sequence of events'? In Manipur, the Meitei media has done just that, specifically the events of May 3.

Who Started It?

The World Meetei Council (WMC) has categorically asserted that it was the Kukis who started the violence to achieve their nefarious political agenda, by which they mean the demand for a separate administration.[145] The Meitei-controlled media went into great detail to prove this.

The Sangai Express, the Imphal-based paper, admits that there was no Meitei media in the Kuki-dominated district of Churachandpur, where the violence first broke out, to report on the events of May 3. It came out with an investigation into the sequence of events of the day by their staff reporter in September. The report is based largely on the testimonies of Meiteis filed before the Manipur Human Rights Commission.

The solidarity rally, or rather rallies, were held in every hill district and were admittedly peaceful. And no incident of violence took place in any of the Naga-dominated districts. However, reports *The Sangai Express*, 'the [Tribal Solidarity March] took an ugly turn in Churachandpur [when,] at around 3.20 pm on May 3, the protesters and the armed men, mostly in black clothes, first tried to storm Waikhurok village, under Kumbi Constituency where there are 33 Meitei villages. However, they decided to "attack Torbung Bangla first" which had a larger Meitei population'.[146] The violence was actually started by the Kukis, it is claimed, and the first person to die in the violence on May 3 was in fact a Meitei.

On the other hand, a Kuki writer, Lien Chongloi, claims that the first victim on May 3 a Kuki from Torbung village. He states that after the 'Anglo-Kuki Centenary Gate at Leisang-Monglenphai was set on fire by unidentified Meitei miscreants…many Meitei volunteers who were held up at Kakwa areas started moving towards Torbung and Kangvai areas and began torching Kuki houses. The first victim of that mob attack was Haopu Kipgen from Torbung Village; he was bludgeoned to death.'[147]

It is often easy to blame one community or the other, especially without looking at the history of grievances that could have turned a spark into a conflagration. Thus, while each death is tragic, instead of focusing on the identity of the person who *first* lost his or her life, the more important question is why the state and central governments could not control the violence in time. Why were the calls to impose President's Rule not heeded?

The evidence provided by accounts from the ground show that the violence was pre-planned, but with what agenda, it is not clear. The question remains: what was the motivation behind the killings? More importantly, why did the government do nothing to stop the violence?

Law and Order

The violence that started in Manipur on May 3, 2023, was unprecedented in the state's history. Out of an estimated population of 32.3 lakhs, as of September, the violence resulted in the displacement of more than 60,000, around 50,000 of whom were living in 350 relief camps without basic amenities. Among the displaced were an estimated 12,694 children living in the relief camps.

On September 14, 2023, in a press conference, the police gave a statement on the details of the loss of life and property during the violence. IGP (Administration) K. Jayanta said the death toll of the ongoing violence stood at 175. He also said that the mortal remains of seventy-nine people had been claimed by then while those of ninety-six others still remained at various hospitals—twenty-six at Jawaharlal Nehru Institute of Medical Sciences, twenty-eight at Regional Institute of Medical Sciences and forty-two at the Churachandpur district hospital. He added that thirty-two people were reported missing while 1,108 had suffered varying degrees of injury amid the violence. As of September 14, of the 5,668 arms that had been stolen from police armouries, 1,329 had been recovered. In addition, 5,172 cases of arson had been reported in the course of the violence. This included 254 churches and 132 temples. Of the thousands of structures set on fire, 4,786 were people's homes. Jayanta also said that 37,286 people had been arrested for violating the curfew which had been imposed and spreading rumours.[148]

The strange thing is that the Manipur government has still not acknowledged that 200 or more Meiteis were killed in the battle in Khamenlok village, a strategically located village belonging to the Kuki community in the Sadar Hills, Kangpokpi district on the night of July 13–14.

This despite the fact that in a press release June 14, the COCOMI 'issued a statement valorizing the "supreme sacrifices" of supposed Meitei "volunteers" who had died in the attacks on Kuki-Zo villages like H Khopibung, Khamenlok, Chullouphai, P Phainom, Aigejang, Thambol, Jordanphai, Songjang and Govajang in Kangpokpi district over [June 13 and 14]. [The Indigenous Tribal Leaders' Forum] stated that all it takes is a simple [Google] search…to know that the villages are tribal Kuki-Zo villages with the nearest Meitei village at least a few kilometres away'.[149]

I heard of the incident from a friend who phoned from Ukhrul to tell us about the incident. Although he had no access to newspapers or the internet, he had the details because there was a Tangkhul Naga village, Hongman, from where the villagers had witnessed the killings; the Tangkhuls later helped remove the bodies.

The details of the event were told to Karan Thapar by Wilson Lalam Hangshing, general secretary of Kuki People's Alliance, in an interview on June 27, 2023.[150] Hangshing said he had got a call from someone from a Kuki village who informed him that the Meiteis had arrived at the foothills in the thousands and there was shelling using 2-inch and 3-inch mortars, which were available only to the security forces and not the insurgents. The person calling told him they could see bulletproof armoured vehicles and the Manipur Commandos. He told Hangshing that the Kukis had barely 200 to 300 volunteers spread over the Kuki villages on the ridge and even though they had weapons they did not have enough ammunition. Please pray for us, he added, before the line got disconnected.

Hangshing says he was crestfallen because he thought the village would fall and the Kuki defence would be breached and the attack could then move to the towns of Saikul and Kangpokpi.

The Kuki village volunteers had evacuated the villages—

of which there were around seven or eight in the area on the hill slopes. The women and children were hiding in the forests. The volunteers ran out of ammunition as night fell. The Meiteis destroyed the villages though one church still stood since it was made of concrete. It was inside the church that the Meiteis celebrated their victory. They slaughtered some animals and cooked them, and they feasted and consumed alcohol, according to the account given to Hangshing. The Kuki volunteers told him they could hear the chatter on their walkie-talkies. After it was dark, they rushed down from the hills with machetes and *daos* (scabbards) and killed 200 to 300 Meiteis and injured as many.

The Sangai Express carried a short report saying nine Meiteis had been killed in Khamenlok.[151] A ritual ceremony was held at Nongshim, a nearby village, for these nine people.[152] According to Hangshing, there was a large exodus of Meiteis after this incident but the Arambai Tenggol stopped the men from leaving. He also said that families were not told of the deaths and it was hushed up.

Such incidents indicate that we likely do not have precise figures for those who have been killed in the violence. The government seems to be hiding these figures from its people.

*

On the second day of the violence, that is, May 4, Manipur Governor Anusuiya Uikey authorized all district magistrates, sub-divisional magistrates and all executive magistrates/special executive magistrates to issue shoot-at-sight orders 'in extreme cases whereby all forms of persuasion, warning, reasonable force etc has [*sic*] been exhausted'.

Internet services were shut down and curfew was imposed.

However, it came out on September 23 that Airtel engineers had been providing internet services to people selectively. The telecom giant in fact tendered an apology after the Manipur government issued a show cause notice to them for providing internet services to *un-whitelisted* mobile numbers. As Kuki journalist Makepeace Sitlhou points out, the ban was of an 'uneven nature: it has offered privileged access to businesses and media close to power, mostly in the valley. Dedicated internet services remained selectively available to particular businesses in the valley and government offices, with the approval of the home department. Notably, in the midst of an internet ban, members of Manipur-based right-wing Meitei groups, such as Meitei Leepun and an armed militia, Arambai Tenggol, have been posting inflammatory hate speech on their social media accounts'.[153]

There were repeated demands by the people in Manipur as well as organizations outside Manipur for President's Rule to be imposed.

The Centre's Role

Then came the news that the Centre had invoked Article 355 of the Indian Constitution. This is part of the emergency provisions contained in Part XVIII of the Constitution and reads: 'It shall be the duty of the Union to protect every State against external aggression and internal disturbance and to ensure that the government of every State is carried on in accordance with the provisions of this Constitution.'

As the media debated the implications of invoking Article 355, constitutional experts wondered how the provision could be invoked without first the imposition of President's Rule. There were debates on national television on the history and scope of the Article and speculation on how the Centre would take over law and order. On the unexpectedness of the move, *The Quint* reported: 'Even as Manipur chief minister N. Biren Singh chaired a meeting to review the unfolding law and order situation, the Central government on Thursday, 4 May, took charge of the security situation by promulgating Article 355 in the wake of arson and violence in the hills and valley areas following Wednesday's Tribal Solidarity March.'[154]

Ashutosh Sinha, Additional Director General of Police (Intelligence), had been appointed by the Ministry of Home Affairs on the night of May 5 as the overall operational commander of the law and order situation. Kuldip Singh, former DGP (Central Reserve Police Force) (and also of the National Investigation Agency), was named security adviser to Chief Minister Biren Singh, who was also the state's home minister.

Despite the invocation of Article 355, the law and order situation kept deteriorating in Manipur. On August 1, 2023, a bench of the Supreme Court led by Justice D.Y. Chandrachud, while hearing a batch of pleas related to the ongoing violence, observed that the state machinery in Manipur had 'completely failed' and that there was no law and order left in the state. *The Economic Times* reported that the Union home ministry's tentative list of business had mentioned a question on Article 355 at first. But the final list which was to be tabled in parliament on August 1 did not mention it.

A day after the Supreme Court's remark on the situation in Manipur, however, an advocate of the Karnataka High Court, Ajay Kumar, told *The Wire* that in response to an RTI query, the Ministry of Home Affairs, 'for the first time, categorically stated that it ha[d] no information on any notification issued by the Centre under Article 355 of the Constitution between January 2023 and June 13, 2023'.

Does this mean that the state was fully under Chief Minister N. Biren Singh and that he was solely responsible for what was happening in Manipur? He seemed to have the full backing of the Meitei community and even his resignation letter was torn up by the Meira Paibis.

On September 28, 2023, a mob of Meitei people, angered by the fact that peace had still not been restored, attacked his private residence in Imphal East. The mob tried to storm his residence and one source told me that some police too joined the mob but it was dispersed.

The questions remain: Why did the Centre not remove Biren Singh and impose President's Rule as has been done in such situations previously? If the Centre were supporting the Chief Minister, then why did they not assist him in controlling the violence? The ultimate responsibility has to be that of the Government of India under our Constitution.

In a book published in 2023 titled *Internal Security in India: Violence, Order and the State*, two US-based scholars, the co-editors of the book Amit Ahuja and Devesh Kapur, come to the same conclusion. They say that the breakdown of law and order in Manipur is an indictment of the central government and a setback to New Delhi's long-term strategy in the Northeast. Ahuja is an associate professor at the University of California, Santa Barbara, while Kapur is Starr Foundation professor of South Asian Studies at Johns Hopkins School of Advanced International Studies.[155]

The right place for a debate on Manipur should have been on the floor of the parliament. Instead of debating on the causes of violence in Manipur and suggesting possible solutions, Lok Sabha and Rajya Sabha saw repeated disruptions over a disagreement between the Opposition and treasury benches on the rule under which the situation in Manipur should be discussed.

The Hindu reported: 'The Opposition's original demand was to hold the debate under Rule 267, which requires suspending the day's business and stipulates the Prime Minister's presence in the House as non-negotiable. The government insisted on a debate under Rule 176, which entails a short duration discussion.'[156]

In July, the Prime Minister spoke to the media on the video of the women being paraded naked in Manipur, saying it had shamed the country. The Opposition pointed out that the Prime Minister had spoken to the media, but still not addressed the House. He chose to remain silent, though, making only the brief comment in parliament on August 10. There was an attempt to stop the parliament from discussing the violence; when the debate did take place, the mic of the Rajya Sabha MP from the Northeast, K. Vanlalvena, was allegedly switched off, as we have seen in the first chapter.

State Complicity

Several journalists and fact-finding teams claimed that the violence was allowed to continue because the state government was complicit in the violence. For instance, a three-member fact-finding team comprising National Federation of Indian Women (NFIW) general secretary Annie Raja, national secretary Nisha Siddhu and Delhi-based lawyer Deeksha Dwivedi that visited Manipur from June 28 to July 1, came to the conclusion that 'it was State-sponsored violence' with the government 'continuing its provocative actions'. The team called for disarming all groups and individuals, restoring peace and the immediate resignation of Chief Minister Biren Singh.

In their press statement, NFIW said that it visited the state following the 'gross breakdown of constitutional bodies, apparent suspension of the right to life and the absolute state apathy towards the crisis'. Speaking to the media, Annie Raja said: 'What is happening in Manipur is not communal violence, nor is it merely a fight between two communities. It involves the question of land, resources, and the presence of fanatics and militants.'

The immediate reaction to NFIW's allegation that the state was complicit was that the police registered a case against the members of the 'fact-finding committee', including Raja. According to a report, 'The FIR was registered at Imphal police station on Saturday night based on a complaint filed by an individual named S. Liben Singh. The sections under which the FIR has been registered include those pertaining to conspiracy to commit offences; provocation with intent to cause riot; defamation; intentional insult with intent to provoke breach of the peace; imputations, assertions prejudicial to national-integration; and promoting enmity between different groups'.[157] It was only because of the intervention of the Supreme Court that they were not arrested.

But there is now some consensus that the violence *was* pre-planned and organized. What there is disagreement over is: who planned it and why?

The Sangai Express, in an article titled 'Planned Aggression: To what end?' on August 23, 2023 stated: 'In [other words], the months long violent crisis is not any spontaneous outburst of pent up anger or grievances but it has all the elements of a pre-mediated and well-planned politico-military offensive, backed by [a] well-oiled and highly aggressive propaganda machinery.'[158]

The article states unambiguously that the violence was planned by the Kukis. It says: 'The media campaign was quite aggressive and successful, at least for the first two months...

it succeeded in influencing a large section of the media and also in articulating several narratives which projected the offenders as victims and the victims as offenders. The media campaign managers of the offenders deserve accolades and commendation, at least for their highly zealous and aggressive working style. The first narrative said that the violent crisis was a clash between tribals and non-tribals. The second narrative claimed that it was [a clash] between Christians and Hindus, and the third one…[that] it was between the majority and the minority. The media campaign was so successful in the initial phase that even the European Parliament adopted a resolution condemning the alleged persecution of minority Christians by majority Hindus.'

On the other hand, in an article titled 'Targeting of Kukis the main reason behind Manipur violence', published on June 27, 2023, in *Frontline*, Angshuman Choudhury, associate fellow at the Centre for Policy Research, writes that '[t]he government's persistent dismissal of Kuki grievances, coupled with its longstanding efforts to label them as outsiders, has led to the crisis'.[159]

He goes on: 'Since early May, when an intense wave of violence and ethnic strife convulsed Manipur, everyone has said practically everything about the north-eastern State. There is a frenzied rush to identify the immediate triggers of the violence. But few have spent time discussing its broader context.

'There is a mistaken belief among large sections of the mainstream policy and media community outside Manipur that this is a petty brawl between two ethnic groups in the "remote north-east" that can be resolved only if both sides make some concessions. This liberal imagination ignores the gross imbalance of social and political power between the

Meitei and Kuki—specifically, how the former enjoys greater agency in decision-making and discourse-setting processes over the latter.'

A July 2023 statement by the organization, Radical Socialist, on the Manipur violence, published in *International Viewpoint*, reads:

'The duplicities of the BJP at the Centre and of [the] Manipur government and the police it controls are self-evident. (i) Well after the earlier outbreaks of violence, on May 17, the Biren Singh government tells the Supreme Court... that the origin of this is the "crackdown on illegal Myanmar migrants...and drug business in the hills". On May 28 Biren Singh again lies declaring that the clashes are not between the two communities "but between Kuki militants and security forces". The nefarious role of two major Meitei vigilante groups with alleged links to the RSS, responsible for the one-sided violence against Kukis, namely Arambai Tenggol and Meitei Leepun, are not brought into the picture. Subsequently, the Chief of Leepun had to be formally investigated by the police for possible crimes but both organizations are not outlawed. (ii) Why has President's Rule not been implemented for so long? Why did Modi himself remain silent for so long? The answer is obvious. There is a BJP government in the state and how can the Centre by such action indict its own party-led government, and implicitly, its biased support to the Meiteis. (No surprise—in this over two-month period Modi ignores domestic church destruction but screams about Hindu temple destruction in Australia.)'[160]

The National Commission for Women received a complaint of sexual assault of Mizo-Chin-Kuki women, including the incident in which two Vaiphei women were stripped naked and paraded, and one was gang raped. The complainant was a Kuki woman living in the USA whose father was a police officer. But the NCW did not react for thirty-eight days. This is inexplicable.[161]

Security Forces

Security experts have been univocal in asserting that, usually, any violence in the country can be dealt with within twenty-four to forty-eight hours, and the fact that this round of violence in Manipur continued for months without signs of abating shows state complicity.

India's police force is one of the weakest in the world. India's police-to-population ratio lags behind most countries and the United Nations-recommended ratio of one police personnel to 220 people. The only states with police forces that meet the global standard are those in the insurgency-hit states in the Northeast and Punjab. It may not be enough even to fill the vacant police posts to bring India's police force up to speed with global standards.[162]

Manipur has tens of thousands of police personnel, with one of the highest ratios of police personnel to the population anywhere in the country, which is at least six times the national average. It is estimated that there are 1,388 policemen per hundred thousand people in contrast to national average is 250 per hundred thousand. In addition, about fifty-odd companies of the CRPF were sent to Manipur after May 2023 along with other paramilitary, apart from the Rashtriya Rifles which has a permanent presence and operational deployment across the state.[163]

Deployment in such great numbers seemed to have little effect on the rioting. Not only were the security forces not able to contain the violence, there were clashes between the police and armed forces.

Ajai Sahni, founding member and executive director of the Institute of Conflict Management, in an interview in July 2023 with Praveen Swami, security advisor to *The Print*, said that the elected representatives have a stranglehold over the police. The latter does not have autonomy and functions in accordance with the wishes of the political power that controls them.

He said categorically in the interview that the reason for the prolonged violence was neither incompetence nor lack of planning but collusion of the state: 'the state is either supporting or orchestrating the violence'.

Sahni pointed out how strange it was that a civil society organization moved the Supreme Court asking them to direct the army to go to Manipur to protect the tribal population. The Supreme Court had responded to the petitioner that this was beyond their competence; it was the function of the executive and not the judiciary to send or not send the armed forces in aid of civil power. This was in stark contrast to the united opposition of all of Manipur to the army and paramilitary forces operating under the Armed Forces (Special Powers) Act.

Analysts were left scratching their heads, to put it mildly, when the Centre declared, on September 27, 2023, the hill districts of Manipur 'disturbed' under the AFSPA even as much of the violence took place in the Valley. An editorial in *The Hindu* on September 30 noted:

'The State government has issued a notification to extend the law's imposition to the whole State, barring the areas falling under 19 police stations in the Imphal Valley... However, given the violent ethnic conflict since this May, between the Meitei and the Kuki communities, the exclusion of the Imphal Valley from its purview even while extending it elsewhere comes across as quite ironical. The Army had sought its re-imposition in the Valley districts, as it felt that the absence of the law is hampering its operations against insurgent groups… It can be nobody's case that AFSPA should remain or its ambit increased; but it is difficult to avoid the question whether, if at all AFSPA is needed for some more time, areas that have witnessed considerable violence in recent months should remain excluded.'[164]

(The police station areas where the Disturbed Areas Act was not be imposed were Imphal, Lamphel, City, Singjamei, Sekmai, Lamsang, Pastol, Wangoi, Porompat, Heingang, Lamlai, Iribung, Leimakhong, Thoubal, Bishnupur, Nambol, Moirang, Kakchin and Jiribam. This meant that the Army and Assam Rifles could not operate in these areas without the consent of the state police.)

The fact is that the police had fractured along ethnic lines, with Meitei policeman flagrantly batting for their community and Kuki policemen abandoning their posts in Meitei areas and heading off to Kuki-dominated areas. But even this was not unique in the history of policing in India where police split down communal and caste lines in Haryana, Punjab and in Jammu and Kashmir, for example. However, when given clear orders and the officers a clear mandate, these divisions are generally overcome. But no such mandate came from the Chief Minister of Manipur.

The ten elected Kuki-Zo MLAs submitted a memorandum to the Union Home Minister in the third week of May in which they alleged that the violence was premediated and 'all Kuki police officers from the DG/Addl DG/Jt DG down to the constables were stripped of all powers, disarmed and rendered inactive much prior to the 3rd [of] May, while Meitei police were let loose upon Kuki-Zo residents of the city as well as of the foothill villages on the 3rd of May and thereafter. As a result of the backlash in the hill areas, all Meitei police staff have abandoned their posts in all hill stations'.

While the Manipur DGP P. Doungel, a Kuki, rejected this allegation, the Governor of Manipur transferred him to the post of OSD (Home), and replaced him with a Tripura cadre IPS officer, Rajiv Singh, with immediate effect.

The order reads: 'Consequent upon the inter-cadre deputation of Shri Rajiv Singh, IPS (TR: 93) from Tripura to Manipur cadre vide OM No. 1.21021/18/2023.IPS-Ill dated 29.5.2023 issued by MHA, Government of India, the Governor of Manipur is pleased to order creation of one post of OSD (Home), Government of Manipur at apex scale of IPS and to order transfer and posting of the following IPS Officers as detailed below with immediate effect and until further orders in public interest...'

P. Doungel, before his appointment as DGP Manipur on December 21, 2021, held the post of additional director general of police (ADGP) DG (Prisons). He is a former Mr India and patron of the All Manipur Body Builders Association (AMBBA).[165]

In his statement denying the allegations against the state police, P. Doungel clarified that 'there is no such action taken by the government or from any quarter'. He also mentioned that all members of the police force, irrespective of their ethnic background, discharged their responsibilities as assigned as per the rules.[166]

With all these contradictory accounts, it is clear that at the very least, an enquiry needs to be made on the conduct of the police force in Manipur. It is only an impartial investigation that can reveal whether the split along ethnic lines within the police was deliberate or an unfortunate consequence of the circumstances.

Violence and Insurgency

The next point of contention is that while the Chief Minister insisted the violence was insurgency-related or due to terrorism, the Chief of Army Staff and of course the Chief of Defence Staff both came out openly and said this was not an insurgency-related issue, effectively calling the Chief Minister a liar.

'The current situation in Manipur has nothing to do with insurgency or counter-insurgency. It is primarily a clash between two ethnicities. It is a law and order situation and we are helping the state government,' CDS General Anil Chauhan said in Pune after presiding over the passing-out ceremony at the National Defence Academy in May.[167]

Another writer who has spent considerable time studying the Northeast wrote: 'One would be justified in concluding from these events that the conflict was well-planned, funded, and executed with precision by people in power. In most cases, the security forces remained mute spectators. Significantly, the chief of the defence staff has stated that Kuki militants were not involved in the conflict.'[168]

In Manipur, insurgency-related violence and law and order cannot be separated too neatly. To begin with, there are more than twenty militant groups with highly trained insurgents who know how to use sophisticated weapons. Even when militants surrender they are still living among the people. We have already pointed out how surrendered militants from Meitei insurgent groups had joined Arambai Tenggol. The looting of arms from police stations would not make sense unless the looters were confident about knowing how to use sophisticated arms.

A report by *The Wire* states, '[A]ccording to an FIR lodged by the Indian Rifles Commando battalion at Heingang Police

Station miscreants stormed their headquarters at Khabeisoi on May 28 at 3 pm. They took away 322 Insas rifles of two versions, 9 AF rifles, assault rifles ExCalibur, and various other modern ammunition. Heingang Police station falls under the Imphal East district.' Another report of the haul gave the following list: '[A]n IRB document listing the weapons taken from...Khabeisoi...includes, 139 self-loading rifles, with 130 magazines and 22,970 rounds of ammunition; 58 submachine guns, with 256 magazines and 6,437 rounds; 68 automatic pistols, with 140 magazines; 28 INSAS light machine guns, with 257 magazines and 30,690 rounds; 165 INSAS rifles, with 237 magazines; 1 Excalibur rifle, with 44 magazines; ten Amogh carbines, with 19 magazines and 1,200 rounds; and eight AK assault rifles, with 164 magazines and 6,610 rounds. The list also includes one MP5 sub machine gun, three tear gas guns, 13 bullet proof helmets, five bulletproof jackets and a pair of night vision binoculars.'[169]

'According to yet another FIR lodged by a subedar of Manipur Police Training College on May 4,' *The Wire*'s report added, 'a mob forcibly entered the gate of the campus at 1.45 pm. They crashed the main gate, opened the locks of armouries and looted 157 Insas rifles, 54 SLRs, 34 9mm carbines, 22 Insas LMGs, 9mm pistols, several magazines, AK-47s, .303 rifles, among others.'[170]

According to various media reporting on the latest disclosures on August 4, 2023, 'mobs had looted around 4,000 weapons and 50,000 rounds of ammunition from police stations and armouries since the conflict began. In a separate incident, around 500 people in more than 40 vehicles looted arms and ammunition from the Indian Reserve Battalion (IRB) camp at Naraseina in Bishnupur district on August 3, 2023'.[171]

Commenting on the looting of arms and ammunition, specifically the May 28 incident at Khabeisoi, Greeshma

Kuthar, writing a cover story for *The Caravan* (August 2023 issue), says: 'It can no longer be disputed that the Meiteis have the support of the state police, and the weapons they were able to loot from police armouries have played a major part [in the violence].'

An article by a frequent contributor to the online publication *EastMojo* talks about the looting of thousands of weapons by Meitei groups from the police armoury: 'The blatant nature of the act was epitomized by the fact that looters were deliberately leaving their Aadhaar cards, informing the authorities of their identity. This clearly shows that these individuals were confident that the authorities would not take action against them and would sympathize with their cause. And indeed, later reports showed that the Manipur police explicitly took sides in the conflict.'[172]

In addition to the arms and ammunition that were looted from police stations is the inexplicable fact about the number of gun licenses that were issued in Manipur. *The Wire* filed an RTI in July 2023 in which they made two requests to the Ministry of Home Affairs:

> Year-wise data: The number of individuals holding licenced guns in each state of the country. Please provide the data for each state separately, indicating the total number of licenced gun holders in that state for each respective year.
>
> Categorization of gun licences: If available, please provide information regarding the categorization of gun licences, such as licences for self-defence, professional requirements, sports shooting, etc., and the number of licences issued in each category, state-wise.

Their report states: 'However, a response was received only about the data for gun licences issued in each state. It showed that as of June 20 this year (2023) there were 37.7 lakh active gun licences. This is over 4 lakhs more than the licences that were active in December 2016—when data was last made publicly available.'

In Manipur, since the BJP government came to power in March 2017, around 8,000 gun licences had been issued. 'In the Northeast, only Nagaland has a comparable growth in gun licences—although more licences were granted in Manipur.'

No collector can issue so many gun licenses without the knowledge and consent of the state government. The portfolio of home affairs in the state was held by Biren Singh in both his first (2017–22) and his second cabinet. It was therefore to him that the district collectors would have had to report.

This was confirmed to *The Wire* by former Manipur civil servant Raj Kumar Nimai: 'The figure of 8,000 weapons [licences] issued in just five years is quite staggering, and [district collectors or magistrates] can't issue weapons in such capacity without letting the state know. If this has happened, then there must have been pressure on the collectors from the authorities.'[173]

In fact, after the violence began, there was also a surge in applications for gun licences in Manipur. An official told Arunabh Saikia of *Scroll*, 'Usually, the average applications we receive in a month is not more than 50. Since the incident, we have received at least 300 but new licenses were not being granted.'

About the weapons in Manipur, the former DGP of Assam G.M. Srivastava told *The Wire*: 'All weapons can't be licensed, there must have been a supply from China and Myanmar. Not from the Myanmar government but from a group in Myanmar; China has an interest in Northeast not from now but from 1947.'[174]

Role of the Armed Forces

Let us turn to the clashes reported between the state police force and the Assam Rifles. These occurred on several occasions, and at least in one case, the police actually filed an FIR against the Assam Rifles for obstructing their work.

In an incident from August 5, 2023, maintains the Manipur police, personnel from the force were heading for a search operation to 'trace out the accused Kuki militants that might have taken shelter' near Kwakta and Pholjang village in the Meitei-dominated Bishnupur area. The operation was being conducted after three people, including a father-son duo, were killed in their sleep by the armed miscreants, suspected to be Kukis from the neighbouring Churachandpur district. They allege that the police was stopped and blocked by Assam Rifles personnel who parked their vehicle in the middle of the Kwakta–Pholjang road, thereby obstructing them in discharging their duty.

'As such an arrogant act of the personnel of the 9th AR giving a chance to the accused Kuki militants to escape freely to somewhere a safer zone for them [*sic*],' the police claimed. They accused the Assam Rifles of disobeying the law and charged it under the IPC sections of disobeying law with intent to cause injury to any person, obstructing public servant in discharge of a public function, threat to injury to public servant, wrongful restraint, assault or criminal force otherwise than on grave provocation, criminal intimidation and common intention.

The Indian Army released a statement on August 9, hours after the Manipur police registered the FIR, saying that these were 'fabricated attempts to malign [the] image of Assam Rifles'.

This tension between the 'local' forces and 'Indian' armed forces has a long history, and the alienation felt by the people of Manipur, especially the Meiteis and Nagas, comes from the fact that they have been victims of human rights violations committed during counter-insurgency operations.

On the other hand, a section of Kukis has been used by the Indian armed forces and Indian intelligence agencies to counter Naga insurgency in the past. According to Home Raikhan, a retired officer of the IRS, writing in *The Sangai Express*, 'Kukis were being trained and supplied with arms and ammunition at Leimakhong, Manipur and Zakhama, Nagaland. The National and State press also reported such suspicions (*The Telegraph* 30-03-1993; *Naga Banner* 16-04-93; *The Week* 23-05-93; *Hindustan Times* 22-07-93; *The Other Media* 31-12-93; *Nagaland Post* 01-06-95; etc.).'[175]

The Meiteis have a long history of resentment against the Assam Rifles, the oldest paramilitary force in India. It became known by its present name in 1917. It is the leading counter-insurgency force in the Northeast.

We have seen in a previous chapter the significance of the Kangla Fort to Meitei culture and how the British came to occupy it after a victory over the Kingdom's forces. After the British left Manipur, the ownership of the land comprising the Kangla Fort was transferred to the defence ministry of the Dominion of India. Post Independence, the Garhwal Rifles replaced the British troops stationed there, only to be replaced later by 4 Assam Rifles. The entire fort area, measuring approximately 236.84 acres, was put directly under the defence ministry of India, represented on the field by the Assam Rifles. The occupation of the Kangla became the focus of campaigns and protests in the state, with the demand for its evacuation being made right from 1949.

Furthermore, the force has been accused by human rights activists of human rights violations, including murder and rape. These violations have allegedly been committed with relative impunity under the AFSPA. Clashes between the civil administration and the Assam Rifles have also been documented by human rights activists as well the government. For instance, during Operation Bluebird in July 1987, the Assam Rifles did not allow the Superintendent of Police and the Deputy Commissioner to enter their own jurisdiction. The situation became so serious that the then Congress Chief Minister, Rishang Keising, felt compelled to write a memorandum to the Union Home Minister in September 1987 complaining that the Assam Rifles were running a parallel administration in the area, and that 'the Deputy Commissioner and the Superintendent of Police were wrongfully confined, humiliated, and prevented from discharging their official duties by the security forces'.[176]

Many writ petitions were filed in the high courts and before the Supreme Court challenging AFSPA. One of the grounds it was challenged on was that under the Act, the Assam Rifles had virtually taken over the civil administration and thus imposed de facto martial law, prohibited by the Constitution. Unfortunately, the Supreme Court upheld the validity of the Act in 1997.

In November 2000, the Assam Rifles shot down ten civilians at Malom Makha Leikai, near Imphal airport. The victims included a 62-year-old woman and an 18-year-old who had been a recipient of a national bravery award.

It was in protest against this incident, and to demand the repeal of AFSPA, that Irom Sharmila—civil rights activist, also referred to as the 'Iron Lady of Manipur'—started her fast which she broke only in 2016.

In 2004, Assam Rifles picked up Thangjam Manorama

(1971–2004), a 32-year-old woman, from her home on the suspicion that she belonged to an insurgent organization and raped, tortured and killed. This act enraged the Meitei women. On July 15 of that year, twelve Meira Paibis, whose ages ranged from 75 years to 45, went to the Kangla Fort, the headquarters of the Assam Rifles, and took off their clothes as an act of protest, holding a banner that said, 'Indian Army Rape Us', and placards that read: 'Indian Army rape us…we all are… mothers [of that woman]' and 'Kill us. Rape us. Flesh us.'[177]

It was soon after that protest that the Assam Rifles finally evacuated the Kangla Fort. The Manipur government passed the Kangla Fort Act that year, whereby the Kangla Fort Board was established with the chief minister as its chairman. But the fight for the repeal of AFSPA continues.

Throughout the violence in Manipur in 2023, the *Imas* (mothers) of Manipur—as the Meira Paibis are sometimes called—have tried to block the Assam Riles and armed forces from carrying out their operations. For instance, the Spear Corps of the Indian Army were forced to hand over twelve insurgents from the Kanglei Yawol Kanna Lup (KYKL) insurgent group whom they had arrested on June 25 after they came face to face with a mob of 1,200–1,500 led by women at Itham village, Kamjong district.

It is only when we know the long and fraught history of the relationship between the armed forces and the people of Manipur that we can understand the actions of the Meitei women during the violence.

This history also gives us clues as to why the Disturbed Areas Act was not imposed under the AFSPA in nineteen police station areas in the Imphal Valley.

It was also reported that under the arrangement, personnel of one paramilitary force would be responsible for maintaining law and order in a district. This was revealed to *Hindustan Times* by a security official in Delhi, 'who added that the move is also aimed at ensuring accountability and reducing possibility of conflict among forces. A unified command led by security advisor Kuldiep Singh is likely to order a rejig of the security personnel across the state for the "one district, one force" arrangement, the official said on condition of anonymity'.[178]

*

The Ministry of Home Affairs, in a gazette notification dated November 13, 2023, banned nine Meitei outfits, stating that they had been engaging in activities 'prejudicial to the sovereignty and integrity of India'. The proscribed outfits under the Unlawful Activities (Prevention) Act were: the Peoples' Liberation Army and its political wing, the Revolutionary Peoples' Front (RPF); the United National Liberation Front (UNLF) and its armed wing, the Manipur People's Army (MPA); the Peoples' Revolutionary Party of Kangleipak (PREPAK) and its armed wing, the 'Red Army'; the Kangleipak Communist Party (KCP) and its armed wing, also called the 'Red Army'; the Kanglei Yaol Kanba Lup (KYKL); Co-ordination Committee (CorCom) and the Alliance for Socialist Unity Kangleipak (ASUK).

'The MHA notification,' a security analyst told *The Print*, 'can either be termed a "precautionary measure" given the ongoing ethnic violence in Manipur or a "balancing act" to bring Meitei insurgents to the negotiating table—similar to the approach the central government took when dealing with armed Kuki groups.

'"It could also be a balancing act on the part of the central government, as it is currently engaged in talks with the Kuki insurgent groups that have signed a Suspension of Operations (SoO) agreement with the government in 2008. The time period of five years could be significant for inking similar agreements with Meitei insurgent groups," said the security analyst, who did not want to be named.'[179]

The central government has been in peace talks with the Naga insurgents since 1997 but has not arrived at a settlement. Would it be able to do so with the Meitei insurgents?

Endless Games

In Manipur, the telling of a folktale or the celebration of a festival can lead to a serious clash of narratives, and potentially to violence. Take the example of the visit of Chief Minister Biren Singh on October 18, 2023, to Ukhrul, the home of the Tangkhul Nagas.

In a public speech he made the announcement of the allocation of development funds along with his intention of making Ukhrul the summer capital of Manipur. In the course of his speech, he quoted an old folktale which says Nagas and Meiteis are brothers; Nagas being older brothers. There is indeed such a folktale, except that the story says that there were three brothers: Naga, Kuki and Meitei.

Imphal Times,[180] a month before the violence started, on April 4, 2023, published these stories, perhaps as a way of reminding the conflicting communities of their common ancestry, under the title 'Legend of Kuki, Meitei and Naga common origin from one ancestor found in folktales'.

A Mao Naga legend says, writes the author of the article: '[O]nce upon a time there was a jumping match across a river among the three sons of [the] same ancestor. The eldest, clearly the strongest, jumped the river and landed on the topmost part of the hills. The second, nearly as good, cleared the river but his foot slipped and he landed on the slopes of the hills. The youngest, however, tumbled and fell on the river. The eldest became the Nagas, the second became the Kukis and the youngest the Meiteis.'

Biren Singh's reference to the folktale aroused both anger and confusion. The Tangkhul Naga Long issued a clarification on the claim by Biren Singh that Nagas and Meiteis are brothers. *The Morung Express* reported that David K. Shimray, president of the TNL issued a statement to 'clear the air in the backdrop of widespread public outrage and confusion regarding the visit of N. Biren Singh...to Ukhrul'.

The statement said: 'TNL welcome and appreciate every move by the state government regarding development works in the district. At the same time, it must be understood that the State government is merely doing its mandated duty and not bestowing any extraordinary largesse to us...' With respect to Singh's reference to Nagas and Meiteis being brothers, it said, 'TNL is compelled to remind that it does not recognize the authority of N. Biren Singh to define the blood relation of the Tangkhul tribe—either as head of a State government or in his individual capacity. Such a declaration holds no bearing for and meaning of [*sic*] TNL...

'TNL also does not dismiss or disregard instances of relationships between certain families or clans of Tangkhul and Meitei communities. However, trying to blanket the entire Tangkhul community under such stray historical and genealogical definition[s] is bereft of any sound logic...

'TNL and the Tangkhul community are competent enough to know our own history. We also belie[ve] in our destiny as an integral part of the Naga nation and do not wish our land to become a Summer, Second or any other Capital of Manipur.'[181]

Behind that apparently innocent reference to the folk story, therefore, there were two objectives: one was to exclude Kukis by emphasizing Naga–Meitei ties; the second was that the demand for a summer capital was opposed by some Naga insurgents, especially the National Socialist Council of Nagalim (Isak-Muivah). The NSCN(I-M) has consistently demanded the integration of the Naga areas since its formation in 1988, including parts of Manipur, a demand strongly opposed by the Meiteis. By announcing that Ukhrul would be the summer capital, Biren Singh was backing a rival insurgent group called the Manipur Naga Revolutionary Front. This group had the backing of the Meiteis because it was an alliance of Nagas and Meiteis and committed to maintaining the unity and integrity of Manipur.[182]

Chief Minister Biren Singh's visit was thus not meant for any kind of reconciliation, to better the relationships between the Hills and the Valley. It was to sharpen the divisions within Manipur: between Meiteis and Kukis, but also within the Nagas by pitting one insurgent group against another.

A Question of Land

Analysing the role of the Centre and the state still does not answer the question: who will benefit from this violence? It is absolutely clear that none of the ordinary people belonging to any of the communities will. The violence has already led to loss of property and livelihood, to say the least.

Some people have assumed that the violence against the Kuki-Zo was an attempt to consolidate Hindu (Meitei) votes by the ruling BJP. But the Kuki-Zo had already joined the BJP or, like the Nagas, had alliances with them. It has been suggested that behind the violence was really a drug war. But then how does it help by branding the entire Kuki community as 'outsiders' or 'illegal migrants' and 'narcoterrorists'?

There is also a theory that the violence against the Kuki-Zo was really a means to get hold of prime land both in the Valley and outside. This view is held by many scholars and people who live in Manipur.

A report published on Land Conflict Watch on April 18, 2023 records:

'On February 20, 2023, the Noney Forest Division and police teams from Noney, Kangpokpi and Bishnupur districts, evicted the residents of K Songjang, a Kuki tribal village in… Churachandpur. The state government notified and carried out the eviction drive, deploying hundreds of police personnel and paramilitary forces to evict around 12 families at K Songjang, saying the village was recently set up and was encroaching on the Churachandpur–Khoupum protected forest stretch. According to the Manipur Forest Department, K Songjang village is a new settlement established in 2021, much after the notification of the Protected Forest in 1966, and violates state forest conservation laws.'

The state government maintained that the eviction drive was not against any one community but against illegal encroachments. During the government's eviction drives carried out between October 24, 2015, and April 18, 2023, 413 families were removed from reserved forest areas; some of these forest areas fell within the hills surrounding the Imphal Valley such as Langol. Of these, 280 families were from the Meitei community (143 Meitei and 137 Meitei Pangal) while fifty-nine were Kukis. During the drive, thirty-eight Naga and thirty-six Nepali families also faced eviction.

However, the Kuki claim that their community has been the main target of the evictions is borne out by the fact that the forest department notification of November 2022, referred to in the report quoted above, derecognized thirty-eight villages in the Churachandpur (which is Kuki-dominated) and Noney districts, claiming they fell within the Churachandpur–Khoupum protected forest. These thirty-eight villages had been excluded from the protected forests by the forest settlement officer way back in the 1970s. But the notification said that the permission for settlement was granted to the villages by an officer who was not qualified to do so.

Kuki groups have pointed out that under Article 371C of the Constitution, which is specifically applicable to Manipur, the state government cannot arbitrarily amend the Indian Forest Act, 1927 in the hill areas of the state. Article 371C provides for the constitution of a committee of MLAs, including those from the hill areas, for the modifications to be made in the state rules.

But the Union government has backed Biren Singh's stand. During a visit to Manipur in March 2023, Bhupender Yadav, Union minister of environment, forest and climate change, emphasized that though the 1927 Forest Act became a state subject after Independence, the 1976 amendment to the Act made the FCA part of the Concurrent List of subjects shared by both the state and Union governments. But he added that the state government retained ownership of the forest and was solely responsible for protecting reserved and protected forest land.

While evictions were going on in and around the Valley, on August 18, 2021, the Prime Minister announced a National Mission on Edible Oil-Oil Palm (NMEO-OP), with an investment of over Rs 11,040 crore for a five-year period.[183] NMEO-OP was a new centrally-sponsored scheme under which the government proposed to add an additional 6.5

lakh hectares for palm oil production by 2025–26. This would involve raising the area under oil palm cultivation to ten lakh hectares by 2025–26 and 16.7 lakh hectares by 2029–30. The special emphasis of the scheme is on India's north-eastern states and the Andaman and Nicobar Islands, due to conducive weather conditions in the regions.

The state government of Manipur had already announced its Oil Palm Mission in 2020. It was constituted on August 20 of that year 'with the Joint Director of Agriculture as the director and three technical staff as members, supported by a consultant. A Sub-Committee on Oil Palm was also constituted with the Principal Secretary to Health as the Chairman'.[184]

Prime Minister Narendra Modi spoke about the palm oil project on his visit to Imphal in January 2022. Then, on March 26, 2022, Chief Minister Biren Singh launched an Action Plan for the state government, '100 Action Points For First 100 Days'. The list included at point 97 holding a high-level seminar on the promotion of palm oil.

Environmental groups have pointed out that the impact of large-scale palm oil plantations on tribal societies would be disastrous. The experience in the countries of Southeast Asia and in neighbouring Mizoram has shown that oil palm is a water-guzzling, monoculture crop with a long gestation period unsuitable for small farmers, and the land productivity for palm oil is higher than for oilseeds, which create the apprehension for more land to be given for oil palm cultivation. This can potentially detach tribal people from their land and identity and damage the social fabric.

Jinine Laishramcha, writing in *Frontier Manipur*, talks about why this project will be disastrous for Manipur: 'Modi's proposal will rub salt into the wound because the palm-oil plantation will accelerate drying up of the water-sources sooner than expected, pushing Manipur to a water scarcity and a water stress zone. Modi is ignoring the already deteriorated environmental reality in the region, he has brought...palm-oil [to] the spotlight. This is contrary to the...policy [of ensuring] water supply for irrigation and household needs.'

As the biggest producer in the Northeast, Mizoram has already planted palm trees on about 29,000 hectares. According to C. Zohmingsangi from Mizoram University, the palm is a high water-consuming crop with each plant needing about 300 litres of water per day. About 45,000 litres of water per hectare every day is also a significant threat to soil fertility.

Out of Rs 11,040 crore outlay approved for the NMEO-OP by the Union government, Rs 8,844 crore was announced to be the share of the Union government and Rs 2,196 crore that of the states. The focus of the programme was increasing the area under cultivation and the productivity of oilseeds and palm trees, said M.S. Khaidem, consultant Oil Palm Mission Manipur, speaking to *Frontier Manipur* in May 2022. Touting the scheme as farmer-friendly, Khaidem revealed that the Assessment Committee, Ministry of Agriculture, GOI had identified 66,652 hectares in six districts of Manipur as potential areas for oil palm cultivation. The area-wise breakdown among the six districts was as follows: 14,516 hectares in Imphal West, 18,475 hectares in Thoubal, 10,389 hectares in Bishnupur, 11,662 hectares in Churachandpur, 6,803 hectares in Chandel and 4,808 hectares Ukhrul.[185]

Godrej Agrovet is among the companies interested in palm oil. By August 2020, it had already signed MoUs with the state governments of 'Assam, Manipur and Tripura...for development and promotion of oil palm cultivation under a central scheme'.[186] According to a *Moneycontrol* report from September 2023, 'In a regulatory filing, Godrej Agrovet said the company has entered into a strategic partnership agreement with Sime Darby Plantation Berhad (SDP), the largest producer of Certified Sustainable Palm Oil (CSPO) in the world. SDP would supply high-quality oil palm seeds to Godrej Agrovet's oil palm business units and would also set up a state-of-the-art seed production unit in India at a later date.'[187]

One can see, then, that an environmental disaster is in the making, one which will affect all communities. If the past is any guide, identity politics will keep people divided and incapable of coming together to fight against corporates looking to take their land.

Perhaps anticipating the possibility of a united opposition to the palm oil project, a Rajkot-based 'fact-checking' platform has alleged that the claim that the Manipur violence was in any way linked to the Palm Oil Mission was 'communist propaganda'; it said in a post on July 26, 2023, that there were no links between (Mukesh) Adani, (Gautam) Ambani and Modi.[188] Strangely enough, no one was making the claim—apart from rhetorical statements by a politician or two or an obscure social media post—and certainly not putting forth a serious argument to that effect. So one wonders why this fact-checking platform was checking claims that were unsubstantiated to begin with.

Perhaps the answer lies in the fact that the man behind the platform is Vijay Patel, who is known to be a staunch supporter of the BJP and against people's movements for justice.[189]

CHAPTER SEVEN

What Is Making People So Angry in Manipur?

Manipur,
People call you 'mother'.
Let me also call you 'mother', please.
But I cannot die for you!
...
If anyone has to die, let those die
Who suck your resources dry.
Deceiving stealing intimidating
Amassing riches for seven generations.
Let them die for you.
Why should I die?

—Thangjam Ibopishak Singh

One of my enduring memories of Manipur is from my time at the Manipur Baptist Convention when I met the famous Meira Paibis. I was watching Doordarshan one night after dinner. Suddenly, a group of ten or twelve women burst in, and without so much as an introduction, took me by my hand and led me outside.

One of them knew Hindi and she started asking questions. They were curious to know about this mayang lawyer who was fighting against the Assam Rifles. We walked out into the night and they quizzed me for an hour and then we walked back to the church.

The movement of the Meira Paibis started in the 1970s with campaigns against smuggling of alcohol into a dry state and drug abuse. By the time I went to Manipur in the 1980s, they had started patrolling the streets to rescue the hapless young men picked up by the armed forces on mere suspicion of being militants. They would force the armed forces to hand the men over to the police or to simply let them go. They saved many men from brutal torture. This was the time when Manipur was first declared 'disturbed' under the Armed Forces (Special Powers) Act, 1958.

In many ways, the Meira Paibis could trace their history to the early 1900s, when Meitei women rose against the British. The first Nupi Lan, or 'women's war', took place in 1904 in response to an order by the colonial authorities to send Manipuri men to the Kabow Valley to fetch timber for re-building the then Police Agent's bungalow. The second Nupi Lan broke out in 1939, in response to the export of rice during the Second World War, which had resulted in a famine-like situation.

An essay on the significance of the Nupi Lan on *EastMojo* gives us another glimpse into the history of the antagonism between the Meiteis and the Assam Rifles, relating a clash that predated the AFSPA: 'Hundreds of women came out on the streets of Imphal on December 12 [1939], demanding a ban on rice exports and...the closure of rice mills. They then marched to the [royal] durbar's office. Since Maharaja Churachand Singh was travelling, they took the president of

Manipur state durbar, T.A. Sharpe, to the telegraph office and sent an "urgent" telegram to the maharaja. Soon, the women revolutionaries swelled to 4,000, and with Sharpe held captive, Assam Rifles arrived at the scene to disperse the crowd. This resulted in a major clash of bayonets and stone-pelting. While the women backtracked, the maharaja took stock of the brutal situation and ordered the rice export to be stopped from next day.'[190]

December 12 is commemorated as Nupi Lan Day and is a state holiday, making Manipur the first state to have its own separate women's day!

While I admired the Meira Paibis' spirit and courage, the women were not feminists and they were not fighting for the rights of women oppressed by patriarchy. They were in fact enforcing traditional norms. For instance, in March 2019, a group of these women descended on a farmhouse in Utlou in Manipur's Bishnupur district. The farmhouse was hosting a party for Yaosang, a spring festival which combines Holi rituals with local traditions. The 'invitation only' party had 80 guests, mostly from the local elite.

They attacked the party because liquor was being consumed, which according to the Meira Paibis was a violation of Meitei culture. 'We had to take steps to correct them from such immorality on time,' declared Borkeina of Machai Leima, one of the oldest Meira Paibi groups. 'Otherwise, what will happen to our future?'[191]

During the violence in Manipur in 2023, there were reports with graphic details and photos of mobs of these Imas, instigating the violence, and often violence against women, including sexual assault, which is most disturbing of all.

An Imphal-based academic told *Scroll* that she would 'refrain from describing Meira Paibis as feminists'. 'Sure, it is a women's movement but most of the causes they espouse are for the community,' she said. 'They hardly talk about themselves, their bodily rights, their reproductive rights. Perhaps the 2004 Kangla Fort protest was one of the few times that they spoke out against sexual violence women faced... It's not as much about women as it is about identity.'[192]

Some reports suggest that the women are often controlled by men, especially politicians. But what concerns me is that these women, Meitei mothers with a proud history of protecting their state from drugs, alcohol and colonial oppression, are now aroused to anger in the name of protecting the Meitei identity.

They claim that they are participating in a war to preserve the unity and integrity of Manipur. It is an issue which unites the Meitei community and any threat or action perceived to undermine this unity brings forth a sharp and violent reaction, for example, the Great June Uprising, which is commemorated each year on June 18—Unity Day.

Great June Uprising of 2001

When I started practising in the Supreme Court, the cases I took up were on behalf of Nagas living in Manipur. This was because I first met the Nagas in Jawaharlal Nehru University when I was a student there during 1977–79. Around 1978, the Naga students were forming a Naga human rights group called Naga People's Movement for Human Rights (NPMHR). To be honest, it hadn't been long since I had first discovered that there were Nagas in Manipur too!

The NPMHR was the perhaps the first ethnicity-based human rights group focused on taking up human rights violations, especially violations by the Indian security forces operating under the AFSPA. Civil liberties and democratic rights organizations in the rest of India had not even heard of the Act and they were anyway reluctant to take up human rights violations by the armed forces. Besides, anyone suspected to be working for the Naga cause would be dubbed anti-Indian.

In 1983, I filed what may have been the first case against the AFSPA in the Supreme Court. From 1983 to 1991, I was basically fighting cases. But then, in 1997, the Indo-Naga peace talks began and my husband and I became involved in those.

The peace talks involved a ceasefire between the Naga insurgent group National Socialist Council of Nagalim (Isak-Muivah) (one of the two major factions of the NSCN led by Isak Chishi Swu and Thuingaleng Muivah) and the Indian security forces. But from the beginning, the talks got stuck on one point—the NSCN(I-M) said the ceasefire must cover all the Naga-inhabited areas, which included Manipur, to which the state government objected. They did not want to concede that there were any 'Nagas' in Manipur, even though Muivah himself was a Tangkhul Naga from Manipur's Ukhrul district.

In 2001, the Government of India conceded the demand and extended the ceasefire to Manipur. This led to an uprising by the Meiteis which is now called the Great June Uprising.

Here's a report of it by the *Imphal Free Press*:

Imphal, June 18: At least 13 persons were killed and more than 50 injured, some seriously, when a large-scale riot erupted in the state capital on the third and last day of the general strike sponsored by the AMUCO [All Manipur United Clubs Organisation] and AMSU [All Manipur Students' Union] today against the extension of cease-fire between the government of India and NSCN(I-M) into the territory of Manipur.

Infuriated protestors set ablaze the Manipur Legislative

 Shooting the Sun

Assembly, chief minister's office, Speaker's residence, offices of Manipur Pradesh Congress Committee (I), Manipur State Congress Party, and residential quarters of ministers and MLAs.

The BJP and Samata Party offices were also damaged by the rampaging mob.

On the last day of the general strike called by the AMUCO and AMSU demanding review of the agreement between the government of India and NSCN(I-M) 'without territorial limit', infuriated mobs converging from different directions in their thousands marched this morning towards the Raj Bhavan where they burnt effigies of Prime Minister Atal Bihari Vajpayee, Union home minister L.K. Advani, PM's special envoy K. Padmanabhiah and NSCN(I-M) leaders Th Muivah and Isak and BJP leader R.K. Dorendra and shouted war cries such as 'death to Vajpayee', 'don't disintegrate Manipur', 'no cease-fire in Manipur' and 'we'll die for Manipur'...

Many among the protestors which included women, children, elderly persons and students were injured in the indiscriminate continuous firing by the CRPF personnel...

Gas cylinder explosion rocked the Lamphel area as the flames licked through the kitchen of the residential areas of these MLAs, making the impact of the destruction more severe. The quarters were badly damaged according to reports.[193]

It was after seeing the events of 2001 that Biren Singh is said to have decided to leave journalism and join politics.

However, there were no clashes between the Nagas and Meiteis and the violence was brought under control fairly soon.

It was in this background that several national television channels asked me to speak on the issue. I made clear I was not speaking on behalf of the Nagas, but as a constitutional lawyer, I could say that the boundaries of states were not sacrosanct and could be changed under Article 3 of the Indian Constitution with a simple majority vote.

It was only in September 2023 that the Ojha Sanajaoba Memorial Trust (OSMT) Manipur and the Centre for Human Rights and Duties Education, Manipur University, submitted a ten-point memorandum to the Prime Minister to safeguard 'the historically evolved multi-ethnic territorial boundary of Manipur by amending Article 3 and Article 371C C(1)&(2) of the Constitution of India so as to empower state legislature to deal with the inherent politico-histor[ical], socioeconomic, and multi-ethnic cultural ethos of Manipur'.

The resolutions included in the memorandum were put together by a panel of experts during the 'One-Day Dialogue on Idea of Manipur: A Historical Legacy of an Asiatic Civilization', organized by OSMT and the Centre, at Manipur University's Department of Commerce conference hall on September 18, 2023.

My 2001 interview on NDTV was banned in Manipur even though all I had stated was a fact about a constitutional provision, more than twenty years before the demand for amending Article 3 was made in September 2023. But it nevertheless infuriated the Meiteis and apparently my effigy was burnt too. My friend Yambem Laba, a journalist, said his daughter had told him she had seen 'Aunty Nandita's effigy being burnt'.

The important thing to remember about 2001 is that despite the fury the Meiteis exhibited, when the ceasefire was extended 'without territorial limits', there was no ethnic conflict as we have seen this time. Meitei artists and writers, however, protested by returning their awards; this included M.K. Binodini, a recipient of the Sahitya Akademi Award for her novel *Boro Saheb Ongbi Sanatombi.* In 2001, she returned her 1976 Padma Shri in protest of the perceived plans to alter Manipur's historical boundaries.

*

A commission of enquiry, headed by C. Upendra Singh, retired judge of the district and session court, was instituted to look into the violence of June 18, 2001. In its report, it was stated:

> Now coming to its people, it is to be noted that Manipur is inhabited by various communities of which Meiteis who are now settled in the Valley, were those people who came down from, and left, the hills now inhabited by their hill brethren. The inhabitants of Manipur are of different communities and out of them about 30 indigenous communities are Aimol, Anal, Angami, Chiru, Chothe, Gangte, Hmar, Kabui, Kaccha Naga, Koireng, Kom, Lamkang, Meitei, Meitei Pangal, Mizo, Maring, Mao, Monsang, Moyon, Paite, Pumai, Purung, Ralte, Sema, Simte, Thangal, Thadou, Vaiphei, Zou, Tarao, Mate, Kharam etc. This communities are known, as a whole Manipuries. *There is no tribe known as 'Naga' in Manipur and it does not find place in the list of communities in the State.* However, only after the coming of the British in the eastern part of India and Manipur, it appears they coined the word 'Naga' to indicate some communities such as Angamis, Kacha Naga, Sema etc. as a whole. Besides these indigenous people, there are some latecomers, which include, the Bengalees, Marwaris, Punjabis, and Nepalis etc. And they are now a part and parcel of Manipuris or people of Manipur. There has been unity in diversity among the different inhabitants of Manipur. There are linguistic, cultural affinities between Meiteis and hill people of Manipur and it is an undeniable fact that there are many similarities

in customs, habits and manners between the Meiteis and the Hill people of Manipur. There has been peaceful co-existence of multi-ethnic communities. Mera Haochongpa [*sic*] is a living example of the integration of hill and plain. There is no single ethnic community clash between Meitei and hill tribes of Manipur. Manipuri or Meitei-lon is the lingua franca of the hill people of Manipur whose mother tongues are other than Manipuri. (Emphasis added)

The commission went on to recommend that 'everyone should keep in mind that this historical state of Manipur is a union of hills and plains and they are two inseparable limbs of a body. In order to cultivate the friendly relationships, to live in amity with each other and bring communal harmony among the different communities in the state, the yearly festivals like Mera Haochongpa should be organized in a befitting manner. It will be helpful to declare this festival as an annual state festival'.[194]

The Mera Hou Chongba festival had been banned by the British, which Meitei scholars say was part of the British policy of divide and rule involving the people living in the Valley and those living in the Hills. The festival was sought to be revived by those who wanted to revive the Sanamahi religion.

The Nagas

While the Nagas have not been involved in the 2023 violence, their demand for the integration of Naga-inhabited areas brings them into conflict with both Meiteis and the Kuki-Zo people. The Meiteis, as we have already discussed, oppose the Naga demand for the integration of Naga-inhabited areas: the state of Nagaland, Naga-inhabited districts in Manipur, Naga-inhabited areas in Assam and Naga-inhabited areas in Arunachal Pradesh. In order to distinguish between the

Nagaland state and the demand for an administration of integrated Naga areas, the Nagas call their 'homeland' Nagalim.

In the 2001 uprising, the Nagas and Meiteis did not physically attack each other although the Nagas gave a call for an exodus—to leave the Valley. But they soon after returned to the Valley and have built homes and businesses there.

This time, although the Nagas have maintained a studied neutrality, many of them no longer feel safe in the Valley after seeing the attacks on the Kuki-Zo community. Many Kuki-Zo have taken refuge in Nagaland and in Naga-dominated districts such as Ukhrul. Nagas have welcomed them and even tried to provide medical and other assistance. However, the Nagas did not allow the Manipur government to open relief camps in their areas. For instance, the Tangkhul Naga Long (TNL), the apex body of the Tangkhul Nagas, said the following in response to an office memorandum issued by the Home Department of the Manipur government on June 9, 2023, regarding the establishment and operation of semi-permanent relief camps in various districts, including Ukhrul:

1. The TNL emphasizes that the relief camps in Ukhrul District should not accommodate displaced persons from other districts. This assertion reflects the TNL's concern over the impact of such a move on the local community and resources.

2. The TNL urges the Manipur government to devise a policy that prioritizes allocating displaced persons back to their original places of residence rather than dispersing them throughout different locations. The Tangkhul apex body believes that this approach will contribute to restoring permanent peace in the state.

3. The TNL declares that any allocation of displaced persons from other districts to Ukhrul District will be opposed vehemently. TNL says it will hold the State Government

accountable for any resulting consequences arising from such a decision.[195]

Although the Nagas are not party to the violence in Manipur this time, there have been several incidents in which Nagas have come under attack despite identifying themselves as Nagas. The attack on four women from Namrei village, Ukhrul district on May 24, for instance. The women were reportedly on their way to Imphal airport to catch flight for Mumbai at 1:20 pm when a group of Meitei men halted their auto on Imphal's Kwakeithel Airport Road. The mob pulled the victims out of the auto and dragged them away even as the auto driver tried to intervene and identified them as Nagas.[196]

The worst was the bludgeoning to death of a Naga woman, Lucy Marem, on July 18, 2023. Initial reports claimed that Arambai Tenggol were involved but they have denied this.

Ukhrul Times reported the terms of the settlement on this murder signed by representatives of the United Naga Council (UNC), the Coordinating Committee on Manipur Integrity (COCOMI) and the Chief Minister's secretary:

> The agreement was arrived at in a meeting held between representatives of the UNC and COCOMI, joined by chief minister N. Biren Singh including his minister and MLAs at 5 pm on July 18, according to the agreement letter. The representatives of UNC expressing their anguish at the brutal killing of Lucy Marem, a Maring Naga woman on July 15 at Sawombung, placed their grievances before the chief minister. "COCOMI, by owning up moral responsibility, expressed regret over the brutal killing of M. Lucy and tendered sincere apology before the Naga delegates led by the UNC," the agreement said.
>
> The following were agreed upon/noted between UNC and COCOMI:

1. It was agreed to ensure that the culprits shall be taken into custody and given befitting punishment in accordance with law. State Government and its agencies will ensure that the investigation is taken up with utmost seriousness and swiftness.

2. State Government will pay an amount of Rs 10 lakh to the next of kin of late Mrs M. Lucy to fulfil the agreement as per Naga customary law.

3. State Government will pay an amount of Rs 5 lakh to meet ritual requirements according to Maring customary law.

4. State Government will pay Rs 5 lakh to meet the educational needs of Ms Marim Shangpui, daughter of late Mrs M. Lucy.

5. State Government will provide employment to Ms Marim Shangpui, daughter of late Mrs M. Lucy, in a government post commensurate with her educational qualification when she becomes eligible in age for such employment.

6. It was agreed that COCOMI shall initiate efforts to ensure that no such untoward incident/harassment is given to any community in future.

7. UNC agreed to suspend all forms of agitation and extend cooperation to the police to facilitate early completion of investigation.[197]

However, not all matters have been so easily settled, like the several incidents in which Nagas have been attacked and injured by Kukis. One such incident took place along the Imphal–Tamenglong road near the Chalwa police outpost around 7.30 am on September 5.

The victim was identified as Z. Hotngambou, former chairman of a local village. The assault took place while he was returning from his farm with his wife and son in his Bolero carrying bananas for sale. The attack reportedly occurred because Z. Hotngambou refused to give 300 rupees to the Kuki Revolutionary Army cadres and mentioned the names of the UNC, the Naga Hoho and NNC (Naga National Council) when asked about the authorities which had banned Naga people from giving in to extortion.[198]

There have also been reports of Naga homes damaged by Kukis, but such matters have been quickly settled by payment of monetary compensation. One Rongmei Naga house was damaged in Noney district and I was told by a very reliable source and retired government officer that Rs 20 lakhs as compensation was paid by the Kukis promptly.

Federation of Haomee

A new organization has come into prominence in this period of crisis in Manipur. The Federation of Haomee (FoH) is an alliance of the Meiteis and the Nagas. The prominent Naga members are Tangkhul Nagas. I have made several enquiries and found that the organization hasn't got the approval of the Tangkhul Naga Long, and its actions and the positions it takes are not necessarily representative of the Nagas in general.

It is this organization which filed cases against Kuki intellectuals for writing books. I discuss these later on in this chapter.

I first heard of the Federation of Haomee in 2021, when I went to Imphal to file a case on behalf of Burmese journalists taking refuge in Moreh. A member of the Haomee had asked me to help them draft something. By that time, I had decided that I would not participate in identity politics and I refused.

After the representative of the Haomee left, my husband asked me whether I remembered the man. I said I did not. Have I met him before? I asked. He reminded me of the time one Tangkhul and a Meitei had come to my home in Delhi. It was just after the passing away of my father in November 1998 and I thought they had come to offer their condolences.

I had casually asked the Tangkhul whether he was studying in Delhi and he had responded saying he was working for an NGO doing social work. My curiosity was aroused and I had asked him the name of the organization. His reply was: 'Rastriya Swayam Sewak'. He was proud he had been able to pronounce the obvious tongue-twister of a name for a Naga. I thought I might have heard wrongly and asked him to repeat and he did so.

The Meitei man had been silent all this while. He did not remove his dark glasses even inside our home. He quickly whisked away his Tangkhul companion.

Then the pandemic came and the same Tangkhul Naga phoned us in Goa and asked whether he could help the Naga migrant workers there. He had learnt that we were trying to find a safe place for the 1,000 or more migrant workers working there, mainly in the hospitality industry. I told him that there were about a thousand Nagas living in two hostels and he promptly organized fresh green vegetables through someone for them and made sure they got what they needed till they took the train back home. It was odd that someone sitting in Manipur could organize the delivery of free vegetables in Goa and that too from a Goan. The person who supplied the vegetables had links to the BJP.

The Haomee was in fact formed sometime in 2017, and claims to be an apex civil society organization of 'indigenous' communities of Manipur. It is not clear how they claim to be representing the Nagas and Meiteis especially when there already exist civil society organizations representing both communities. The FoH is perhaps the first organization of the Meiteis and Nagas against the Kuki-Zo community.

The first Indigenous People's Assembly organized by the FoH on August 6, 2023, at Adimjati Amity Hall in Imphal declared 25 ethnic communities as the 'First Settler/Aborigines/Indigenous and Native People of Manipur'.[199] As per a resolution of the Assembly, the 25 communities are: Anal, Aimol, Chiru, Chothe, Inpui, Lamkang, Liangmei, Kabui, Kharam, Khoibu, Kom, Koireng, Maring, Mao, Maram, Meetei, Monsang, Moyon, Paomei, Purum, Rongmei, Thangal, Tangkhul, Tarao and Zeme. The resolution stated that the ancestors of the 25 communities had recorded history of ancient origin. By family lineage, the 25 communities are the only indigenous communities of Manipur, according to them. In other words, they do not consider the Kuki-Zo indigenous to Manipur because they arrived in Manipur much later than the Nagas and Meiteis.

The Kuki-Zo and the Seven New Districts

I have represented the Nagas in my capacity as a lawyer. I had been involved in the Indo-Naga peace process as well. As an advocate, I had internalized the Naga narrative, and so, when I wrote an article published in *Mainstream* in June 2010 titled 'Constitutional Crisis in Manipur', I presented a Naga point of view. Immediately, there was a reaction from the Kukis demanding an apology for misrepresenting their case. In response to the criticism, a following issue of *Mainstream* published the viewpoints shared by the Kukis with the following note: 'In our issue of June 19, 2010 we published an article by Ms Nandita Haksar entitled "Constitutional Crisis in Manipur". The article was reproduced in many papers and websites in the North-East and has generated a lively debate. We have also received some responses directly. We are reproducing some extracts from various points of view so that our readers may get a feel of the volatile situation in Manipur.'[200]

I mention this because it was this experience which made me realize that I should ensure that my role as an advocate representing Nagas in the peace process should not cloud my judgement while writing on a controversial subject unless I expressly state that I am writing to present a particular point of view.

The objection the Kukis had to my article was that I had presented the Naga viewpoint when stating that four hill districts[201]—Chandel, Tamenglong, Senapati and Ukhrul—of the total of five were Naga-inhabited while the fifth hill district was Kuki-inhabited. I had not mentioned that there were Kukis living in the Naga-inhabited districts and that there was a sixth district which the Nagas did not recognize, the Sadar Hills district.

In 2016, the state government created seven new districts, which has been seen as an attempt to manipulate the demographics as part of a divide-and-rule policy.

Writing for the Institute for Defence Studies and Analyses issue on March 15, 2017, Brig Sushil Kumar Sharma, then posted as the DIGP (CRPF) in the Northeast Region, explained how:

'On December 9, 2016, the Manipur government issued a gazette notification creating seven new districts by carving out and bifurcating the state's existing nine districts. This took the total number of districts in the state to 16. The seven new districts were: Kangpokpi ([based on] a longstanding demand by the Kukis for a separate Sadar Hills district carved out from parts of the predominantly Naga populated district of Senapati); Tengnoupal (carved out from the predominantly

Naga district of Chandel); Pherzawl (earlier a part of Kuki-dominated Churachandpur); Noney (earlier a part of Naga-dominated Tamenglong), Jiribam (carved out from Imphal East), Kamjong (carved out from Ukhrul) and Kakching (in the Imphal Valley, to which some areas of Chandel have been added)...

'While Chief Minister Ibobi Singh reiterated that the creation of these new districts is a response to the longstanding demands of the local people as well as for reasons of administrative convenience, Naga leaders feel that it was an attempt to divide the Naga people by merging them with non-Naga areas to form the new districts. Further, they have also taken exception to the Manipur government not consulting the Hill Area Committees before taking the decision.'

While the United Naga Council protested by blockading the national highway the Naga insurgents made their displeasure felt by a series of ambushes.

'On December 14, the day Chief Minister Ibobi Singh was to inaugurate the new Tengnoupal district (earlier part of Chandel district), three police commandos were killed and 11 injured in two ambushes. And on December 17, 70 NSCN(I-M) militants reportedly attacked a police post in Tamenglong district and took away nine automatic weapons and ammunition.' [202]

While the Nagas opposed the creation of the new districts, the Kuki-Zo communities welcomed the decision. *India Today* reported: "For people residing in Sadar Hills, the news of the creation of Kangpokpi district is a long-cherished dream having come true. The people of Kangpokpi ecstatically danced all night, on the national highway that runs through Kangpokpi," said Kamboi, a Kangpokpi-based journalist. For the residents of Sadar Hills, the creation of the new district comes after a long struggle and at the cost of seven lives lost during the agitation for the same.'[203] The formation of a separate district for the Sadar Hills—Kangpokpi—was a step in the journey towards the dream of the Kuki-Zo to have their Kukiland.

Anglo-Kuki War, 1917–19

One grievance the Kukis have is that their contribution to India's freedom struggle is not given due recognition. In fact, Kukis were very much part of India's freedom struggle. Of the total 193 freedom fighters of Manipur listed in the Indian National Army Museum at Moirang in Manipur, 159 belonged to the Kuki community. In *Bande Mataram: Freedom Fighters of Manipur*, published by the Congress party in 1986, 79 out of the 112 individuals are Kukis.[204]

The grandson of Subhas Chandra Bose, Sumantra Bose, reminds us that all communities living in Manipur came together to fight the British. He writes: 'It was March 18, 1944. The First Division of the Indian National Army entered Manipur from Burma, mainly through the Tamu–Moreh border. For the next four months, until mid-July, virtually the entire southern half of Manipur, an area of 10–12,000 square kilometres, was under the authority of the Provisional Government of Free India (*Arzi Hukumat-e Azad Hind*) proclaimed by Subhas Chandra Bose in Singapore on October 21, 1943...

'The Meiteis, Pangals, and Kukis of Manipur, all extended support to the INA and its struggle. Their own experiences of colonial rule shaped this cooperation and solidarity. The Meiteis had not forgotten the public hanging of Prince Tikendrajit Singh and his general in Imphal at the conclusion of the Anglo-Manipur War of 1891. The Kukis could hardly have forgotten the British atrocities during the 1917–1919 Anglo-Kuki War.

'The Naga people were not an exception either. Ukhrul, where Shah Nawaz Khan's Subhas Brigade operated, is a predominantly Tangkhul Naga area of Manipur. Angami Zapu Phizo, the pioneer of Naga nationalism, joined the INA in 1944 and retreated with his Naga comrades to Rangoon, just like the Meitei youths of the Imphal Valley.'[205]

If one day sanity is restored in Manipur, all the communities would find common ground. But there are parts of the history of each community which are controversial, such as Kuki accounts of the Anglo-Kuki War of 1917–19.

In Kuki-Zo villages, the chiefs were powerful and their word was the law; in contrast to a more democratic form of governance in Naga villages. Every villager was bound by this unwritten rule and would abide by the chief's decisions. One of the primary duties of every villager was defending their land, which essentially meant the village. This duty was an expression of loyalty and solidarity.

In general, the village chiefs acted independently of each other. It was during 1917–19 that the chiefs of different Kuki villages united together politically to resist the British attempt to recruit them into the Labour Corps, to serve as labourers and porters in France during the Second World War. Many Nagas did join the Corps, but the Kukis refused. When the surviving Nagas came back they formed the Naga Club which was the first modern political organization and the foundation of the Naga national movement.

Vibha Arora and Ngamjahao Kipgen, in their essay on Kuki nationalism in the edited volume *Democratisation in the Himalayas: Interests, Conflicts, and Negotiations* (Routledge, 2017), write that the principle causes 'fuelling [the Kuki] rebellion were general hostility towards the alien British; resistance to British presence as it threatened their independence; and the British imposition of land revenue and house tax and practice of forced labour (pothang in the Meitei language), which contradicted Kuki customary practices and laws. Nonetheless, the immediate trigger for the armed uprising was the recruitment of Kuki villagers as labour corps and their deportation to France.

'According to archival sources, Chengjapao (the clan chief of Doungel) convened a meeting of various Kuki chiefs and Shajam Lha was performed in early March 1917 and later in various Kuki enclaves in many parts of Northeast India.'

Shajam Lha is a Kuki custom to mark solidarity. It involves the slaughter of a buffalo followed by the distribution of the animal's flesh among the various chiefs. The sharing of its heart and liver symbolizes the commitment to a common cause.[206]

'The Kuki rebellion effectively crystalized the political unity of the Kuki community and served as the foundation of their ethnic nationalism,' write Arora and Kipgen. '[M]any chiefs and politicians referred to the Kuki uprisings of 1917–19 as turning point of Kuki political history, attesting to its extended significance and its memory as a reminder of the spirit of oneness and their political unity as a distinct and historic nationality.'[207]

The All Tribal Students' Union of Manipur (ATSUM), Manipur's influential student body, alleges that the 2023 clashes between the Meiteis and Kukis started after some miscreants burned a portion of the Anglo-Kuki War Memorial gate at Churachandpur. Whether this was the cause of the violence is difficult to establish but whoever tried to damage the memorial knew of its importance to the Kukis.

The Anglo-Kuki War is a subject of intense disagreement

between the Nagas and Kukis. Books published on the subject by two Kuki academicians from Jawaharlal Nehru University and another by an officer of the Indian army have sought to be banned by the Federation of Haomee. It in fact lodged FIRs on August 7, 2023, at the Imphal West police station.[208]

The academicians in question were Jangkhomang Guite and Thongkholal Haokip, the editors of the 2018 book, *The Anglo-Kuki War, 1917–1919: A Frontier Uprising Against Imperialism During the First World War*. Guite is an assistant professor at the Centre for Historical Studies, JNU. He specializes in the history of the tribes in Northeast India, and has published many scholarly articles in both national and international journals, and in edited volumes. Haokip is an assistant professor at the Centre for the Study of Law and Governance, also at JNU. He was formerly with the Department of Political Science, Presidency University, Kolkata. He has authored *India's Look East Policy and the Northeast* (2015), and edited *The Kukis of Northeast India: Politics and Culture* (2013). He is the editor of *Journal of North East India Studies* and executive editor of *Asian Ethnicity*.

The second FIR was against Col (Dr) Vijay Chenji for his book titled *The Anglo-Kuki War 1917–19: A Military Perspective* (2022).

The editors and author moved the Supreme Court for protection against arrest, which the Court granted.

What is the grievance of the Nagas against these accounts of the Anglo-Kuki War of 1917–19? The Nagas point out that during their rebellion against the British, the Kukis attacked Nagas and destroyed their villages. As one senior Naga insurgent said in an interview to me: 'My earliest memories are of stories told by my parents about the Kukis. If ever I cried, my grandfather or grandmother would tell me to keep quiet so the Kukis don't hear me… My grandparents told me how the chief of Chassad village raided Tangkhul villages. The entire village was wiped out during a Kuki raid. My grandmother told me how our people, the Tangkhuls, were persecuted by the Kukis who carried off the entire village and converted them.'[209]

In 2019, the Kukis announced that they would be organizing the commemoration of 100 years of the Anglo-Kuki War and a part of their commemoration was the erection of memorial stones with the inscription 'in defence of our ancestral land and freedom'. This outraged the Nagas and they wrote to the then Chief Minister protesting against said proposal.

The general secretary of the Tangkhul Naga Long wrote an open letter to the Kuki chiefs Ref TNL/PR/19/16 dated October 7, 2019, stating:

> 1. That without going into the details and veracity on the genuineness of the historical facts, Tangkhul Community have no objection in your endeavour to commemorate the Anglo-Kuki War 1917–19 on 17th October 2019.
>
> 2. However, in your commemoration, your decision and act of erecting memorial stones in all the Kuki villages with the inscription '…in defence of our ancestral land and freedom…' is highly objectionable and not acceptable.
>
> 3. Because, all of us know that in the period 1917–19, there was not even a single Kuki village established in Tangkhul land. It is also [a] well known fact that Kuki Community in Manipur (particularly in Tangkhul areas) is not the indigenous people and have been receiving payment of refugee allowance as late as 1968.[210] It is also a fact that most of you and your fathers have been paying 'loushal or lamban' to the Tangkhul Naga Village Headmen for cultivation and settlement in lands under Tangkhul Naga village settlement.

A few days later, there was a report about four Naga tribal bodies—the Inpui Naga Union, the Liangmai Naga Council, Rongmei Naga Council and the Zeme Naga Council—dismissing the very fact that there ever was an Anglo-Kuki *war*:

'"There is [a] Kuki Rebellion (1917–18) in history. It was started in December 1917 and brought under control in November 1918, a period of about one year," the joint statement…pointed out.

'Therefore, the design of the so called commemoration of "Anglo-Kuki War 1917–1919" is highly provocative and objectionable because it is an attempt to claim ownership over the Nagas' ancestral land in the Naga areas'.

According to their statement, the Kukis had carried out attacks and killed civilians and burnt down houses in the Naga villages and in which they killed 289 Nagas and four Meiteis and burnt 34 Naga villages.[211]

Indeed, the atrocities committed by the Kukis against Nagas rarely find mention in accounts of the 1917–19 war. Take for instance Col Vijay Chenji writing on the Anglo-Kuki war: 'The British had resorted to inhuman and unethical actions like burning down of villages… [In contrast] the Kuki War Council exercised emphasis on strict adherence to… conventions [of war]. There was not a single instance of war excesses by the Kukis during their two year long armed struggle against the British.'[212]

In 2020, there was an attempt by the Nagas and Kukis to resolve the issue. A major Kuki rebel group, the Kuki National Organsiation (KNO) signed an accord with the Working Committee of Naga National Political Groups (NNPG), a major stakeholder in the Naga peace parleys with the Union of India, to respect and accept the history and identity of one another. The accord was purportedly signed on January

10, 2020, in Imphal following thorough deliberations on contentious political, social and inter-community matters.[213]

Yet the book, *Zalengam: The Kuki Nation* (published in 1998 with a reprint in 2008), by KNO president P.S. Haokip, became a subject of controversy in November 2020. The Federation of Haomee in fact burnt an effigy Haokip alleging distortion of the history of Manipur in his book. FoH also alleged Haokip was of Burmese origin, claiming that his native village was Mongloi in Myanmar. In chapter ten of his book, they pointed out, Haokip claims that Zalengam existed before AD 33 and that it was with the help of Kuki Achouba and Kuki Ahongba, two Kuki chiefs, that Pakhangba was made the king of Kangleipak.[214]

More recently, in October 2023, there was controversy in Nagaland too over the way the book portrayed the relationship between the Angami Nagas and Zeliang Nagas. But there the concerned organizations were able to sit down together and pass a resolution putting the matter to rest. According to a report: 'The Nagaland Zeliang Peoples' Organisation (NZPO) convened a joint meeting with the Kuki Inpi Nagaland on October 11 at Jalukie and discussed what it termed the "controversial writings of P.S. Haokip"… A press release from the NZPO President Kevipele Iheilung and Kuki Inpi Nagaland (KIN) President L. Singsit informed that the delegates "after prolonged deliberation condemned and declared their rejection of the book which is without basis and devoid of facts of history". The NZPO and KIN jointly declared that the book in question "is borne of his personal figment of imaginations [*sic*] and has no bearing on the relationship between the Zeliang and Kuki people of Nagaland."'[215]

In August 2023, the United Naga Council issued a statement setting out the differences between the Kukis and Nagas, but they ended on a reconciliatory note, saying: 'Nagas believe that nothing in this regard is too late to set the wrong...right.' It is an important document, setting out the potential areas of conflict between the Nagas and the Kuki-Zo. I reproduce it here in extenso:

While the Nagas [understand the] hardships, distress... borne by the Kuki-Zo peoples as a consequence of the present ethnic conflict, it has become all the more inevitable for the Nagas to register [their] opposition to the issues raised and incorporated in their memorandum submitted to different authorities as it is poses a big threat to the very existence and inalienable rights of the Nagas, particularly in the state of Manipur.

The United Naga Council has been [making] all possible efforts to end the ongoing ethnic conflict between the warring Kuki-Zo and Meitei communities through dialogue but unfortunately things are not turning positive as expected. The Nagas are also taken aback by the blatant lies, lopsided history and fabricated information contained in every statement and memorandum issued by the Kuki-Zo community which is tantamount to a distortion of Naga history and an insult to the Naga people.

With regard to land, the Nagas' opposition to the creation of new districts in 2016 remains alive as an unfinished issue. Of the districts, ones carved out from the Senapati and Chandel districts are the handiwork of the Congress government's appeasement policy carried out in the name of administrative convenience. Hence the demand [for a] separate administration [by the Kuki-Zo] which incorporates the so-called two new districts is necessarily opposed. The Nagas' stand on the opposition remains unchanged. The bifurcation of the so-called two districts is an issue virtually with the Kukis only not with Zo peoples.

In this regard the Kuki-Zo people's representation to the Union Government, Israel's Prime Minister, European Parliament, UNO, etc. is [based] on a false territorial foundation and an attempt to befool those authorities because in the context of Manipur, the name Kukis [was] first heard sometime between 1830 and 1840 and therefore, 'Kuki hills' that appears in the fourth para of the mentioned memo to the Prime Minister of Israel is non-existent and a utopian concoction.

... The doctored [*sic*] statement is mentioned in the memorandum submitted to the United Nations Organization. [T]he advent of the British in the history of Manipur... brought about many unwanted changes. One of the many problems that we inherit from...British colonial rule is the issue of the planting of the Kuki tribe in the Naga hills. As a mercenary tribe the British found the Kukis quite useful. Their total lack of attachment to any land and landscape was immediately recognized by the British, thus making them instrumental to crushing the indigenous communities of Manipur. [The] UNC would like to set the record straight that the recent blatant attempt of Kukis at distorting the history of the Kuki rebellion of 1917–1919 [and presenting it as the] Anglo-Kuki War to legitimize their imagined Kuki homeland within the Naga ancestral homeland is a classic example of their habitual lies.

It may be recalled that Kuki Rebellion of 1917–1919 was a savage episode of murdering, torching of houses, plunder and enslaving of women and children of the indigenous Naga community in Ukhrul, Chandel and Tamenglong in Manipur.

... It is also pertinent to bring to the notice of all conscientious individuals and authorities that the state of Manipur is now flooded with illegal immigrants from Myanmar and Bangladesh... Columns of illegal camps are being built at an alarming rate near the town of Moreh and its surrounding areas to facilitate the settlement of those intruding [*sic*] Kukis from Myanmar. If the flow of illegal immigrants is not stopped by the Government of India and the Government of Manipur, the day will not be long when the Indigenous population will be reduced to a minority.

… [The names of nine] Naga tribes of Chandel district are incorporated in the Kuki Constitution as Kuki tribes. The Nagas urge the Kukis to show them the basis of the inclusion. The Nagas will not remain mute over the issue.

Having said all this the Nagas believe that nothing in this regard is too late to set the wrong…right.

(Issued by UNC Information & Publicity Secretary, August 21, 2023)[216]

Throughout the violence in Manipur, the Nagas have been on edge. As tribals and Christians, they have sympathy for the Kuki-Zo. But at the same time, they also fear that the central government may concede the demand for a separate Kuki administration, which would result in a new conflict over territory.

Conflict Resolution

As I have already said, tribal identities in Manipur have tended to be rather fluid, and there have been conflicts within the Kuki-Zo group as well. There have been attempts to break away from the dominant tribe and claim a separate homeland. For instance, in a Paite initiative, the Hmar, Zou, Vaiphei, Gangte, Simte, Zomi and Paite (notably excluding the Thadou Kuki) had once wanted to establish a homeland in Churachandpur called Zogam, or the 'Land of Zo', under the leadership of the Zomi Re-unification Organization (ZRO). This was in 1995.

Similar processes have been seen within the Naga group of tribes as well.

                    Shooting the Sun

Conflicts between the Kuki-Zo communities have in the past sometimes taken a violent turn, for instance, the Thadou–Paite clashes that took the lives of hundreds of people and uprooted thousands from their homes. These clashes took place in 1997–98. The government had to send in the army to bring the situation under control. However, it was only with the intervention of the church leaders that peace was restored.

An MoU was signed on March 26, 1998, followed by a ceasefire agreement which was extended thrice. After a six-month period of relative calm, real negotiations took place at the end of September 1998. Peace talks were held under the leadership of Chief Minister Nipamacha Singh, assisted by his cabinet colleagues and the Churachandpur district administrator.

It was recalled during these talks that the turning point of the conflict was the attack on Saikul village (now in Kangpokpi district) on June 25, 1997, in which ten Paites were killed. After hearing what the Paites had to say, the Kuki Inpi leaders apologized to the Paites and even arranged for an apology banquet on September 29, 1998, by killing a cow. It was part of their tradition of making peace. The Kuki Inpi Churachandpur and Zomi Council leaders shared the meal. In response, the ZC leaders arranged a banquet by killing a pig on September 30, 1998, to show their acceptance of the apology.

After these gestures of peace, the KIC and ZC leaders signed a written agreement on October 1, 1998, in the presence of the Chief Minister. With it the district which had become a battlefield changed once again into a peaceful place. Signed on behalf of the Kukis and Zomis, the points of agreement laid down by the KIC and ZC were:

1. That every individual or tribe should be given the freedom to be either Kuki or Zomi or have any other identity. No force should be used against those who make this choice.

2. Those who have, during the conflict, occupied the property or houses of those who fled should return them to the rightful owner.

3. The Kuki and Zomi militant groups should not 'levy taxes' on any one other than persons of their own tribe. This included government employees, the public in general, contractors and businessmen.

4. The MoU was meant for all tribes, individuals and organizations and was to be followed by all...[217]

I have given the details of the memorandum signed at the end of conflict as an example of how local customs can be drawn upon for conflict resolution.

Demand for a Kuki Homeland

The demand for a Kuki homeland is the most contentious issue in Manipur and many believe the root cause of the violence in 2023.

The Kuki-Zo in Manipur have been united on wanting autonomy. This began with the demand for the recognition of Sadar Hills as a full-fledged revenue district. Thongkholal Haokip[218] traces the history of the demand:

'SADAR is an abbreviation of Selected Area Development Administrative Region as found in the land records of Manipur. Likewise there are a number of SADARs in many states of India particularly Uttar Pradesh which were established by the British during their colonial rule in India. Thus, Sadar Hills [are] the hills overlooking and encircling the Imphal Valley. Sadar Hills was conceived way back in 1933 by J.C. Higgins, the then British Political Agent in Manipur...

'The demand for the creation of Sadar Hills district first came from the Kuki Chiefs' Zonal Council in its meeting held on September 3, 1970. The leaders of Kuki Chiefs' Zonal Council met the then Home Minister K.C. Pant in July 1971, and placed their demand for a separate district comprising of Sadar Hills. The delegates of the Kuki Chiefs' Zonal Council again held a meeting with [the] Security Commissioner on October 6, 1971 at Kholjang village. The Nayal Commission in 1974 not only recommended the creation of [a] Sadar Hills district, but also suggested the inclusion of some adjoining areas of Senapati and Ukhrul for administrative convenience and development. However, all these demands, talks and recommendations failed to produce any result.

'Under the [auspices] of the Kuki National Assembly the Sadar Hills District Demand Committee (SHDDC) was formed in 1974 to demand full-fledged revenue district status for the Sadar Hills Autonomous District Council, consisting of Saikul, Kangpokpi and Saitu subdivisions. Ever since Manipur attained full-fledged statehood in 1972 several state ministries made attempts to declare Sadar Hills as a full-fledged revenue district. The first attempt was made by the Rishang Keising's Congress government in 1982. The ministry put up an ordinance to the Governor to declare Sadar Hills as [a] district and the same was duly signed by the Governor but the ordinance was withdrawn due to opposition from the then Manipur Naga Council.'

The demand for the Sadar Hills district brought the Kukis into direct conflict with the Nagas who, as we have seen, have asserted their right to the lands claimed by the Kukis on the ground that they were the original settlers.

While more recently the Kukis in Manipur have demanded a separate administration, what this will entail has not been spelt out. A section of the Kukis want an autonomous district within Manipur under the Sixth Schedule while others have demanded Union territory status, and then there is a section of the Mizo-Chin-Kuki who want Zai'langam, a separate homeland. After the violence in Manipur, the demand for a Greater Mizoram, or a Zofate, too has been revived and supported by Mizoram. (We will go into the impact of the violence in Manipur in Mizoram and Myanmar in the next chapter.)

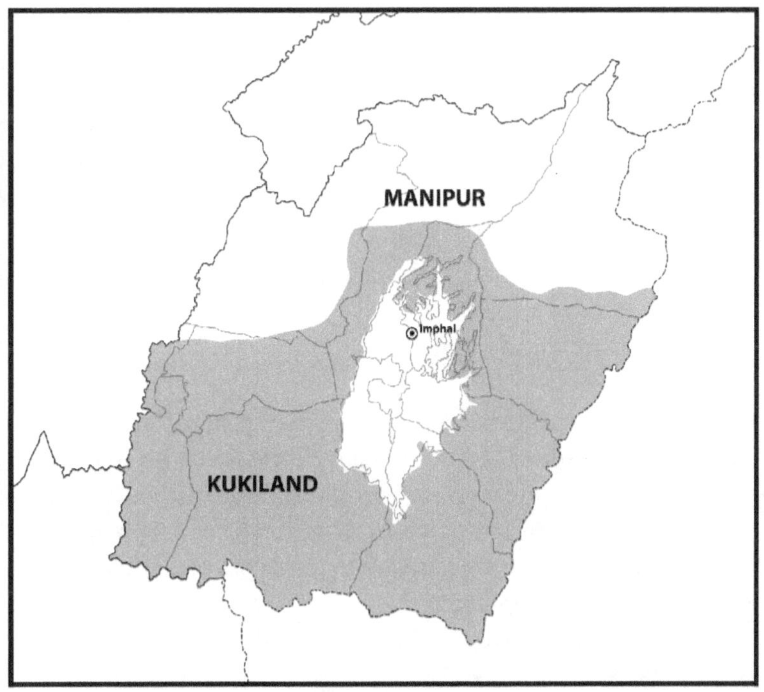

The ethnic homeland demanded by Kuki groups. Reproduced from the boundaries given on Scroll.in (scroll.in/article/916961/manipurs-ethnic-divisions-mean-candidates-are-likely-need-support-of-armed-groups-to-win-elections).

The land claimed by the Kukis brings them into conflict with the Meiteis as well. The Meiteis look upon the Kuki demand for a separate administration, even within Manipur, as a threat to the 'unity and integrity' of Manipur, the justification being that both the Hills and Valley were part of the erstwhile Manipur Kingdom which joined the Indian Union. This claim has been, as we have seen, disputed by the Kukis and the Nagas (ATSUM), who maintain that the Hills were never under the Maharaja.

What we must realize, however, is that the demand for a separate administration is both a political as well as an economic demand. While it is amply clear that there are disagreements between the two on questions of culture and history, the demand for economic development in the hill areas is shared by both the Nagas and Kukis.

Development Funds and Autonomy

The Nagas and Kukis have in the past demanded that the provisions of the Sixth Schedule be extended to the Hill districts of Manipur. A letter written by L.K. Advani, the then deputy home minister, to Chief Minister Ibobi Singh reveals the politics of manipulation which has deprived the people of Hill areas of development.

The letter, DO No. 11012/41/2001-NE-IV, dated April 7, 2003, states:

> Reports received [by the central government] reveal that no election has been held to [the] Autonomous Councils [in the Hills] during the last 10 years. Further, the Councils do not enjoy any legislative or judicial powers. The Councils are not able to exercise the executive and administrative powers vested in them because of many controls. Reports

also indicate that even though separate fund allocation has been made in the State budget, in respect of the major development departments for the hill areas of the state, most of the funds had not reached the interior villages and the beneficiaries.

Whether more autonomy would automatically bring development to the hill areas is a question that needs debate and discussion. But it is important to understand the grievances of the people as articulated by them. A Kuki writer speaks on the grievances felt by his community:

'Tribal leaders continually complain and point towards the lack of infrastructural development, the poor condition of the education and health services, endemic poverty, lack of employment opportunities, and of access to resources for their development. A survey of budget allocation for the hill districts in 2004–05 is indicative [of] this situation: in education only 26 per cent was allocated to the hill districts, while this was 25 per cent in health and 22 per cent in the public works department. Four out of five hill districts figure at the bottom of the heap on the human development index. These districts also have a larger proportion of the poor than the valley areas.

'As a Kuki villager lamented, "Above all, we [Kukis] are deprived of government development funds and have become strangers in the land of our ancestors." The tribal communities inhabiting Manipur have often complained of their poor representation in government jobs and of the paucity of personnel and poor functioning of public offices in the hills. While it is mandatory to have at least 31 per cent tribal employees in all government departments, few departments have been able to meet this target, sometimes due to shortage of adequately qualified candidates, but mostly on account of a lack of political and bureaucratic commitment.

'Tribal leaders attribute these problems to the concentration of power and resources in Meitei hands. The head of Sipukawn village, Churachandpur District lamented, "Inadequate access to government and private jobs, poor functioning of local government in the hills, and reluctance of state government to devolve power to tribal representatives, have directly resulted in feelings of alienation and lack of democratic accountability."

'The Kuki chief of Gelnel village (Senapati district) remarked, "Most departments are centralized with almost all development schemes being formulated and implemented from Imphal and they neglect our needs."'[219]

In October 2023, the Indigenous Tribal Leaders' Forum (ITLF) exposed another scandal by which central government funds worth three crores rupees for tribals were allegedly being diverted to Meitei NGOs based in the Valley. In his proposal to Union Minister of Tribal Affairs Arjun Munda on October 23, 2023, Chief Minister N. Biren Singh stated that there are tribal inhabitants in all the 16 districts of Manipur which constitute a major part of the population of the state. And that therefore the empowerment of tribal communities would have a significant impact on accelerating the overall socio-economic development trajectory of Manipur.

He further stated: 'Towards this objective, Manipur Khadi and Village Industries Board, a statutory body established under the Manipur Khadi and Village Industries Board Act, 1966, has prepared a Detailed Project Report for "Integrated Empowerment of Schedule Tribe Communities in Manipur" for submission of the same through the state department of tribal affairs.'

However, according to a report by *EastMojo* on October 30, '[A]s per the letter issued by Manipur Khadi and Village Industries Board vice chairman, Wahengbam Dineshchandra

Singh, none of the six NGOs recommended for different projects meant for the tribal populace are either owned by tribal people nor based in hill districts inhabited by the tribal community.'

In addition to the above allegation, adds the report, the ITLF also expressed concern about the revival of the Meitei community's somewhat sudden demand for Scheduled Tribe quota benefits, despite their existing classification and protection under the Scheduled Caste and Other Backward Classes categories.[220]

Job Reservations

The tribals have consistently complained that the quota for jobs for the SCs and STs have never been fulfilled. John H. Pulamte, a civil servant, has written in detail about the problems of job reservations for tribals in Manipur.[221] In a 2007 article in *The Sangai Express*, he gave the history of how the state government scuttled the law relating to job reservations for fifteen years:

'A Bill known as "Manipur Reservation of Vacancies in Posts & Services (for SC and ST) 1976" was passed by the state's Legislative Assembly on December 12, 1976 and [received the Governor's assent] on February 21, 1977, but the same is inoperative till date in the absence of Rules under the Act.

'The Rules framed and published by the then Commissioner of Tribal Welfare Department in Gazette No. 474 (B) on December 10, 1990 "for immediate enforcement" [were] rescinded by Gazette No. 618 published by the Chief Secretary on February 2, 1991 "with immediate effect" and reinforced by another Gazette No. 639 published on February 5, 1991 rescinding once again and stating that, "the same shall be treated as to have not been issued and existed".

'The main reason cited by the government for this cancellation is that no proper channel and mandatory state's Cabinet approval [was] sought and obtained by the Tribal Development department before going ahead for publication in the Gazette.'

Why does it take such a long time to make the first attempt to frame the rules to make the Act operational? asks Pulamte. 'With no effective watchdog to oversee the rights and privileges of the tribal peoples,' he writes, 'they are continuously marginalized and exploited in matters of recruitment for services, admission in Government institutions and seats in Government sponsored courses such as medical, engineering and other technical courses. For instance, had the one-third reservation for SC/STs in all Government jobs [been] followed in letter and spirit, there [would] definitely be at least 10,000 more tribal employees in the state at present.

'Education (S), the department that ha[s] maximum employees after Home department and the one that gives maximum room of employment to tribals, has just 3,037 STs out of the total 1,21,40 employees, a shortage of more than 700 posts. The State's Legislative Assembly secretariat, which is the centre of a democratic system, has only 24 tribals out of the total 305 regular employees—a clear shortage of some 70 posts.'

It should be noted that since Manipur joined the Indian Union, the chief minister's post has been filled by men (not women) from different communities. For instance, the list includes Mohammed Alimuddin and two Tangkhul Naga chief ministers. However, ever since the late 1990s, the post has invariably gone to a Meitei.[222]

Insurgency and Identity Politics

The Northeast region of India has for long been associated with insurgency. There is no conflict in Manipur which is not related to insurgents and insurgency. It has the largest number of armed groups in this region, some of which are active while others are involved in peace talks.

One list of these organizations compiled by the South Asia Terror Portal (SATP) states that there are six proscribed militant organizations, six others which are active but not proscribed, and twenty-five armed groups which are not active. And then there are five groups which are engaged in peace talks.[223]

Each of these insurgent groups are committed to preserving their identities. Most often this has meant controlling 'their' women and making sure they wear the traditional dress, occasionally issuing diktats that marriage to men from other communities would be disapproved, boycott of Hindi films, giving orders to 'outsiders' to leave the state (which means migrant workers are targets of violence from time to time). In the case of Meiteis, the preservation of their identity also entails reviving their old culture and language. There are also attempts to change the exonyms of places, mountains, rivers and tribes, some of which were imposed by colonial rulers and some by the Indian armed forces, for example, the naming of Lairouching in Senapati district as Jwalamukhi. But most often, it is the tribals in Manipur who are changing Meitei names to names in their own languages. This battle of names is integral to identity politics. The naming of villages, rivers or mountains has tremendous symbolic significance.

On October 7, 2023, the state government warned civil society organizations against changing existing names of places, districts and institutions. The government order stated that there had been deliberate attempts to change the names of places and institutions and that this could add to the tensions between communities amid the ongoing conflict.

The Kukis call Churachandpur Lamka. Tracing the history of the name Churachandpur, Ginza Vualzong of the ITLF points out: 'Lamka and Churachandpur are two different locations altogether and have different stories of origin. However, due to the political manipulation of the Meitei people of the valley, the two have been amalgamated into one. It might sound confusing but if you know the histories and origins of both these places, the two are not the same and should not be confused. The real Churachandpur is a hillock 15 kms west of Lamka, which was previously known as Songpi. Songpi was later changed to Churachandpur to honour the Maharaja Churachand. Lamka, the current District headquarters, on the other hand existed separately and had no connection with Songpi. Songpi was the old sub-divisional headquarters which was abandoned in 1930. After 10 years of this abandonment, the new sub-divisional headquarters was moved to the present Lamka town, which was incorrectly put [on] paper as Churachandpur by the people from the valley.'[224]

The militant groups which are leading the identity movements have a vision of leading their people to an imagined homeland where the people will live in peace and harmony, without 'the other'. However, the territory claimed by each of these groups often overlaps. Most times the territorial claims are not borne out by the historical evidence, and the imagined nation is increasingly rooted in race and religion. There is no programme for social, economic or cultural rights. What is more, in the name of tradition, women are denied their right to dignity.

The Nagas and Kukis want a theological state where their versions of Christianity become the official religion; the Meitei Pangal militant groups dream of a Caliphate and the Meiteis want to revive their pre-Hindu past with the help of Hindutva ideology.

The militant groups have also over the years undermined democratic institutions in Manipur. They give calls for boycott of elections and at the same time back political parties and put up candidates. They run parallel governments and indulge in extortion, but do not have any programmes which could benefit the people in their daily struggles. They are also responsible for closing the democratic space for discussion and debate. Open, free discussion on most issues is almost impossible. All differences, it seems, tend to be settled by threat and intimidation and even assassinations to silence dissidence. The extremist elements, backed by armed force, have usurped the right to speak for their people even though the vast majority of people have been alienated by this destructive identity politics.

As I have shown, the warring parties can, and indeed have, come to the negotiating table, using traditional mechanisms for conflict resolution. But there appears to be no such mechanism for settling disputes between the state and the people.

The state—Manipur as well as the Centre—has used all manner of divide-and-rule methods to keep the people from coming together. The intelligence agencies have played their part in this. In all likelihood, international intelligence agencies have also used the Northeast region, including Manipur, as their playground.

There have been deadly conflicts in the past over control over the arms and drug trade. The most dramatic example are the decades-long clashes over the control over the illegal trade in Moreh, the town on the India–Myanmar border. Moreh is now in Tengnoupal district, around 110 kilometres from Imphal, and it became a survey land[225] in December 1989. Prior to 1990, the major communities in the town were the Tamils, the Meiteis and the Nagas, with a significant number people from other communities such as Kukis, Malayalis, Bengalis, Jains, Punjabis, Meitei Pangals and Nepalis. After many communal clashes—the Kuki–Naga clash (1992), Kuki–Tamil (1995), Kuki–Paite (1997), Kuki–Meitei (2007, 2010, 2015, 2023), the Kuki community now dominates Moreh.[226]

But then all this was predicted long ago. Way back in 1981, Nibedon Biswas, the youngest son of the late Nirod Kumar Biswas, the bishop of Assam, writing under the name, Nirmal Nibedon, published a book titled *Northeast India: The Ethnic Explosion* (1981). In the preface he predicted: 'It is an ethnic explosion. Make no mistake about it. Have no doubts about it. World governments, more so India and Southeast Asian countries, will have to closely study the case of the ethnic minorities, whether they are Kachins and Karens of Burma, the Mizos or the Ahoms of India. The ethnic minorities of India, particularly those of the Mongoloid stock, will deserve more attention. For, gone are the days when small bands of proud tribesmen fought and defended themselves with poison-tipped arrows. Today, in the 1980s the ethnic minorities are wielding sophisticated weapons and engaging national armies in combat, increasingly. In brief, they are zealously guarding their ethnic identity... It is going to be a long war for all sides, frighteningly effective and cripplingly expensive for both. None may emerge victorious. Both may be losers.'

In June 2023, a retired high-ranking Army officer tweeted about the dire state of affairs in the state. Lt Gen (retd) L. Nishikanta Singh tweeted: 'I'm just an ordinary Indian from Manipur living a retired life. The state is now "stateless." Life and property can be destroyed anytime by anyone, just like in Libya, Lebanon, Nigeria, Syria, etc.'

To this, former Army chief General V.P. Malik replied, 'An extraordinary sad call from a retired Lt General from Manipur. Law and order situation in Manipur needs urgent attention at highest level.'[227]

Identity politics has deprived Manipur of people who can speak for the entire state, which now stands deeply and tragically divided. But the question that still needs an answer is: how did things come to such a pass? Who was really behind the violence in Manipur? And what did they want to achieve?

The state government has blamed the insurgents in Myanmar for infiltrating into India. They have also blamed the Kuki-Zo people for harbouring illegal migrants and the insurgents from both Myanmar and Manipur for backing narcoterrorists.

CHAPTER EIGHT

The Myanmar Factor

It's OK. Never mind. Don't take it too seriously or even
personally. Shit happens.
Anyway, it's not your shit, is it?
It's not your problem that our country
will soon be
the world's unceremonious cemetery.
Come join us one day.
Bring along your departed, too.
Gloriously we'll sing together
'We are the world. We are the civilians.
Slaughtered for our fight for freedom.'
In the meantime, stay safe. Stay home.
Watch the news. Cheat on partner.
The world has never been our oyster.

—written in English, March 3, 2021,
by Zeyar Lynn (b. 1958), among the most
influential living poets in Myanmar

Beards looking for a Chin like words for a poem
Beard is the war-torn town of the Chin in civil war
In the history of Chin, beard is the defeated truth

—'The Ways of the Beard' by Zeyar Lynn
(translated by Ko Ko Thett)

The second poem by Zeyar Lynn above speaks of the plight of the Chin, among the most persecuted and dispossessed ethnic groups in Myanmar.[228]

From the start of the violence in Manipur, and even before that time, the central and state governments have been insisting that Manipur is facing a threat from the influx of illegal migrants from across the Indo-Myanmar border. The Government of India, in early October 2023, announced its intention of building a 100-kilometre-long smart fence along this border to boost surveillance.[229] This enterprise is supported by Manipur's Chief Minister and a section of Meiteis who think the wall would be the answer to all the causes of the violence: insurgency, drugs and illegal migrants.

Building a smart fence along the Indo-Myanmar border would go against the Prime Minister's Act East Policy which aims to set up better road and rail links between India and Southeast Asia.[230] Myanmar is the only Southeast Asian country with which India has a border.

In 2018, India and Myanmar decided upon having a Free Movement Regime (FMR). Manipur suspended the FMR in 2020 during the Covid pandemic. Efforts were made to open the border for trade again but the date kept getting extended. The justification for this prolonged suspension of the FMR was that it could lead to a further increase in 'the number of illegal entry of Myanmar nationals into India in view of the current law and order situation in Myanmar', as stated by a Home Department order of November 2022.[231] What we got instead of a resumption of the FMR was a decision to put up a fence. In a post on X (formerly Twitter) on September 24, 2023, Biren Singh spoke of an 'additional 70 km of border fencing along the Indo-Myanmar border…[i]n view of the rise in illegal immigration and drugs smuggling from the neighbouring country'.[232]

The Indo-Myanmar border must be seen in the context of the geography of the entire region. The north-eastern region of India, comprising the states of Assam, Meghalaya, Tripura, Mizoram, Manipur, Nagaland and Arunachal Pradesh, is spread over an area of 2.55 lakh square kilometres which accounts for 7.8 per cent of the total landmass of India. The region shares international boundaries with four foreign countries, viz. China, Myanmar, Bhutan and Bangladesh. The entire area is connected to the Indian mainland by a twenty-two-kilometre land corridor through Siliguri in the state of West Bengal, popularly known as the 'Chicken's Neck'.

The border between India and Myanmar runs for 1,643 kilometres along four Northeast states: Mizoram (475 kms), Manipur (425 kms), Nagaland (200 kms), and Arunachal Pradesh (525 kms).

There are over 250 villages with over 300,000 people living in them within ten kilometres of the border, and many of these people frequently cross the border through 150 small and large formal and informal border crossings. These people have families across the border; their fields too have been separated by the border. Yet they have maintained their relationships with their families and friends across the border and there also exists a brisk informal trade among the people. Children from Myanmar cross the border every day to study in the schools in India and many villagers come here to access medical facilities.

What will the effect of the proposed smart fence on the lives of these people be? And can a 100-kilometre wall solve any problems? Can it ensure that Manipur will be safe from ethnic conflicts and violence in the future?

The answer to the question is a simple no.

The smart fence is not being built in response to a demand by the state of Manipur. It is a project that is part of the Narendra Modi government's plan to completely seal India's border with Pakistan, Bangladesh and Myanmar. Smart fencing allows security forces to maintain the surveillance system through a monitor sitting inside their control rooms. The alarms go off as soon as there is any infiltration attempt.

According to a report titled *A Walled World: Towards a Global Apartheid* brought out in November 2020 by the Transnational Institute, over the last fifty years, 63 border walls have been built worldwide leading to growing militarization of borders. It is claimed in the report that the 'drive and profiting from this surge in wall building is an entire Border Industrial Complex. This industry has reinforced a narrative in which migration and other political and/or humanitarian challenges at the border are primarily framed as a security problem, where the frontier can never be secure enough, and for which its latest military and security technologies are always the solution'. A table ranking countries by border walls built between 1968 and 2018 shows Israel as having built six with India coming in next with three. 'Of India's 15,106 km of land borders,' the report states, 'an estimated 6,540.7 km of barriers have been erected, making 43.29% of its borders walled.'[233]

The smart fence on the Indo-Myanmar border will increase the militarization of Manipur. In order to understand how dire the situation can potentially become, let us turn to the political situation in Myanmar.

Army Rule in Myanmar

The Northeast region of India and Myanmar share a history going back several centuries. Known by its colonial name till 1989, the latter is the largest country by area in mainland Southeast Asia. It had a population of about 54 million in

2017. It is bordered by Bangladesh and India to its northwest, China to its northeast, Laos and Thailand to its east and southeast, and the Andaman Sea and the Bay of Bengal to its south and southwest, respectively. The country's capital city was Yangon (Rangoon) till 2005, when a new planned city named Nay Pyi Taw (popularly known as Naypidaw) became the administrative capital.

The majority of the population is ethically Burman and Buddhist. There are 135 ethnic nationalities recognized by the state, many of which are predominantly Christian. There is a small percentage of Indian-origin people who are mostly Hindu, and then there is the Muslim population which includes the Rohingyas of Rakhine State, who have been stripped of their citizenship and are stateless refugees.

The ethnic minorities have a long history of fighting against the central government in support of their demand for more autonomy or for independence from Myanmar. The government has looked at the presence of armed resistance by these ethnic nationalities as a threat to the union, and throughout the country's contemporary history it is largely the army which has been in control.

Independent Burma came under military rule in the 1960s, which soon gave way to one-party rule which lasted until 1988. In 1988, the entire country rose in a national uprising, but it was a military junta that took power this time. It was only in 2010 that the government allowed elections. In the 2012 by-elections, the National League for Democracy, led by its charismatic leader Daw Aung San Suu Kyi, won an overwhelming majority. She had been placed in long periods of detention under the junta.[234] Even after her victory at the polls, she was not allowed to assume the office of president, since her husband and children were foreign citizens.

In 2016, the military regime started a slow process of democratization and Aung San Suu Kyi served as State Counsellor of Myanmar (equivalent to a prime minister) and Minister of Foreign Affairs till 2021. After the elections in 2020, Suu Kyi's party once again won an overwhelming majority, but the parliament was still controlled by the military, and instead of handing over power and establishing a real democracy, the military staged another coup in February 2021 and arrested Suu Kyi, among other political leaders, journalists and essentially anyone who showed the courage to challenge the repression.

The opposition formed a National Unity Government of Myanmar (NUG) in exile which included elected members of parliament, ethnic insurgent groups and other minor parties. It had a minister for human rights who was openly gay but it did not include anyone representing the Rohingyas.

The European Parliament has recognized the NUG as the legitimate government of Myanmar. Many of its members are taking refuge in Mizoram.

In India, we have for the most part been unaware of the extent of military repression in Myanmar. In a pamphlet published in July 2023 jointly by Burma Affairs and Conflict Study (BACS) and New Delhi-based India for Myanmar, the impact is summed up in the following manner:

'On February 1, 2021 the Myanmar military overturned the 2008 Constitution, which [they] had drawn up [of] their own accord without the will of the people, and forcibly and unlawfully seized control from the elected government. In the span of 30 months since the coup, the aggressive Myanmar military has apprehended and incarcerated over 24,462 citizens, including prominent figures such as public leader Daw Aung San Suu Kyi and Myanmar's elected president U. Win Myint. Among the detained were more than 653 children and over

4,897 women, while the number of individuals sentenced to death reached 101.[235]...

'Hundreds of thousands have sought refuge in neighbouring countries, with an estimated 50,000 seeking shelter in India. As a consequence of the coup in Myanmar, more than 40 per cent of the population has plunged below the poverty line.'[236]

These 50,000 Burmese citizens who have sought refuge in India are refugees as defined by international law and by the Indian courts which have ruled on the rights of refugees. Even though India is not a signatory to the UN Refugee Convention, the Indian Constitution guarantees rights to all foreigners, including refugees who do not have the required travel papers, to life (Article 21) and against arbitrariness under the law (Article 14).

In the past, the United Nations High Commission for Refugees (UNHCR) and the Government of India have offered Burmese refugees basic protection, ultimately helping many resettle in Europe, America or Australia.

Refugees Crossing Into Mizoram

The majority of these refugees are crossing to India from Sagaing Division and Chin State, and so, are Chins, who are ethnically and culturally related to the Mizo-Kuki-Zo tribes in India.

The Mizoram government has declared that they would offer refuge to the Chins coming in and not treat them as illegal migrants. More recently, as we saw in chapter four, the government has also refused to carry out biometric surveys of the refugees because many of them have expressed fear that the biometric data would be shared with the Myanmar military.

However, even in Mizoram, where the government and

the people have welcomed the Chin refugees, there has been some conflict between the Chins from Myanmar and Indian citizens who are Mizo. In part, the tension lies in the fear of being overwhelmed by the refugees and local populations having to share economic resources. But in the absence of a refugee policy, the refugees have no rights at all, and many resort to illegally acquiring papers identifying them as Indians. One of the most well known of these cases was that of a famous Chin singer who took refuge in Mizoram. His name is Benjamin Sum.

Sum is a singer and youth icon from Myanmar. After the coup, his opposition to military rule meant he was blacklisted. He crossed into Mizoram over the course of a dangerous three-day journey soon after the coup. He became popular in Mizoram too for his music, in particular the song, '*Chhaili Di Lenna*', which brought him into the spotlight. He garnered over four million views on YouTube. His fan base set up an Instagram account under the name 'Summers'.

EastMojo reported about the controversy that erupted online in April 2023, after Zmp Tlau, a journalist 'known for filing PILs and questioning government policies', wrote a Facebook post along with a screenshot of Benjamin Sum's motor vehicle registration details.

The Mizo journalist stated how he planned to find out if Sum had an Aadhaar card or a voter ID and 'which local council helped him state that he ha[d] a garage'. The post had over 6,000 likes and almost 2,000 comments, with the majority showing support for Tlau while questioning the legality of Sum's documents.[237]

This incident exposed the limits of the tolerance of the Mizos for the refugees.

However, there's no denying the fact that Mizo-Kukis

and Zos in India are sympathetic to the genuine refugees. In Manipur, the burden of protecting the refugees has fallen on the Kuki community which itself is economically poor.

Burmese resistance groups complain that India has been selling arms to Myanmar and that these arms are used against the people fighting the brutal military repression. While the Indian state sells arms to the military junta there are also allegations that arms are smuggled from India to the Burmese insurgents as well.

The resistance to the Burmese military has indeed grown stronger with militant groups uniting to fight for democracy in their country. This too has had an impact on neighbouring Northeast India.

Armed Resistance in Myanmar

After the coup of 2021, the various armed groups in Myanmar came together under a joint command to form what is called the People's Defence Force, or PDF. People's Defence Force is an umbrella term for three types of armed groups that have emerged since the coup: the PDFs, Local Defence Forces (LDFs) and People's Defence Teams (PaKhaPha/PDTs).

The PDFs are generally larger armed units formed or recognized by the National Unity Government. The PDFs mainly operate under joint command systems established by the NUG and several ethnic armed organizations, many of which have been fighting the Myanmar army for decades. They are more regularized military units than the other two categories, operating across townships and states/regions. The LDFs and PDTs are self-defence or community security militias operating at the community level.[238]

According to estimates, there are roughly 65,000 to 70,000

total PDF troops. Approximately 20 per cent of PDF troops are equipped with military-grade weapons and another 40 per cent have homemade weapons. As of October 2022, there were around 300 PDF battalions with 200 to 500 troops each. Sixty-three additional battalions were awaiting NUG recognition.

A report by the US Institute for Peace explains the command structure of the armed resistance groups:

'The PDFs operate under the command of the Central Command and Coordination Committee (C3C) and Joint Command and Coordination (J2C), which were established by the NUG and its EAO [ethnic armed organization] allies. Most PDFs are primarily loyal to or were formed by the NUG, whereas others, including the powerful Chinland Defense Force (CDF), Karenni National Defense Force (KNDF) and Kachin People's Defense Force (KPDF), operate under the C3C but are not otherwise aligned with the NUG. Regardless of their national-level affiliation, PDFs work most closely with military division commands (MDCs), which operate semi-autonomously of the C3C and J2C. Recent PDF deployment and operations indicate that MDCs are becoming more involved in PDF operational strategy.'

Myanmar's government-in-exile, the NUG, has warned Burmese citizens 'temporarily sheltering' in India to stay away from local political matters and ethnic-based conflicts.[239] However, the NUG does not always have control over the armed groups and there have been incidents where the Burmese armed groups have tried to smuggle arms across from Mizoram to Myanmar.

The Chin State has the highest poverty rate among the states in Myanmar at 73 per cent of its population. There are 53 different subtribes and languages in Chin State but they share a history and culture with the neighbouring Chins. As Rini Ralte and Sanjay Valentine Gathia write in *The Irrawaddy*, 'Ethnic affinity is one of the strongest points of welcoming refugees in Mizoram, as they are our brothers and sisters, claiming the same ancestry as the Zo ethnic group. They were divided by British rule [and] as a result they were given different names. In Myanmar they are Chin, in Manipur they are Kuki and in Bangladesh they are Chin-Kuki and in Mizoram they are Mizo.'

The shared history includes a history of insurgency on both sides of the border. The National Investigating Agency has conducted raids at the houses of the suspects linked to the transportation of explosives and arms from Mizoram to Myanmar.

One NIA probe revealed in July 2023 that a Chin, in connivance with two Mizos, had illegally purchased arms by using the latter's arms dealer's license. These arms were being transported across the border to Myanmar. The NIA spokesperson stated that said it was investigating other links of the accused in the arms and explosives smuggling racket.[240]

The rule of the military junta in Myanmar has also had an impact on poppy cultivation on the borders. The United Nations Office of Drugs and Crime's (UNODC) 2023 report does document that the increase of 14 per cent in opium production in the Chin State can have an impact on India. This gains greater significance when we note that the Chin State was never part of the previous Opium Surveys by UNDOC as a hotspot for opium. It is the military repression and the resistance to it which are factors for the growth of drug trafficking on the Indo-Myanmar border. A Burmese rebel group which has influence in the region, Zomi Revolutionary Army (ZRA), is based in Churachandpur.

'Estimates suggest that [poppy] cultivation and total

production…increased in 2022, reversing recent historic downward trends,' according to the Myanmar Opium Survey, 2022 by UNDOC. The report further states: 'Myanmar's economy in 2022 faced a series of external and domestic shocks. The war in Ukraine…caused steep increases in global prices of fuel and fertilizer, disproportionately affecting Myanmar's poor and rural populations. Continued political instability in the post-coup environment, a weak economy, inflation, and very high farm-gate prices for opium are shaping household decisions. Taken together, these economic signals can provide a strong incentive for farmers to take up or expand opium poppy cultivation.'

Several experts point to Chinese involvement in the drug cartels in Myanmar which, it is claimed, control the insurgents who in turn run a large portion of the narcotics business in the region.[241] The Chinese government has effectively ensured that the ethnic militant groups play ball and do not threaten Beijing's bigger agenda—Myanmar as a de facto tributary state allowing for the construction of the proposed 1,700-kilometre China–Myanmar Economic Corridor (CMEC) transport route connecting southwest China with the Indian Ocean, as part of the Belt and Road Initiative (BRI). China thus has a relationship with both the junta as well as the militant groups. India continues to support the junta, and its Act East policy has been adversely affected by the Manipur violence and the plan to build a smart border.

It is of course difficult to state whether the Chinese government has any direct involvement in the illegal narcotics trade. Chinese businessmen, however, are known to be involved in many illegal activities in Myanmar such as cyber crime and gambling, and allegedly in the drug trade as well.[242] Many are in fact wanted by the Chinese government for criminal activities. I have myself with dealt one case of trafficking in which more than thirty Indians from Kerala were trafficked to Myanmar to work for a Chinese businessman who had made his fortune in illegal gambling.[243]

Threat of the Illegal Migrant

The Manipur government and some Meitei organizations have alleged that the refugees coming from Myanmar are linked to poppy cultivation. However, there has not been any incident to link those seeking asylum with drug trafficking. In fact, many of them wish to come to Delhi to get the protection of the UNHCR and dream of resettlement in the West.

Yet, because of the illegal migrants coming from across the border, there have been reports about a 'sudden increase' in the population of the Kuki-Zo. We have already seen in the previous chapters how several Meitei politicians and intellectuals have made such claims in the media. They, however, falter on substantiating their claims.

A report in *The Sangai Express* published on September 4, 2023, on the issue of illegal migrants is full of contradictions. The report was about the findings of a three-minister cabinet sub-committee in February 2023 set up by the Manipur government headed by Tribal Affairs Minister Letpao Haokip. It stated that there had been a 'sudden increase in the size of population of certain communities in Manipur over the *last few decades*', and then goes on to say only 2,187 'illegal migrants' were detected.[244] Although, to be fair, it was claimed that the verification drive in five districts bordering Myanmar identified many immigrants 'within a short period', suggesting that given more time, they could identify many more.

But then, according to *The Sangai Express*, the state government 'then took up steps to provide shelter to these immigrants on humanitarian ground[s]'. The fact that the Manipur government had decided to provide shelter to 'illegal migrants' shows that they considered these people as *refugees* escaping persecution in Myanmar, which has been under military rule since February 2021! Besides, this seems to contradict what is stated later in the report by the *Sangai Express*: 'Significantly, the report [of the cabinet sub-committee] said that the illegal immigrants from Myanmar were found to have established their own villages.'

New, Unrecognized Villages

There have been a large number of new villages which have sprung up in the Kuki-dominated districts of Manipur. At a press conference in June 2022, leaders of the Co-ordinating Committee on Manipur Integrity (COCOMI) and United Naga Council (UNC) held a joint media conference to express their concern over the rise in the number of new villages in Chandel, Tengnoupal, Kangpokpi, Churachandpur and Pherzawl districts. Their district-wise break-up of unrecognized villages was as follows: Chandel (205), Tengnoupal (130), Kangpokpi (304), Churachandpur (281) and Pherzawl (14). In all, there were 934 new villages.[245]

The question is whether these new, unrecognized villages have been set up by illegal migrants or refugees coming from Myanmar. From what I have been able to gather through reliable sources in Manipur, these are not villages set up by the Chins (the ethnically related tribes from Myanmar).

The Kukis too maintain that it has long been their custom to set up new villages. Here is a brief description of how the traditional practice works by Haoginlen Chongloi, author of *History, Identity and Polity of the Kukis* (2020):

'When any member of a family proposes to establish a village, it is customary to approach the village chief or the elder clan members of the intention. If a new village is to be carved out from the village he resides, it requires the approval of the chief to allow or disallow the request. However, if it happens that a proposed village is in a newly annexed land, the intending individual approaches his clansmen for the project. If the plan is agreed amongst its clan members, a new village is set up and the head of the clansmen till a certain generation is made the chief of the village...

'There exists no limitation for a commoner to establish a village of his own. Any influential commoner with a strong kinship has the freedom to establish a village and head the village himself or appoint his elder kinsmen. Such chieftains deserve the same respect and privileges as those of the established ones. It must be understood that if such settlement assumes the administrative setup of Kuki chieftainship, the chief and the villagers have the obligation of fulfilling the needs of each other. In howsoever may the land be acquired, be it through cash and kind or annexation, it shall exhibit the evolutionary character to ensure the land is well protected against enemy forces.'[246]

From the above description, it is clear that the Kukis establish new villages. It is the contention of the UNC and the COCOMI, however, that the establishment of these new villages may be part of the plan to carry out a demographic change in pursuance of the dream of Thadou Kukis to have a homeland. It is claimed that this is not an overnight phenomenon, but has been going on since the 1940s.

One reliable source told me that there is a possibility that these may indeed be illegal migrants from Myanmar who're living in these new villages and who could have acquired papers proving Indian identity, thus making them difficult to identify. As we saw earlier, the people coming in from Myanmar are often forced to acquire false Indian identity cards because the government does not recognize genuine refugees and register them as such. With the Mizoram government having refusing to record the biometric details of the Burmese refugees, there is certainly a possibility that many refugees could slip into neighbouring Manipur, and become a part of the Kuki community.

Even if this is the case, and even if the biometric data of the refugees is not collected, they should be registered, for their own safety as well as to reassure the Nagas and Meiteis who feel they may become minorities in their own land. If our brief review of the history of ethnic conflict in the state of Manipur has taught us anything, we cannot dismiss this as an unjustified fear.

*

In November 2023, rebel groups in Myanmar, such as the PDF, the Chinland Defence Force and Chin National Army captured the junta's outposts in the border areas. The army, in response, bombed these areas, resulting in thousands of villagers losing their homes and more people fleeing to India. It was reported that seventy-four army personnel fled to Mizoram too. The Assam Rifles airlifted them to Moreh and handed them over to Myanmar at the border.

Lalthiamsanga Sailo, joint secretary of the Home Department of Mizoram told *Hindustan Times*: 'The number of refugees in south Myanmar is around 90. They will return soon. Of the recent 5,000 people who had crossed over to Champhai in the last two weeks, nearly two-thirds have already returned home. These people realized that their villages in Myanmar are no longer controlled by the Myanmar army but the groups fighting against the army, so they found it safe to return.'[247] As this book goes to the press, it seems that the PDFs may be soon able to take over Myanmar and end military rule and hopefully initiate a democratic process.

Mizoram's approach to the problem of refugees has been exemplary. That of Manipur, however, has not won India friends. It has only served to alienate our neighbours and many within our borders too.

Can there ever be a solution to the Manipur imbroglio, or will we continue to witness violence spiralling out of control again and again?

Afterword

Can There Be Peace in Manipur Again?

The hate and the spirit of revenge is tangible on the streets of Imphal. The latest illustration of it was the attack on a hospital on November 23 in the city.

Khoantum, a resident of Thanan in Myanmar's Sagaing region, died at the Jawaharlal Nehru Institute of Medical Sciences hospital in Imphal, of bullet injuries that he suffered during the fighting in Myanmar.[248]

The death itself was sad, but what was alarming was that a mob of Meitei women stormed into the compound of the government hospital to protest against his treatment, because he was thought to be a Kuki militant. They were angry that the government had allowed a Kuki militant to get medical attention. Police used teargas to disperse the mob.

This incident shows how deeply identity politics has entered into the psyche of the people of Manipur. Those who once fought against the Armed Forces (Special Powers) Act are now unable to show solidarity to the people in Myanmar, who are fighting one of the most brutal military regimes in the world.

It is ironic that India is returning Burmese soldiers who entered into Indian territory safely back to their military authorities, but pushing back refugees fleeing persecution. The same forces who are fighting the Myanmar junta may well rule the country one day. And they will then not see India as a friend. China is taking advantage of this and is supporting both the ethnic armed groups as well as the junta.

The hate against the Kuki-Zo community and the Burmese refugees in Manipur is turning the people of the state blind to their sufferings. It has dehumanized an entire society.

People have lost their loved ones, their homes and their means of livelihood. Children have not been able to go to school; the youth to attend college or university. The dreams of thousands lie shattered in burnt homes and relief camps.

Every person who has suffered in Manipur is demanding justice. Who will deliver it?

Hundreds of FIRs have been filed for serious crimes such as murder and rape. But the police have not even begun investigations in many cases. The people who have dared to speak out are silenced by intimidation. The homes of lawyers have been vandalized, forcing lawyers to withdraw from cases. The courts cannot function.

The battle lines have been drawn and no one is backing down. In fact, even communities who were not directly involved are preparing to defend themselves in anticipation of a possible solution by the central government which would impinge on their land and identity.

So, is there hope for peace and normalcy?

There cannot be peace without justice. And the first step towards justice is to bring those who are guilty to account. As this book does to the press, however, the commission of enquiry announced in September 2023 to comprehensively investigate the violence is yet to hold any public hearings, either in Delhi or Manipur.[249]

Both the state and the central governments have been complicit in the tragedy that has unfolded. Who will hold them to account?

Unless every home destroyed is rebuilt, every vandalized church or other religious structure restored, livelihoods given back, and until the children can safely go back to school, the youth can return to college, doctors can work again without fear, there can be no peace.

Building smart borders will not stop insurgents. They have only to dig under the fences as the recent discovery of underground tunnels in the no-man's land between Bangladesh and Myanmar illustrates. The tunnels were allegedly being used by the Arakan Rohingya Salvation Army (ARSA).[250]

Borders can be safe only if the people across them can be friends and allies.

The central government must enforce a legal regime to protect refugees and differentiate between refugees and illegal migrants. Manipur must adopt a humanitarian approach to the refugees, register them, provide humanitarian assistance while ensuring that they do not settle permanently or own land. Mizoram has shown the way.

Then there is the complex problem of narcoterrorism. The Government of India with the possible help of the United Nations Office on Drugs and Crime must investigate and expose the people involved in it.

However, crucially, the people party to the conflict too have a role to play to bring about peace.

The Meiteis will have to acknowledge that they have dominated state politics and the people in the Hills have been discriminated against in all fields: economic, political and cultural. They will need to apologize and also condemn extremist organizations among them, which will have to be disarmed and banned.

Tapta will have to apologize publicly and learn to sing songs of peace and reconciliation.

Can the communities living in Manipur come together as equals, to live with dignity?

The one possible way that they can is for there to be a common social and economic programme, which brings the benefit of development to the poorest people across communities; and a cultural programme, whereby each community's rich history, culture and language is respected and celebrated without a need for separate homelands.

Can the insurgent groups abjure identity politics?

The insurgent groups must realize that the demands for imaginary homelands based on race, religion and ethnicity are a reflection of the bankruptcy of such politics. If ethnic violence is to be a thing of the past then identity politics must be replaced by a politics that brings all ethnic communities together. And by all communities, I mean those 'mayang' communities too who have been living in Manipur for at least a century, like the Marwaris, or the Nepalis, among others.

A politics which encourages demographic engineering, which is rooted in divide and rule, and which is dependent on conflict and feeds on divisions must be eschewed.

There is a need for a more inclusive politics; a socio-economic programme which ensures economic prosperity for all sections of people; and a vision that celebrates cultural diversity, language and histories.

So far, the ethnic communities and the insurgents have channelized their energies towards death and destruction. Can they learn to work together against those who have an eye on the land and resources of Manipur? Can their courage and tenacity now be used to create an inclusive, vibrant and democratic Manipur based on the values enshrined in the Constitution of India?

This book was written because I have hope and faith that the people of Manipur can and will find a way to come together, that they have the courage and determination to make the sun shine again, to make Manipur a place where there is peace, prosperity and justice.

Nandita Haksar
New Delhi

Acknowledgements

This has not been an easy book to write. But as I said, I have been driven to write it because Manipur has given me so much. My experience of working in the state has shaped my politics, and my understanding of many aspects of culture and history.

Without the journalists who reported on the events that unfolded, grappling with a complex reality and under very difficult circumstances, both the local Manipuri base and those who came from outside, this book could not have been written.

Three friends have supplied me with facts, documents and answered my queries constantly. None of them want to be named. So, thank you, dear friends, and you know who you are.

Ravi Singh suggested that I write this book, trusting me with this volatile subject, and Nazeef Mollah has done a very meticulous and sensitive edit of the manuscript. I also thank Maithili Doshi Aphale for her cover design.

But this book would never have got written if my friend and partner, Sebastian Hongray, had not pushed me to keep going. His abiding faith in my writing gave me the courage to write this book. He believed that I would be able to write without hate or prejudice towards any community. I hope he will not be disappointed.

This book is written not as a requiem for Manipur but in the hope it can recover from the trauma and heal.

Endnotes

1   The founder of the Ningthouja dynasty of Meitei monarchs in AD 33.

2   Taken from a *History of Manipuri Literature* by Ch Manihar Singh (Sahitya Akademi, 1996).

3   See Nandita Haksar and Sebastian Hongray, *The Judgement that Never Came: Army Rule in North East India* (2011). The book is dedicated to N. Surendra Singh and others.

4   Mayang is a derogatory term for 'outsider'. It is also racist because Mongoloid people are not usually included in the category. It was widely used interchangeably with 'Indians'. The term historically has been used to denote the Bishnupriya Manipuris and Bengalis, who are considered by Meiteis to be outsiders in Manipur. The term was later casually used to denote 'foreigner' or outsider, i.e. Indians.

5   Since Article 356 was enshrined in the Constitution in 1950, President's Rule has been imposed a total of 134 times across 29 states and UTs; President's Rule has been imposed in Manipur 10 times, including the time it was imposed from December 31, 1993 to December 13, 1994 (347 days), after hundreds of people died in the Naga–Kuki conflict.

6   Makepeace Sitlhou, 'The many costs of internet shutdowns amid violence in India's northeastern state', *South Asian Avant-Garde* (available on: https://www.saaganthology.com/article/chokepoint-manipur, accessed November 29, 2023).

7   In the 2011 Census, there were 49,081 Hmars in Manipur.

8   From the Foreword by K.S. Singh, p. xvii.

9   Aniruddha Dhar, 'Manipur violence: Swati Maliwal meets assaulted BJP MLA Valte, claims "he was given electric shocks"', *Hindustan Times*, July 29, 2023.

10   On August 4, 2023, *The Sangai Express* carried a story with a headline: 'Manipur not a resting place of dead foreigners: Retd Judge "Set up Kukiland somewhere else"'.

11   Saptarshi Basak, '"We Won't Stop The War": Meet Tapta, the Voice Behind Manipur's "Genocide Song"', *The Quint*, July 12, 2023.

12   'Manipur Tribal Women Group Seeks Withdrawal of Solicitor General's Remark in SC', *Newsclick*, August 7, 2023.

13   'Watch | Meitei Pride Group's Threat: 'Kukis Mainly Illegal, Modi Must Intervene or There'll Be Civil War', *The Wire*, June 6, 2023.

14   Vijaita Singh, 'Manipur Police file case against Meitei Leepun chief Pramot Singh', *The Hindu*, July 12, 2023.

15   Rustom Bharucha, 'Politics of Indigenous Theatre: Kanhailal in Manipur', *Economic and Political Weekly*, vol. 26, no. 11/12, Annual Number (March 1991).

16   'In December 2005, the Zomi Human Rights Foundation issued an open statement calling for the clearance of mines laid by rival militant groups in Thanlon, Singngat, Henglep and Tipaimukh sub-divisions of Churachandpur district, Manipur. The Foundation also organized a seminar on problems for hill tribes in Manipur, at which they invited Nandita Haksar, Advocate of the Supreme Court of India, to speak on the topic of banning landmines in the region.' See the Landmine & Cluster Munition Monitor (website) (http://archives. the-monitor.org/index.php/publications/display?url=lm/2006/india. html, accessed on November 29, 2023).

17   See the entry on the People's Liberation Army on the South Asia Terrorism Portal website (https://www.satp.org/satporgtp/ countries/india/states/manipur/terrorist_outfits/pla.htm, accessed on November 29, 2023).

18   Iboyaima Laithangbam, 'Newspapers, the last holdouts of Bengali script in Manipur, given ultimatum to switch to Meetei Mayek next month', *The Hindu*, December 04, 2022.

19   Sairem Nilbir, 'Sanskritization Process of Manipur Under King Gharib Niwaz', in *New Insights Into the Glorious Heritage of*

Manipur, volume 2, edited by H. Dwijasekhar Sharma, New Delhi: Akansha, 2009.

20 Ibid.

21 Page 5, second edition of 1992.

22 Naorem Sanajaoba, *Manipur: Past and Present*, volume 4, New Delhi, 2005, p. liii.

23 Quoted in *Arambai: The Weapon of War that Scripted History* by Homen Thangjam (2016), pp. 86–87. James Johnstone's *Manipur and the Naga Hills* was originally published under the title *My Experiences in Manipur and the Naga Hills*, London: S. Low, Marston and Co., 1896.

24 Excerpt from Chapter II of *Chainarol: Way of Warrior*, published on *E-Pao* on April 19, 2012.

25 'State forfeits controversial book on Manipur merger', *Imphal Free Press*, November 14, 2022.

26 Sandip Kumar Mishra, 'The Colonial Origins of Territorial Disputes in South Asia', *The Journal of Territorial and Maritime Studies*, vol. 3, no. 1 (January 2016).

27 H. Dwijasekhar Sharma and A. Brajakumar Sharma, 'Economic History of Manipur During the British Raj', in *New Insights Into the Glorious Heritage of Manipur*, volume 3, New Delhi: Akansha, 2009, p. 542.

28 Abhinay Lakshman, 'Registrar-General of India office says it cannot reveal stance on Meiteis', *The Hindu*, May 21, 2023.

29 Pushpita Das, 'The Unfolding Kuki–Meitei Conflict in Manipur', Institute for Defence Studies and Analysis, May 26, 2023.

30 'Scheduled Tribe Demand Committee', *The Sangai Express*, November 20, 2012, reproduced on *E-Pao* (http://e-pao.net/ GP.asp?src=7..011212.dec12, accessed on November 29, 2023).

31 Sekholal Kom, 'Identity and Governance: Demand for Sixth Schedule', *Indian Journal of Political Science*, vol. 71, no. 1 (Jan-March 2010).

32 'Manipur tribal groups slam CM Biren's remarks on land', *The Hindu*, June 13, 2022.

33 See the STDCM website (https://stdcm.org/genesis.html, accessed on November 29, 2023).

34 'Assertive scheduled tribes and militants push Meiteis to precarious situation', *The Sangai Express*, August 21, 2023.

35 It is obligatory for Indian citizens from outside those states to obtain a permit to enter the protected state. The document is an effort by the government to regulate movement to certain areas located near the international border of India. An ILP is usually significantly easier to obtain than the analogous Protected Area Permit which is the document required by non-citizens to enter the same areas. This inner-line permit is needed for some areas of Arunachal Pradesh, Nagaland, Lakshadweep, etc.

36 'Change in Criteria for inclusion in ST', Union Ministry of Tribal Affairs press release, December 28, 2017.

37 'Centre Still Employs "Obsolete" Criteria to Categorise Groups Under ST Lists: Report', *The Wire*, January 12, 2023.

38 Mohit Sharma, 'VHP urges Centre to exclude tribals who 'converted to other religions' from list of tribes', *India Today*, December 26, 2021.

39 'NE will be like J&K if ST tag is removed from Christians, warns lawyer', *The Meghalayan*, February 8, 2023.

40 'More teeth given to ST demand for Meiteis', *The Sangai Express*, January 3, 2023.

41 Abhinay Lakshman, 'ST status for Meiteis was considered and rejected in 1982 and 2001, government records show', *The Hindu*, October 17, 2023. Abhinay Lakshman's observation on the ST status of Meiteis have been challenged by three Meitei researchers as misleading and incorrect: K. Yugindro Singh, Sh. Janaki Sharma and M. Manihar Singh; a Naga scholar has challenged the three Meitei researchers.

42 Churches had been vandalized even in 2009, when three churches located in Imphal West district were set on fire twice by unidentified miscreants. 'Miscreants set ablaze churches', *The Sangai Express*, May 1, 2009, reproduced on *E-Pao* (http://e-pao.net/GP.asp?src=7..130509. may09, accessed on November 29, 2023).

43 Manipur had also seen attacks on the Catholic community by the Baptists.

44 'A Look At Recent Attacks Against Churches In Manipur: Timeline', *Hub News*, June 17, 2023.

45 Afrida Hussain, 'Gunfight erupts between Arambai Tenggol militants and 37 Assam Rifles in Manipur', *India Today NE*, May 30, 2023.

46 Rinku Khumukcham, '6 major organizations of Manipur derecognizes titular king Leishemba Sanajaoba', *Imphal Times*, June 14, 2020.

47 'Arambai Tenggol dissolved', *Imphal Free Press*, May 26, 2023.

48 Interview with Bhasha Singh. See https://www.youtube.com/watch?v=jVdL8IpDOfY, accessed November 29, 2023.

49 'Arambai Tenggol dissolved', *Imphal Free Press*.

50 Jaideep Mazumdar, 'Manipur CM Biren Singh Outwitted The Centre, But Here's How He Can Still Be Checkmated', *Swarajya*, July 2, 2023.

51 'Minority religion status sought', *The Sangai Express*, October 14, 2021.

52 Rabi Banerjee, 'Frightening Faith', *The Week*, September 20, 2020.

53 'Fanatic Christian Missionary Daniel Stephen Courney Who Was Deported In 2017 Found To Be In Manipur', *The Commune*, August 15, 2023.

54 'Apology Tendered by Takhellambam Ramananda Meitei', MAMI TV, see https://www.youtube.com/watch?v=S0_PoOZBL3U, accessed November 29, 2023.

55 'Youths storm house of pastor in Manipur', *Nagaland Post*, April 3, 2023.

56 Ibid.

57 'Apology Tendered by Takhellambam Ramananda Meitei', MAMI TV.

58 'All Manipur Christian Organisation expresses concerns over demolition of churches', *Imphal Free Press*, April 13, 2023.

59 To the best of my knowledge, the mosque was not demolished during this period.

60 Luke Coppen, 'Manipur archbishop: 249 churches destroyed in 36 hours', *The Pillar*, June 19, 2023.

61 'Archbishop of Imphal claims 249 churches burnt in Manipur: "Religious attack carried out"', *The Indian Express*, June 17, 2023.

62 Rittick Sharma, 'Remove our churches from SC petition: Meitei Christians tell Kuki groups', *EastMojo*, June 11, 2023.

63 Padmakshi Sharma, 'Supreme Court Hears Meitei Christian

Community's Plea Regarding Destruction Of Churches In Manipur', *LiveLaw*, September 1, 2023.

64 Rohan's main work involves feeding the hungry, which he started during the Covid pandemic. These include mentally challenged people, drug abusers, sex workers, the elderly, the homeless and migrants. He began by procuring food with his own money, but has since been able to raise more funds through crowd-funding websites and his network of fellow Christians. Rohan had a difficult childhood. His father was given to substance aduse and his parents divorced when he was still very young. He was brought up by his grandmother, and it was this background that made him sensitive to the sufferings of others.

65 '393 Temples burnt in course of ethnic clash "Idols and places of worship spat upon"', *The Sangai Express*, August 13, 2023.

66 Lien Chongloi, 'Dispelling Some Misleading Claims About the Violence in Manipur', *The Wire*, May 27, 2023.

67 Shivnarayan Rajpurohit, '"A pen can do more harm than a gun": In Manipur, Meitei-owned media is winning the "perception" war, *Newslaundry*, June 9, 2023.

68 Snigdhendu Bhattacharya, 'Hindutva Is A 'Friend' That Manipur's Meiteis Would Be Better Without', *Outlook*, July 24, 2023.

69 'Citing Burnt Churches in Manipur, Mizoram CM Says Won't Share Campaign Stage With Modi', *The Wire*, October 24, 2023.

70 Jaideep Mazumdar, 'Why conflict in Manipur is ethnic and NOT religious', *The Sangai Express*, July 26, 2023.

71 'European Parliament Adopts Resolution on Manipur, India Says it Reflects "Colonial Mindset"', *The Wire*, July 13, 2023.

72 'Fiona Bruce Speaks Out: Manipur Violence Takes Center Stage in UK', INVC News, July 22, 2023.

73 'No evidence of religious violence in Manipur: US-based think tank', *Deccan Herald*, August 25, 2023.

74 'Bnei Menashe community member killed, 2 synagogues torched in India violence', *The Times of Israel*, May 5, 2023.

75 Joydeep Hazarika, 'Far from home, Kukis from Manipur fight for "homeland" Israel', *India Today NE*, October 14, 2023.

76 Wahengbam Rorrkychand Singh, 'Zalengam: Kuki's deadly dream—a threat to Nation', *The Sangai Express*, July 31, 2023.

77 Bismee Taskin, 'Formed post 3 May horror, Kuki-Zo outfit banned by Manipur govt has "students, teachers, writers"', *The Print*, November 8, 2023.

78 'AMCO felicitates UPSC successful candidate', Hueiyen News Service, reproduced on *E-Pao* (http://www.e-pao.net/GP.asp?src=24..180713.jul13, accessed on November 29, 2023).

79 Sayima Ahmad, 'How Manipur Muslims are bridging the divide amid ethnic strife', *The Siasat Daily*, October 1, 2023.

80 Senjam Raj Sekhar, 'Cookie Cutter approach will not work in Manipur: The complexity of Kuki ethnicity, *India Today NE*, May 31, 2023.

81 Lien Chongloi, 'Dispelling Some Misleading Claims About the Violence in Manipur'.

82 'Rahul Gandhi listens, but does not act: Manipur CM Biren Singh', *India Today*, October 6, 2018.

83 Angana Chatterji et al., 'Detention, Criminalisation, Statelessness: The Aftermath of Assam's NRC', *The Wire*, September 9, 2021. See also Harsh Mander and Navsharan Singh (eds.), *This Land Is Mine, I Am Not of This Land*, New Delhi: Speaking Tiger, 2021.

84 Nandita Haksar, 'Man on a mission: How Soe Myint went from being a hijacker in India to a media tycoon in Myanmar', *Scroll*, August 28, 2018.

85 Article 14 protects all people residing within Indian territory, including foreigners, a right against arbitrariness; and Article 21 gives them a right to life and personal liberty. These are fundamental rights guaranteed under the Constitution of India.

86 Nandita Haksar, 'A lawyer's diary: How I fought for justice for 7 Myanmarese refugees in the midst of the pandemic', *Scroll*, May 15, 2021.

87 Abraham Thomas, 'SC stays Manipur HC order permitting seven Rohingya to seek refugee status', *Hindustan Times*, April 26, 2022.

88 Sumir Karmakar, 'Not acceptable to Mizoram: CM Zoramthanga writes to PM Modi on Myanmar refugees', *Deccan Herald*, March 20, 2021.

89 'Mizoram govt refuses to follow Centre's order to collect biometric data of Myanmar refugees', India TV, October 1, 2023.

90 'As at 2023, India was hosting over 74,600 refugees from Myanmar, more than an estimated 54,100 of whom arrived since the coup in February 2021. As at 1 May 2023, over 40,000 refugees from Myanmar were living in Mizoram, and 8,250 were living in Manipur state. Since 1970, Rohingya refugees have been coming to India in different instances from Myanmar and Bangladesh. According to the Indian Government's public estimates from 2017, around 40,000 Rohingya refugees were living in India, of whom at least 13,000 entered between 2012–2016. Over 20,000 are registered with the UNHCR. Most of the Rohingya live in camps and informal settlements in Delhi, Hyderabad, Jammu, Noida, and Nuh cities.' See 'ACAPS Briefing note: India–Myanmar refugees', Reliefweb, July 28, 2023 (https://reliefweb.int/report/india/acaps-briefing-note-india-myanmar-refugees-28-july-2023, accessed on November 29, 2023).

91 'Manipur was given to us by our forefathers, not by India: Meitei Leepum chief Pramot Singh', *India Today NE*, July 30, 2023.

92 Tora Agarwala, '"Everyone should know what happened to us": Four Kuki women recount brutal assaults they survived', *Scroll*, July 21, 2023.

93 Paotinthang Hangsing and Paolin Chongloi, 'Our Daughters Were Killed in Imphal on May 5. We Haven't Even Been Able to Retrieve Their Bodies', *The Wire*, May 29, 2023.

94 Meenakshy Sasikumar, '"Police Drove Kuki Women Towards Meitei Mob": Villagers Recount Manipur Horror', *The Quint*, July 20, 2023.

95 Rujuta Thete, 'Fact-Check: This Image Doesn't Show a Nurse "Raped & Murdered" in Manipur', *The Quint*, May 10, 2023.

96 Tanmay Chatterjee, 'Meiteis, Kukis keep moving to safer areas as tensions persist in Manipur', *Hindustan Times*, May 23, 2023.

97 Yaqut Ali, 'The Manipur Crisis: Four Months of Unending Violence', *The Wire*, September 14, 2023.

98 'Manipur violence: Zomi Mother's Association condemns incident of rape of Meitei woman by miscreants in Churachandpur', *India Today NE*, August 13, 2023.

99 Praveen Donthi, 'What's Behind the Manipur Violence and Why Stopping It Poses a Test For Modi', *The Wire*, July 27, 2023.

100 Seikhongam, 'Opinion: Did Imphal-based media add fuel to the Manipur violence?', *EastMojo*, August 10, 2023.

101 'Aimol tribe should not be depicted as Kukis: Aimol Tribe Union Manipur', *Ukhrul Times*, August 21, 2023.

102 'Aimols Declare "We Are Not Nagas, Aimol Will Be Aimol" Against Naga Monolith', *Kangla Online*, November 20, 2015.

103 Yaqut Ali, 'Manipur: Defence Service Corps Soldier Abducted, Killed in Imphal West', *The Wire*, September 18, 2023.

104 'Death penalty for drug peddlers in Manipur', *Hindustan Times*, September 7, 2006.

105 Khelen Thokchom, 'Manipuri girls bow to rebel dress code', The Telegraph, October 14, 2002.

106 Binalakshmi Nepram, 'Drugs, Guns And Four Stories From The Northeast', *Outlook*, September 25, 2020.

107 'Manipur: In throes of drug crisis', *Tehelka*, September 16, 2023.

108 India is the world's largest manufacturer of legal opium for the pharmaceutical industry according to the CIA World Factbook. India is one among the 12 countries in world where legal cultivation for medical use is permissible within the ambit of the United Nations Single Convention on Narcotic Drugs 1961. In India, legal cultivation is done primarily in Madhya Pradesh, Rajasthan and Uttar Pradesh.

109 Vino Raman, 'Dynamics of Ganja Cultivation in Manipur: Case Study of a Village in Ukhrul District', *Economic and Political Weekly*, vol. 49, no. 33 (August 16, 2014).

110 R.K. Nimai, 'Cannabis Plantation In Manipur: Breaking The Law', *The Frontier Manipur*, August 25, 2022.

111 Ngamjahao Kipgen, 'Why Are Farmers in Manipur Cultivating Poppy?', *Economic and Political Weekly*, vol. 54, no. 46 (November 23, 2019).

112 Thounaojam Naresh Singh1 and Nongmaithem Kishorchannd Singh, 'The Poppy Menace in Manipur: Causes, Consequences and Responses', *Eur. Chem. Bull.*, vol. 12, Special Issue-5 (Part-A) (2023).

113 'Manipur CM N Biren Singh calls Kukis a terrorist group: KPA president Tongmang Haokip slams BJP govt', India TV, August 7, 2023.

114 Savio Rodrigues, 'The Narcos Manipur: A story of Rs 70000 crore narcotics business', *The Goa Chronicle*, September 15, 2023.

115 Thangjanganba Luwang, 'Cannabis Eradication: The Missing Piece In Manipur's War On Drugs', *The Frontier Manipur*, September 24, 2023.

116 Dr Marc Nongmaithem, 'Have Manipur Lost The War Against Drug Cartels And Militants?', *The Frontier Manipur*, October 22, 2023.

117 Samir K. Purkayastha, 'Manipur launches another drug-free drive, but on ground it's a different story', *The Federal*, April 1, 2022.

118 'Drug mafia responsible for Manipur violence', *NE Now*, May 10, 2023.

119 Arunabh Saikia, 'Why Manipur's civil war is being linked to the narcotics trade', Scroll, June 13, 2023.

120 Ibid.

121 Binalakshmi Nepram, 'Drugs, Guns And Four Stories From The Northeast', *Outlook*.

122 Thangjanganba Luwang, 'Examining Allegations Of Assam Rifles' Involvement In Drug Trade With Kuki Militants, Role Of The Home Ministry', *The Frontier Manipur*, September 16, 2023.

123 Javed Parvesh, '"People from all communities involved in narcotics trade": Ex-super cop Brinda', *The Week*, July 16, 2023.

124 'Manipur: Is CM Biren Fighting A War Against or For Drugs? Asks Ex-Cop Th Brinda I Tamal Saha', NTT (see https://www.youtube.com/watch?v=XLPuP42T9wM, accessed on November 19, 2023).

125 'FIR Against Manipur's Top Cop | Alleged Coercion To Retract Her Statement', Mojo Story (see https://www.youtube.com/watch?v=0Czqu0Nkmlg, accessed on November 19, 2023).

126 Khorjei Laang, 'hina, India And Manipur: Emerging Illegal Drugs Economy And National Security Question', *The Frontier Manipur*, August 4, 2022.

127 '1,200 Chinese nationals arrested by Myanmar militia over alleged scam links amid rising cybercrime concerns in Asia', *South China Morning Post*, September 10, 2023.

128 Shivnarayan Rajpurohit, '"A pen can do more harm than a gun": In Manipur, Meitei-owned media is winning the "perception" war, *Newslaundry*.

129 'Urban Poverty Highest In Manipur, Goa Has Lowest Poverty Rate', GoNews (see https://www.gonewsindia.com/latest-news/news-and-

politic/urban-poverty-highest-in-manipur-goa-has-lowest-poverty-rate1-21881, accessed on November 19, 2023).

130 Hanjabam Ishworchandra Sharma, 'Understanding Underdevelopment in Manipur: A Critical Survey', *Economic and Political Weekly*, vol. 47, no. 46 (November 17, 2012).

131 Donald Takhell, 'Manipur farmers blame institutional failures for low yield and demand compensation', *Mongabay*, January 6, 2023.

132 Mamta Lukram, 'The Thoubal Multipurpose Project and Tumukhong Village road', *E-Pao*, December 10, 2018.

133 Daniel Kamei, 'Development or destruction?', *Imphal Free Press*, September 12, 2023.

134 Loitongbam Hena Devi and Utpal Kumar De, 'Multidimensional Deprivation in the Development of Manipur, a North-Eastern State of India', available at Research Square (https://doi.org/10.21203/rs.3.rs-1937056/v1).

135 'Manipur's budget is beautiful, but how would the Hill Areas grow?', *Ukhrul Times*, August 31, 2021.

136 Janghaolun Haokip, 'Communal Mistrust In Manipur Via-à-Vis The ADC Bill, 2021', *The Frontier Manipur*, August 15, 2022.

137 'Interrogating Governance and Financial Implications of 'Smart Cities'—Part I Report', available at Environment Support Group (https://esgindia.org/new/campaigns/interrogating-governance-and-financial-implications-of-smart-cities-part-i-report/, accessed on November 29, 2023).

138 Ngangbam Indrakanta Singh, 'Protest against smart city plan—Thadou students oppose land acquisition in Moreh', *The Telegraph*, November 13, 2014.

139 'Manipur: Over 167 households residing along Imphal River served eviction notice by district administration for city expansion project', *India Today NE*, March 25, 2023.

140 Vaishnavi Rathore, 'Mega "Eco"tourism Project Questions Wetland Ownership and Livelihoods in Manipur's Loktak Lake', Centre for Research and Advocay Manipur, February 26, 2021.

141 Ngamjahao Kipgen, 'Why Are Farmers in Manipur Cultivating Poppy?', *Economic and Political Weekly*.

142 Ibid.

143 Sravasti Dasgupta, 'In a 2-Hour-Long Speech in Parliament, PM Modi Spoke for Less Than 10 Minutes on Manipur', *The Wire*, August 10, 2023.

144 Prabin Kalita, 'More central forces sent to Manipur amid Meitei outfit's appeal to boycott Biren govt', *The Times of India*, August 7, 2023.

145 'Blow by blow account of start of clash from May 3 detailed Kukis started the violence: WMC', *The Sangai Express*, June 21, 2023.

146 'May 3, 2023: How it all started at Torbung', *The Sangai Express*, September 24, 2023.

147 Lien Chongloi, 'Dispelling Some Misleading Claims About the Violence in Manipur', *The Wire*, May 27, 2023.

148 '175 killed, 4786 houses burnt down: Police', *The Sangai Express*, September 15, 2023.

149 'How do those supposedly innocent civilians die in tribal Kuki-Zo villages on June 13; asks ITLF', *The Hills Journal*, June 15, 2023.

150 'Kuki Leader Who Once Backed Biren Manipur Govt Claims '200 Meiteis Killed' in Khamenlok, June 13/14', *The Wire* (see https://www.youtube.com/watch?v=fV2PpL8m2s4, accessed on November 29, 2023).

151 'Curfew hours', *The Sangai Express*, June 15, 2023.

152 'Massacre at Khamenlok; Mangani Leihun (Ashti) held at Nongshum foothills', HY News (see https://www.youtube.com/watch?v=0TRrh97N-PA, accessed on November 29, 2023).

153 Makepeace Sitlhou, 'The many costs of internet shutdowns amid violence in India's northeastern state'.

154 'Manipur: Centre Invokes Article 355, Takes Over Security in Violence-Hit State', *The Quint*, May 5, 2023.

155 Keshav Padmanabhan, 'Manipur violence an "indictment" of Centre, setback to long-term strategy in northeast, say scholars', *The Print*, June 21, 2023.

156 Sobhana K. Nair, 'Manipur debate in Rajya Sabha lost in a maze of rules', *The Hindu*, August 9, 2023.

157 Sukrita Baruah, 'For calling Manipur violence state-sponsored, CPI's Annie Raja, 2 others face FIR', *The Indian Express*, July 10, 2023.

158 'Planned aggression: To what end?', *The Sangai Express*, August 21, 2023.

159 Angshuman Choudhury, 'Targeting of Kukis the main reason behind Manipur violence', *Frontline*, June 27, 2023.

160 'Radical Socialist Statement on Manipur', available at International Viewpoint (https://internationalviewpoint.org/spip.php?article8181, accessed on November 29, 2023).

161 Prateek Goyal, 'Exclusive: NCW ignored complaint linked to Kuki women video filed 38 days ago', *Newslaundry*, July 20, 2023.

162 Sriharsha Devulapalli and Vishnu Padmanabhan, 'India's police force among the world's weakest', *Livemint*, June 19, 2019.

163 'Why isn't violence in Manipur being stopped in spite of heavy police, military presence?', Praveen Swami interview with Ajai Sahni, The Print, July 2023 (see https://www.youtube.com/watch?v=WOlp9OODy60, accessed on November 29, 2023).

164 'Extended exclusion: On AFSPA in Manipur', *The Hindu*, September 30, 2023.

165 'Manipur DGP P Doungel removed; Tripura cadre IPS officer new Police chief', *Ukhrul Times*, June 1, 2023.

166 'Manipur DGP Rubbishes Allegations Regarding Removal of Kuki Officers from Duty', *The Sentinel*, May 20, 2023.

167 Kalyan Ray, 'Manipur not an insurgency issue: CDS', *Deccan Herald*, May 31, 2023.

168 Walter Fernandes, 'A land in trouble', *The Telegraph*, June 25, 2023.

169 Greeshma Kuthar, 'Fire and Blood, *The Caravan*, August 1, 2023.

170 Banjot Kaur, 'Manipur: FIRs Show the Type and Quantity of Weapons Taken from Police Armouries', *The Wire*, June 19, 2023.

171 'Manipur Police confirms reports of arms, ammunition loot', *Livemint*, August 6, 2023.

172 Bhogtoram Mawroh, 'Opinion: Can "disarmament" solve the Manipur crisis?', *EastMojo*, July 30, 2023.

173 Yaqut Ali, 'Exclusive: In Past 7 Years, Biren Singh Govt Has Issued Highest Number of Gun Licences in Northeast', *The Wire*, July 12, 2023.

174 Ibid.

175 Home Raikhan, 'Resolving Kuki-Zo-Chin and Meitei conflict', *The Sangai Express*, July 24, 2023.

176 See my article 'Assam Rifles: Manipur Police's FIR Underscores the Meiteis' Long-Held Resentment', *The Quint*, August 10, 2023.

177 See Teresa Rehman, *Mothers of Manipur*, Delhi: Zubaan, 2017, for details of the protest.

178 'Manipur violence: "One force, one district" policy may be adopted for better coordination', *Hindustan Times*, September 28, 2023.

179 Karishma Hasnat, 'Banned by MHA for 5 years: A look at active Meitei insurgent groups in Manipur & their demands', *The Print*, November 15, 2023.

180 Phanjoubam Chingkhei, 'Legend of Kuki, Meiteis and Nagas common origin from one ancestor found in folktales', *Imphal Times*, April 4, 2023.

181 'Tangkhul Naga Long clarifies on CM's visit to Ukhrul', *The Morung Express*, October 21, 2023.

182 K.S. Solomon Naamai, 'The Question Behind the Tangkhul Naga Long Demand for Ukhrul to Be the Summer Capital of Manipur', *My Perception and I* (blog) (see https://thohepou.wordpress. com/2009/09/15/the-question-behind-the-tangkhul-naga-long-demand-for-ukhrul-to-be-the-summer-capital-of-manipur/, accessed on November 29, 2023).

183 'Cabinet approves implementation of National Mission on Edible Oils—Oil Palm', official press release, available at Press Information Bureau (https://www.pib.gov.in/PressReleasePage. aspx?PRID=1746942/, accessed on November 29, 2023).

184 'The launch of Oil Palm Project, Manipur', November 26, 2020, available at Government of India website (https://blog.mygov.in/ the-launch-of-oil-palm-project-manipur/, accessed on November 29, 2023).

185 Based on my article 'Double-Engine: The Union and State Government Must Answer for Manipur', *The Wire*, August 3, 2023.

186 'Oil palm cultivation: Godrej Agrovet signs MoUs with Assam, Manipur and Tripura', *Economic Times*, August 23, 2022.

187 'Godrej Agrovet gains on tie-up with Malaysian firm for palm oil seeds', *Moneycontrol*, September 29, 2023.

188 Vikrant Singh, 'Communist Allegations Debunked: No Link Between Adani, Ambani, and Manipur Violence Over Palm Oil Production', *Only Fact*, July 26, 2023.

189 Prateek Goyal, 'Alt News, CIA, "Hinduphobic" media: The fixations of a rightwing "fact-checking" enterprise', *Newslaundry*, July 9, 2022.

190 'Manipur: Why we celebrate "women's war" on Nupi Lan Day', *EastMojo*, December 12, 2020.

191 Makepeace Sitlhou, 'Why were people attending a Manipur spring festival party assaulted by women's groups?', *Scroll*, March 26, 2019.

192 Tora Agarwala, 'Feminist icons or violent vigilantes? The contentious role of Meira Paibis in Manipur's conflict', *Scroll*, August 4, 2023.

193 '13 Killed in Firing as Protestors Go On Rampage', *Imphal Free Press*, reproduced on *E-Pao* (http://e-pao.net/GP.asp?src=8..190601. jun01, accessed on November 29, 2023).

194 A. Kamson, 'The Mera Haochongpa Festival—the traditional hill-valley interface: The Carnival of Manipur', in *New Insights Into the Glorious Heritage of Manipur*, volume 1, pp. 155–56.

195 'TNL expresses concerns over setting up of semi-permanent relief camps; Opposes Proposed UCC', *Ukhrul Times*, July 8, 2023.

196 '4 women from Ukhrul attacked by mob in Imphal', *Ukhrul Times*, May 24, 2023.

197 'Settlement arrived at between UNC & COCOMI in Lucy Marem's murder case, signs agreement; CM Biren assures justice', *Ukhrul Times*, July 18, 2023.

198 'Kuki Revolutionary Army cadres allegedly attack Liangmei Naga man; total shutdown imposed in Naga areas of Kangpokpi Dist', *Ukhrul Times*, September 5, 2023.

199 '25 communities are native people of Manipur: FoH', *Imphal Free Press*, August 6, 2022.

200 'Manipur: Reactions to Nandita Haksar's Article', *Mainstream*, vol. XLVIII, no. 33 (August 7, 2010) (available at: https://www. mainstreamweekly.net/article2224.html, accessed on November 29, 2023).

201 Subsequently, each Hill district was bifurcated: Tamenglong district has been bifurcated into Noney and Tamenglong districts; Churachandpur into Pherzawl and Churachandpur; Chandel into Tengnoupal and Chandel districts; Ukhrul into Kamjong and Ukhrul districts; and Senapati into Kangpokpi and Senapati districts. Kangpokpi district is also the other name of the Sadar Hills district.

202 Sushil Kumar Sharma, 'How Nagas Perceive the Creation of Seven Additional Districts in Manipur', Institute for Defence Studies and Analysis, March 15, 2017.

203 Manogya Loiwal, '7 new districts formed in Manipur amid opposition by Nagas', *India Today*, December 19, 2016.

204 Haoginlen Chongloi, 'Narratives of hate behind Manipur violence', June 13, 2023.

205 Sumantra Bose, 'How Manipur's Kukis, Meiteis and Nagas Were United to the INA's Cause to Free India', *The Wire*, July 31, 2023.

206 Seilen Haokip, 'The Kuki Rising, 1917-1919', blogpost (available at https://tklenhaokip7.wordpress.com/2017/02/19/the-kuki-rising-1917-1919/, accessed on November 29, 2023).

207 Vibha Arora and Ngamjahao Kipgen, 'Demand for Kukiland and Kuki Ethnic Nationalism', in *Democratisation in the Himalayas Interest Conflicts and Negotiations*, edited by Vibha Arora and N. Jayaram, New York: Routledge, 2017.

208 'FH lodge FIR against two Kuki-Zo academicians and Author of Anglo-Kuki War 1917-1919 book', *Ukhrul Times*, August 10, 2023.

209 Interview with V.S. Wungmatem in July 1999, published in Nandita Haksar and Sebastian Hongray, *Kuknalim: Naga Armed Resistance*, New Delhi: Speaking Tiger, 2019.

210 Harshavardhan Konda, 'Viral letter does not mention all Kukis in Manipur as refugees from Myanmar', *Factly*, July 25, 2023.
     'Claim: Kuki tribes living in Manipur came from the Burma (Myanmar) as refugees and were later granted ST (Scheduled Tribe) quota in India in 1968.
     'Fact: The letter does not mention the entire Kukis in Manipur as refugees. Previous letters related to the viral letter indicate that the District Commissioner of Manipur was implementing the humanitarian aid provided by the Indian Government to the Kukis of Myanmar, who were forced to flee to Manipur in 1967 during the Khadawmi operation in Myanmar. Moreover, the Kuki tribes were granted the ST status in India as early as 1950 and and they have existed in the Manipur kingdom for many centuries. Hence, the claim made in the post is misleading.'

211 'Four Naga tribes on "Anglo-Kuki War" issue', *The Morung Express*, October 13, 2019.

212 See p. 127 of his book.

213 'KNO, NNPG sign Imphal AccordBoth agree to accept history and identity of each other', *The Sangai Express*, January 19, 2020.

214 Rinku Khumukcham, 'Haomee burns effigy of KNO President P.S. Haokip and ban his book Zalengam: The Kuki Nation', *Imphal Times*, November 13, 2020.

215 'NZPO & KIN reject claims made in "Zalengam" book', *The Morung Express*, October 13, 2023.

216 'United Naga Council sets the record straight on Nagas' Land in Manipur; No "Anglo Kuki War" in history', *Ukhrul Times*, August 21, 2023.

217 Rebecca C. Haokip, 'Kuki-Paite Conflict in Churachandpur District of Manipur' in *Conflict Mapping and Peace Processes in North East India*, edited by Lazar Jeyaseelan, Guwahati: North Eastern Social Research Centre, 2008.

218 Thongkholal Haokip, 'Decades of Sadar Hills Demand', *Hueiyen Lanpao* (English Edition), September 6, 2011, reproduced on E-Pao (http://e-pao.net/epSubPageExtractor.asp?src=news_section.Sadar_Hills_District_Demand_201108.Decades_of_Sadar_Hills_Demand, accessed on November 29, 2023).

219 Vibha Arora and Ngamjahao Kipgen, 'Demand for Kukiland and Kuki Ethnic Nationalism'.

220 Vangamla Salle K.S., 'Manipur: Tribal body condemns govt for supporting non-tribal NGOs', *EastMojo*, October 30, 2023.

221 John H. Pulamte, 'Tribal reservation in Manipur: A boon or a bane', The Sangai Express, March 16, 2017, reproduced on E-Pao (http://e-pao.net/epSubPageExtractor.asp?src=news_section.opinions.Tribal_reservation_in_Manipur_A_boon_or_bane, accessed on November 29, 2023).

222 Lien Chongloi, 'Dispelling Some Misleading Claims About the Violence in Manipur', *The Wire*.

223 See 'Terrorist/Insurgent Groups—Manipur' (Data Updated till December 24, 2017)' South Asia Terrorism Portal (https://www.satp.org/satporgtp/countries/india/states/manipur/terrorist_outfits/index.html, accessed on November 29, 2023).

224 Ginza Vualzong, 'The Story Behind Songpi, Churachandpur and Lamka', available at Zogam.com (https://www.zogam.com/articles/articles-i/general-articles/3022-the-story-behind-songpi-churachandpur-and-lamka.html, accessed on November 29, 2023).

225 The land system in the state comprises of surveyed and unsurveyed land. All the Valley districts are surveyed land, where people have to pay revenue. Tribal lands in the hill districts have not been surveyed and the law forbids the transfer of land from from tribals to non-tribals. People here just pay the house tax. However, Moreh, which is in the hills, is a revenue town now and yields rich dividends because of the trade—legal and illegal.

226 'After Thangjing to Thangting : Change of names to Kuknise Moreh comes to the fore', *The Sangai Express*, October 12, 2023.

227 Debanish Achom and Ratnadip Choudhury, '"Extraordinary Sad Call": Ex Army Chief On Retired Officer's Manipur Tweet', *NDTV*, June 17, 2023.

228 Reproduced from *Verses of Resistance: The Activist Poetry of Myanmar* by John Charles Ryan.

229 Vijaita Singh, '100-km smart fencing along Myanmar border in the pipeline to boost surveillance: Home Ministry', *The Hindu*, October 9, 2023.

230 See also my article 'Borders As Walls', available at *Force* (https://forceindia.net/guest-column/borders-as-walls/, accessed on November 29, 2023).

231 '"Avoid Unnecessary Along Movement Indo-Myanmar Border"', *The Frontier Manipur*, November 15, 2023.

232 Snehashish Roy, 'Manipur CM meets top officials on 70-km fencing across India-Myanmar border; "urgent necessity"', *Hindustan Times*, September 24, 2023.

233 Ainhoa Ruiz Benedicto, Mark Akkerman and Pere Brunet, *A Walled World: Towards a Global Apartheid*, Barcelona: Transnational Institute, 2020, available online (https://www.tni.org/en/publication/a-walled-world, accessed November 29, 2023).

234 'Burma: Chronology of Aung San Suu Kyi's Detention', Human Rights Watch, November 13, 2020.

235 As far back as December 2022, according to reports by Human Rights Watch, military tribunals in Myanmar had sentenced 138 people to death since the February 2021 military coup, including 41 *in absentia*. See 'Myanmar: Junta Sentences 10 Prisoners to Death', Human Rights Watch, December 5, 2022.

236 Burma Affairs and Conflict Study and India for Myanmar, '30 Months of Myanmar Military Coup—A Comprehensive Analytical Report on India's Approach and Relations With Myanmar', available at Progressive Voice Myanmar (https://progressivevoicemyanmar.org/2023/09/05/30-months-of-myanmar-military-coup-a-comprehensive-analytical-report-on-indias-approach-and-relations-with-myanmar/, accessed November 29, 2023).

237 Kimi Colney, 'Chin rockstar Benjamin Sum's "Aadhar" card fuels refugee debate in Mizoram', *EastMojo*, April 24, 2023.

238 Ye Myo Hein, 'Understanding the People's Defense Forces in Myanmar', United States Institute of Peace, November 3, 2022.

239 'Myanmar Govt in Exile Asks Refugees in India to Stay Away From Political, Ethnic Conflicts', *The Wire*, July 7, 2023.

240 'Mizoram: NIA arrests 3 including Myanmar national in arms seizure case', *Livemint*, July 25, 2023.

241 Praveen Swami, 'In Myanmar, a new 'criminal' State is rising. And China is paying to build it', *The Print*, May 11, 2022.

242 Tom Kramer, 'The Current State of Counternarcotics Policy and Drug Reform Debates in Myanmar', Transnational Institute, 2016 (available online: chrome-extension://efaidnbmnnnibpcajpcglclefindmkaj/https://www.brookings.edu/wp-content/uploads/2016/07/Kramer-Burma-final.pdf, accessed November 29, 2023).

243 See my article 'On Pravasi Bharatiya Divas, India must reunite citizens trafficked to Myanmar with their families', *Scroll*, January 8, 2023.

244 'Expert panel notes sudden increase of population', *The Sangai Express*, September 5, 2023.

245 K. Sarojkumar Sharma, '"5 Manipur hill districts have 934 unrecognised villages"', *The Times of India*, June 6, 2022.

246 Haoginlen Chongloi, 'Reinterpreting Kuki Chieftainship of Northeast India in relation to Colonial Historiography: Media Theory Perspectives', *Media Watch*, vol. 9, no. (2018) (DOI: 10.15655/mw/2018/v9i3/49494).

247 Prawesh Lama, 'Refugees now reach south Mizoram amid fresh airstrikes by Myanmar army', *Hindustan Times*, November 23, 2023.

248 Sukrita Baruah, 'Mob storms Imphal hospital treating man injured

in Myanmar fighting, he later succumbs', *The Indian Express*, November 24, 2023.

249 Vijaita Singh, 'Manipur conflict inquiry panel yet to hold any public hearing', *The Hindu*, November 24, 2023.

250 'Underground Tunnels Found at Bangladesh-Myanmar Border Used by Separatist Armed Group: Sources', *Borderlens*, January 31, 2023.

Kuknalim

Naga Armed Resistance

Testimonies of Leaders, Pastors, Healers and Soldiers

Nandita Haksar and Sebastian M. Hongray

This first-of-its-kind book tells the story of the Naga national movement from the inside. Based on extensive interviews of the Naga nationalists, conducted in the late 1990s in Bangkok, Kathmandu, Dimapur and Delhi, it explains why the Indo-Naga conflict has lasted more than seven decades, and why successive prime ministers of India, from Jawaharlal Nehru to Narendra Modi, have personally met the Naga leaders and tried to resolve the conflict.

In *Kuknalim*, leaders and members of ten Naga tribes spread across India and Myanmar speak directly to the reader about their childhood experiences, reasons for joining the armed struggle, and their personal triumphs and tragedies. They recount their journeys from small, impoverished mountain villages through the jungles of Myanmar to China—from where they carried back arms to fight for an independent Nagaland—and finally the journey to the negotiating table. These stories relate to the period of the Naga movement from World War II to 1997, when Naga nationalists under the NSCN (IM) entered into a ceasefire agreement with the Indian state and began peace talks. And in the introduction to the book and the different sections in it, the authors also write about subsequent events, besides providing the political context for each interview.

A groundbreaking work, *Kuknalim* offers invaluable insights into the world of Naga insurgency and its geo-political significance. Without asking the reader to agree or disagree with the people and movement it profiles, the book also examines complex questions of identity politics; the role of religion in nationalism; and the sentiments that drive men and women to take up arms and endure extreme hardship in pursuit of their dreams.

www.ingramcontent.com/pod-product-compliance
Lightning Source LLC
Chambersburg PA
CBHW031450160726
47994CB00005B/1959